The Catholic Connections Handbook

for Middle Schoolers

Catholic Connections

Pray It! Study It! Live It!® *resources
offer a holistic approach to learning,
living, and passing on the Catholic faith.*

Saint Mary's Press®

The Catholic Connections Handbook

for Middle Schoolers

Janet Claussen

Pat Finan

Diana Macalintal

Jerry Shepherd

Susan Stark

Chris Wardwell

The Subcommittee on the Catechism, United States Conference of Catholic Bishops, has found this catechetical text, copyright 2009, to be in conformity with the *Catechism of the Catholic Church.*

Nihil Obstat: Rev. William M. Becker, STD
                Censor Librorum
                October 2, 2008

Imprimatur: † Most Reverend Bernard J. Harrington, DD
                Bishop of Winona
                October 2, 2008

The nihil obstat and imprimatur are official declarations that a book or pamphlet is free of doctrinal or moral error. No implication is contained therein that those who have granted the nihil obstat or imprimatur agree with the contents, opinions, or statements expressed, nor do they assume any legal responsibility associated with publication.

The publishing team included Maura Thompson Hagarty and Brian Singer-Towns, development editors; Lorraine Kilmartin, reviewer; prepress and manufacturing coordinated by the production departments of Saint Mary's Press.

Shutterstock, cover images

Printed in Canada

2150 (1833)

ISBN 978-0-88489-994-5

Library of Congress Cataloging-in-Publication Data

The Catholic connections handbook for middle schoolers / Janet Claussen ... [et al.].
      p. cm.
      Includes index.
ISBN 978-0-88489-994-5 (pbk.) — ISBN 978-0-88489-995-2 (hardbound)
      1. Catholic Church—Doctrines—Juvenile literature. I. Claussen, Janet.
BX1754.5.Y68 2008
248.8'3088282—dc22

                                                    2008014771

CONTENTS

Part 4: Liturgy and Sacraments

Part 5: Christian Morality and Justice

Part 6: Prayer

Appendixes

List of People of Faith

INTRODUCTION

Come with Me

"Come with me" (Matthew 4:19). Jesus said this to his first disciples, and it is his message to us today. Following Jesus is at the heart of being Catholic. Even though following Jesus isn't always easy, it's the most fulfilling and meaningful way to live life.

   The Catholic Connections Handbook for Middle Schoolers is a guide for young teens on what it means to follow Jesus and to be Catholic today. This handbook offers a summary of what God has revealed to us through his Son, Jesus Christ, and what the Church has passed on from generation to generation through the working of the Holy Spirit. The handbook is a companion to the Bible and aims to help you learn about the Catholic Church and its beliefs about God—Father, Son, and Holy Spirit, the sacraments, Christian morality and justice, and prayer.

Study It!

This handbook is divided into the following six sections, each a different color so you can more easily find the part you are looking for:

Part 1: God, Revelation, and Faith

Part 2: Jesus the Christ

Part 3: The Holy Spirit and the Church

Part 4: Liturgy and Sacraments

Part 5: Christian Morality and Justice

Part 6: Prayer

The handbook is a great tool for study, but it is more than that. It includes many prayers and lots of guidance for living the Catholic faith.

Each of the handbook's forty-three chapters has a number of special features. These are short articles set in special boxes. Along with the main text in the chapters, these articles are intended to help you further study, pray, and live the Catholic faith. Following are descriptions of the special articles you'll see throughout the handbook:

Pray It!

Faith becomes more alive by praying. In each chapter you'll see a short prayer just right for times when you are by yourself or when you are with a group of peers.

Pray It!

Liturgy Connection

Faith is celebrated in the Church's liturgy and sacraments. The "Liturgy Connection" articles you'll see in many chapters will help you see the relationship between Catholic beliefs and worship.

Live It!

Being Catholic has to do with beliefs, but it also has to do with the way you live. The "Live It!" articles suggest ways you can put your faith into action.

Think About It!

Every chapter has a "Think About It!" article with questions for you to ponder on your own or discuss with your friends or family members.

Did You Know?

The many "Did You Know?" articles take topics from the chapter they appear in and explore it in more depth.

Looking Back

Sometimes a little history provides a better understanding of aspects of Catholic beliefs and practices. The "Looking Back" articles appear occasionally to provide you with this type of historical insight.

FUN FACT

The "Fun Fact" articles in every chapter are brief notes designed to inform and amuse.

PEOPLE OF FAITH

Try to imagine the Church without faithful people. It's impossible. This handbook introduces you to or reacquaints you with approximately twenty of the many people who have strengthened the Church and inspired others with their faith.

© 2009 Saint Mary's Press/Illustrations by Vicki Shuck

Catholic Prayers, Beliefs and Practices, Key Words, and Index

Several handy sections at the end of the handbook provide the following easy-to-access information:

- a collection of Catholic prayers

- a brief summary of core Catholic beliefs and practices

- a glossary of the handbook's key words

- an index for those times when you are searching for information about particular topics

The authors, and everyone at Saint Mary's Press who had a hand in creating this book, wish you many blessings as you use it to explore more deeply what it means to follow Jesus and to be a member of the Catholic Church.

PART I

God, Revelation, and faith

*I believe in God,
the Father almighty,
creator of heaven and earth.*

REVELATION, SCRIPTURES, AND TRADITION

It's Saturday morning. You wake up, turn on the TV, and start flipping through the channels. On the way to your favorite show, you find a preacher on one channel. He explains that the Creation story in the Bible happened just as it is written in the Bible. He insists that the world was created in only six days and that this should be taught in schools. Later that day, in the grocery store checkout line, a magazine cover tells why scientists support the idea that our universe began billions of years ago in a huge explosion. Inside, another article talks about how apes slowly changed over time to become human beings. At school on Monday, you find out that your newest friend at school is an atheist—someone who doesn't believe in God. His mother has told him that people made up the idea of God so they wouldn't feel bad when people died.

In the beginning God created the world. A powerful hand shows God's role in the creation of the universe.

© Mike Agliolo/Corbis

There are so many different ideas. You begin to wonder about the things you have been taught. Is God really out there? How can you know?

Revelation

One place where you can begin to look for answers to these questions is under your own two feet. The earth itself is a sign of God's existence. In fact, you can find the evidence of God's handiwork everywhere: the trees that give you shade, the sun that warms your back, the dogs that bark in the distance, and of course, all the people around you. Though we do not fully understand God and his ways, we can use our minds to see that God truly exists because of the wonder of creation itself.

In fact, throughout all history, God has made himself known to human beings in a number of ways. He continues to do so today through the signs of creation around us, through the voice of the Church, and through the voices of our consciences speaking from within us. You may already have had an experience where God became known to you. Maybe after going to confession, you have felt the relief of having God remove the burden of your

PRAY IT!

Lord God,
I ask,
    When I am lost, make
    yourself known to me.
    When I celebrate,
    make yourself known
    to me. When I am
    lonely, make yourself
    known to me. When
    I am confused, make
    yourself known to me.
    When I am sick, make
    yourself known to me.
    When I am joyful, make
    yourself known to me.
    When I doubt you, make
    yourself known to me.
    When I am in need, make
    yourself known to me.
    When I pray, make yourself
    known to me.
                    Amen

17

FUN FACT

Did you know that the Catholic Bible contains seven more books than many other Christian Bibles? The Old Testament books of Tobit, Judith, 1 Maccabees, 2 Maccabees, Wisdom, Sirach, and Baruch are all inspired by the Holy Spirit, and so they are included in all Catholic bibles.

guilty feelings and your sins. Maybe you have felt God's presence in the prayerful quiet of the church before Mass. If anything like this has ever happened to you, you know it comes as a gift. God makes himself known to us, because he loves us. Even more amazing, he wants to give himself to us so we know we are never alone.

What God has made known about himself and his plan for humanity is called **Revelation.** Throughout history God's Revelation has been made known through creation, events, and people but most especially through Jesus Christ. While it is certainly possible for one to have a personal experience of God, Revelation is communicated to the whole world in two main ways: the Scriptures and Tradition.

"Moses! Moses!" He answered, "Yes, here I am." God said, ". . . I am the God of your ancestors, the God of Abraham, Isaac, and Jacob." (Exodus 3:4,6)

Did You Know?

The Case of the "Missing" Gospels

From time to time, in the newspaper or in other news media, you might hear about a newly discovered "gospel" or other ancient book that somehow mysteriously never made it into the Bible. Often, these articles or programs make it sound like leaving these books out of the Bible was an evil plot to hide a dark secret of the Church. Actually the truth is far less dramatic: early in the Church's history, these books were considered misleading or incomplete; they did not express the true faith of the Church. Eventually they were just forgotten.

The Scriptures and Tradition are distinct, yet very close-ly related. Both communicate or transmit the Word of God. The Scriptures and Tradition have been given to the Church to be kept safe and passed on so all generations will know God's Revelation. All be-lievers share the responsibility for helping hand on what God has revealed through the Scriptures and Tradition.

God fully revealed himself by sending his only Son, Jesus Christ. There is nothing new that God needs to reveal until Christ comes again to establish a new heaven and new earth. But what the Father revealed through his Son needs to be explained and taught to all people. Teaching what God has revealed through Sa-cred Tradition and the Scriptures became the responsibility of the Apostles and their succes-sors, the popes and bishops of the Church.

The Scriptures

Sacred **Scriptures** are the seventy-three inspired books and letters we recognize as the Word of God. The Bible is an-other name for Sacred Scriptures. The Bible contains the forty-six books of the Old Testament and the twenty-seven books that make up the New Testament. God is the ultimate author of the Bible. The Holy Spirit inspired the human

THinK AbouT It!

Sometimes people say God speaks to them. If you were to ask them, though, whether they hear voices in their heads, they would probably say, "Of course not! I'm not crazy!" How does God communicate with us without using an actual voice? What are some things God might use to make his wishes known to us?

Break Through!

The **Bible** for Young Catholics

PRAY IT
STUDY IT
LIVE IT

Saint Mary's Press

The Bible helps us discover who God is and how he relates to us. Do you ever get the chance to read the Bible?

PRAY IT!

Liturgy Connection

We listen to God's Revelation every time we go to Mass. When we celebrate the Liturgy of the Word (the part of Mass when the Bible is proclaimed), God is revealed to us in a special way. In these readings we hear about what God has done for our salvation. We listen to how God led Moses and the Israelites out of slavery, how the prophets reminded the people of their promise to follow God, what Jesus taught and did, the stories about Jesus' death and Resurrection, and how the early Christians carried on Jesus' mission. In all these readings, God is revealed to be all powerful, loving, and forgiving. God always cares for his people, no matter what.

authors to communicate what God wants us to know for our salvation. That is, we learn how to be fulfilled in this life and how to spend eternity with God.

Four special books in the New Testament are called the **Gospels.** The word *gospel* means "good news." The Gospels are special because they tell us about the life, teachings, Passion (suffering), death, Resurrection, and Ascension of our Lord, Jesus Christ. God's Revelation is complete in Jesus Christ.

The Bible often has accurate scientific facts and history, but we must be careful in looking for that kind of information. That is not what the original authors were trying to teach. Rather we look to the Bible for those truths that will assist our salvation. It is 100 percent correct when it tells us what we need to know for our salvation. God inspired the many different writers of the Bible to write down those truths he wanted to teach us. **Inspiration** is the fact that the Holy Spirit guided the Bible's authors to record without error what God wants us to know for our salvation.

Remember that even though the Holy Spirit guided these writers, they were still human beings. They wrote in ancient languages and lived in cultures different from ours. Just like us, they

had an incomplete understanding of the world. This sometimes makes the Scriptures hard to understand. Scholars study the Bible closely to find out exactly what its human authors intended to say. The Pope, our bishops, and our priests help us in understanding the Bible. Above all, we must ask the Spirit to guide us in understanding God's message of salvation.

Tradition

Unlike some other Christians, however, Catholics do not rely only on the Scriptures to discover God's Revelation. We also look to Tradition (with a capital T), which is sometimes called Sacred Tradition. **Tradition** is based on a word meaning "to hand on." So, Tradition means both the central content of the Catholic faith and the way in which that content has been

Live It!

Despite what magazines in the grocery store checkout lines claim, prophets are not psychics who predict the future. Prophets are people who speak God's Word. In the Bible, the prophets reveal God's will to the people. Jesus Christ is the Word who became flesh, the ultimate prophet who was sent by the Father and anointed by the Holy Spirit. In Baptism, we are anointed to share in Christ's prophetic ministry. We are all called to be prophets in some way. We are all called to speak God's Word.

That doesn't mean we have to preach on street corners, but it does mean our words and actions should reveal the faith we claim as our own. If someone were to follow you around for a day, would they be able to see God in the way you interact with your classmates? If it were illegal to be a Catholic, how many of us would be found guilty?

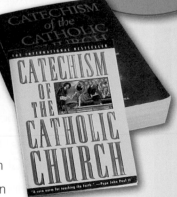

This handbook is based on the *Catechism of the Catholic Church*, a summary of the central teachings of our Tradition. Read the handbook along with your Bible to discover who God is.

handed down through the centuries under the guidance of the Holy Spirit.

Did You Know?

The Flat Earth Under the Dome

The Holy Spirit inspired the human authors of the Bible, but they still had the same mistaken ideas about the earth as everyone else during the times they lived. For example, when the Book of Genesis was written, people believed the world was flat and covered by a giant dome. They believed water surrounded the dome. When the Creation stories were written, this incorrect scientific information was described. Whether the earth is as flat as a pancake or as round as a ball is not important when it comes to our salvation. God's creation of everything in the world out of love is important to our salvation. That truth is part of God's Revelation.

Tradition is not the same thing as traditions (with a lowercase t). You probably take part in a number of traditions. They might include things like when your family eats a certain kind of pie every year for your Thanksgiving meal, or school traditions where everyone wears the school colors to all the sporting events. The Tradition of the Catholic Church has some things in common with these, but it is still different.

Sacred Tradition started with the preaching of the Apostles. Some of this preaching was later written down in the Bible, but the Bible does not contain all of Sacred Tradition. Tradition includes our belief in the Trinity, the Incarnation of Jesus Christ, the Seven Sacraments, and many other matters revealed through the teachings of the Pope and bishops under the guidance of the Holy Spirit. Through the Church's Scripture and Tradition, God actively helps us move toward salvation.

Key Words

Revelation
Scriptures
Gospels
Inspiration
Tradition

God's Mystery

While God does make himself known to us, we cannot expect to fully understand all of God's ways. We can come to know a lot about God, but we cannot completely grasp him. God is just too big for us to understand.

The Book of Job tells the story of a man named Job. Job was trying to understand why bad things were happening to him. At the end of the story, God asks him questions that no one but God could answer (see Job, chapter 38). Job then realizes something important. Even if we stand face to face with God, we will still never be able to understand some things (see Job 42:1–6).

"At God's command amazing things happen, wonderful things that we can't understand. . . . God's power is so great that we cannot come near him; he is righteous and just in his dealings with us. No wonder, then, that everyone is awed by him." (Job 37:5,23–24)

Looking Back

The Scriptures, Tradition, and the Ecumenical Councils

In the early 1500s, a German priest named Martin Luther began to teach that the Scriptures were the only necessary source of Christian truth. Shortly afterward all the bishops in the world gathered at the Council of Trent (1543–1565), in Italy, to respond to Luther's ideas. The bishops made clear that both the Scriptures and Tradition were necessary ways of passing on, or transmitting, God's Revelation. Ecumenical Councils such as the Second Vatican Council are official meetings of all the world's Catholic bishops with the approval of the pope. These councils are how the Church addresses important issues or questions that come up from time to time. The councils do not occur often. In fact, throughout the entire history of the Church, there have only been twenty-one Ecumenical Councils.

God
THE FATHER

When you picture God in your mind, what do you see? Many people see an old man with white hair and a beard sitting on a throne in a cloud up in the sky. Is this what God really looks like? Not really. It seems that many of us have adopted this image of the Greek god Zeus, whom the stories about the ancient Greek gods describe just like this.

Michelangelo painted God as an old man with a white beard. What image comes to your mind when you think of God? What are some other ways to think about God?

You might be curious why you have the image of this Greek god in your head when you think about the one, true God. Centuries ago, artists needed some way to portray God in their works, but the Bible contained no physical descriptions of God the

24

Father. Some painters used Zeus as the model because he was the most powerful of the Greek gods. The image of Zeus helped many people connect to some of the traits of God. That image has stuck with us. It is not wrong to picture God like this, just remember that it is an incomplete image of God. If God is not an old man with a white beard in the clouds, then who is God?

Who Is God?

If you were asked to describe a friend, you might answer in a few different ways. You could say something about her relationships to others (she is a daughter, a sister, and a friend). You might talk about what she does (she is a student and a softball player). Maybe you would say what kind of person she is (she is smart and kind). We get to know people through their relationships with others and by observing what they do and listening to what they say.

Whatever we know about God, we know because he revealed it to us. God first revealed his name to Moses. It is pretty simple, but very powerful: I AM. The Hebrew word for I AM is **Yahweh.** The name I AM or Yahweh reminds us how immense

PRAY IT!

God, our Father, I understand so little about you, but I know a few things. You exist beyond the farthest star, but I also know you are here with me now. I do not know everywhere I will go in the future, but I do know I came from you. I do not always understand your ways, but I do know I can trust you. I cannot even guess how you came to be, but I do know you will always be with me. Thank you, God, for being you. Amen.

and beyond us God truly is. I AM may seem like an incomplete sentence ("I am . . . what?"), but that is what makes the name so powerful. Think about all the possibilities that could complete

> God said, "I am who I am. You must tell them: 'The one who is called I AM has sent me to you.'" (Exodus 3:14)

this sentence: the who, what, when, where, how, and why. There are an infinite number of ways for God to be. God sustains every person, place, time, and condition that exists. At the same time, God exists beyond all people, places, times, and conditions.

Many of our Jewish brothers and sisters do not even say this name of God. The ancient Israelites believed that naming someone or something gave one power over the person or thing. Out of respect for the name of God and for how beyond us he truly is, they substituted "LORD" for the name "Yahweh."

Though God is so great and beyond us, he is still close to and intimate with us. He knows every hair on our heads and every passing thought that flows through our minds. The Book of Psalms says it best:

FUN FACT

In the Bible, God often appears in the form of a cloud. When the Israelites escaped from Egypt, they followed a cloud. (See Exodus 13:20–22.) They camped in one place as long as the cloud covered the Tent of the Lord's presence. (See Numbers 9:15–23.) In the New Testament, a cloud came over Jesus, Peter, James, and John and said, "This is my own dear Son!" (Matthew 17:5).

LORD, you have examined me
    and you know me.
    You know everything I do . . .
Where could I go to escape
    from you?
    Where could I get away
      from your presence?
If I went up to heaven, you
    would be there;
    if I lay down in the world
      of the dead, you
      would be there . . .
When my bones were
    being formed,
    carefully put together in
      my mother's womb,
when I was growing there
    in secret,
    you knew that I was there—
you saw me before I was born.

    (Psalm 139:1,2,7–8,15–16)

Live It!

When reading the Bible, you'll notice that God did not just create us and then run off. He continues to care for us with truth and love. We are also called to follow God's footsteps here. Our relationships with our friends, classmates, teachers, and family are not just created and left on their own. These relationships must also grow. The only way that will happen is if, like God, we are truthful and loving. We cannot have a real relationship with someone if it is based on lies and selfishness. Those relationships fall apart. Relationships based on love and honesty last . . . just like our relationships with God.

The author of Psalm 139 expresses how deeply God knows and loves each one of us—from the earliest days in our mother's womb.

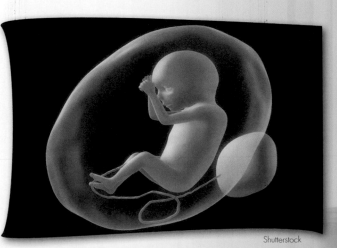

The Trinity

Long after God told Moses his name was Yahweh, he revealed much more about himself. He revealed that he is the Father, Son, and Holy Spirit—one God in three equally divine Persons who is the Holy Trinity. This is the central belief of all Christians. If this sounds confusing, don't be alarmed. (See more on the Trinity in chapter 3.) Even when God reveals himself to us, he remains a **mystery.** As hard as we try, we can't fully understand God.

Did You Know?

"Abba": Jesus' Name for His Father

In the Gospels, Jesus sometimes calls the Father **"Abba."** The language Jesus spoke was Aramaic, and *abba* is the Aramaic word for "father." This gives us an idea of the special bond Jesus has with his Father. The Father loves Jesus, much as a human father loves his children by protecting, feeding, and teaching them. Yet even the Bible sometimes portrays God's motherly characteristics. "As a mother comforts her child, so will I comfort you," says the Lord (Isaiah 66:13, NRSV). Jesus teaches us to begin our prayers with "Abba" and to share in his special close relationship with God, "our Father."

The Father

Let's explore the first Person of the Trinity—God the Father. He is far beyond any image we can conjure up in our minds. When we pray the Creed, we call the Father "almighty." No creature in the universe possesses more power. God the Father is all knowing and is everywhere. Try to imagine that. Contrary to how he is often portrayed, the Father does not have a white beard. In fact, "he" is not even a man. On the other hand, God is not a woman either. The Bible portrays God as having both masculine and feminine qualities, but still God is neither male nor female. We praise God as a loving, powerful Father, at the same time recognizing that our picture of him is incomplete.

You might wonder why we call God "Father" and "he" if he is not male. Jesus calls him "Father," and we do the same, referring to him as "he." In calling God "Father," Jesus expresses his unique relationship with him. "My Father has given me all things. No one knows the Son except the Father, and no one knows the Father except the Son and those to whom the Son chooses to reveal him" (Matthew 11:27).

We also call him "he" because we do not want to call God "it." An

"My thoughts," says the LORD, "are not like yours, and my ways are different from yours. As high as the heavens are above the earth, so high are my ways and thoughts above yours." (Isaiah 55:8–9)

THiNk About It!

Jesus called the Father "Abba" or "Father" (see the article "Abba: Jesus' Name for His Father") and said we should also do this when we pray. Jesus tells us we should rely on God as children rely on their parents. How do you rely on your parents? How do they provide for you? What are some good things you have seen fathers do for their children? How is your relationship with God like a child's relationship with his or her parents?

"it" names an object, not a person. God the Father is most certainly a distinct and special person, but unlike us, he is not a human being. Though this might seem obvious, it is important to note this difference between God and us. We should remind ourselves that God's ways are not human ways.

God the Father is not even old. The universe has been around for billions of years. You might think that because—as we confess in the Creed—he is the creator of the universe, he must be at least several billion years old, right? (See more on creation in chapter 4.) The only problem with this idea is that time itself is a part of God's creation. God lives outside time, and because he created it, he is not limited or confined by it. If this boggles your mind, do not worry. It can baffle the most intelligent minds on our planet.

Logically, one could say that God created everything in the universe, but the next step backward is the difficult one. Who made God? The answer is that no one made God. God is not a created being, but rather one who is, always was, and always will be.

Pray It!

Liturgy Connection

In Mass, have you ever noticed that most of our prayers are directed to God the Father? While our prayers do address Jesus Christ, his divine Son, they are mostly aimed at the Father. If you think about it, it makes sense. During Mass, we recall all the good things God the Father has done for us, including sending his Son. His Son, Jesus, is the greatest way for human beings to get to know the Father. We also thank God for doing this. But again, Jesus is a key part of our gratitude. We offer thanks to the Father in the same way we come to know the Father: "through Jesus Christ, our Lord."

Looking Back

The One God of the Old and New Testament

In the second century AD, a man named Marcion thought the God of the New Testament could not be the same as the one in violent stories of the Old Testament. He argued that the loving and forgiving God was revealed only by Jesus in the New Testament. Marcion did not consider what the human authors of the Old Testament thought about God. The Old Testament writers pictured him this way because they thought of God as a warrior who protected his people when they were good. Without considering the intentions of the human authors, people like Marcion can misunderstand the Scriptures. The Church Fathers (the leaders of the early Church) declared that Marcion was incorrect and emphasized that there is only one true God of both the Old and New Testaments.

If this somehow doesn't make sense, again do not worry. This is why we call God a mystery. A religious mystery is not like a story the reader has just not figured out. Rather this kind of **mystery** refers to a truth so big that no human being can completely know or understand it.

God Is Truth and Love

Throughout time, God has revealed himself to us. He is Yahweh. God is Father, Son, and Holy Spirit, three divine Persons in one being. He is Truth and Love.

God is Truth simply because what he tells us is true. We can trust God's Word. God is someone we can count on, more than even the most trusted human being you know. God always keeps his promises.

God is also Love. First and foremost, God created us out of love. God is like a husband and wife

"Whoever does not love does not know God, for God is love." (1 John 4:8)

who become parents so they can share their love with their child. God's love does not end at creation, though. The Bible is filled with stories describing what God has done for us. Even though we human beings have failed to keep our part of the bargain, God forgives us and continues to be faithful to his people. Most important, God became man out of love for us. The Father gave his only Son and sent his Spirit to be with us always. There is no greater sign of love than this.

Imagine being held in the arms of God! God holds each one of us in his loving embrace, as a mother loves her child.

Illustration by Elizabeth Wang, "the Father loves each one of us with a passionate love, and holds us in His tender embrace," copyright © Radiant Light 2008, www.radiantlight.org.uk

THE HOLY TRINITY

Think of the many different ways you have reached out to God in the past. There may have been times when you wanted the comfort of the all-knowing Father, who could help you see everything was going to be okay. Maybe you wanted someone who could move mountains and change lives. Other times you may have reached out to God when you were confused. Maybe you wanted God to inspire you or reveal his wishes to you. Of course there were times when you just wanted God to know you were in pain. Alone or sad, you wanted God just

> The grace of the Lord Jesus Christ, the love of God, and the fellowship of the Holy Spirit be with you all. (2 Corinthians 13:13)

We share in the life and love of the Trinity. Pictures like this one help us to imagine our relationship with the Father, Son, and Holy Spirit, three Persons in one God.

Illustration by Elizabeth Wang, "Sharing the life of the Holy Trinity," copyright © Radiant Light 2008, www.radiantlight.org.uk

THiNK ABoUT It!

When making the Sign of the Cross, we say, "In the name of the Father, and of the Son, and of the Holy Spirit." We also move our hands in the shape of a cross on our head, chest, and shoulders. Why do you think the Sign of the Cross connects the Trinity and Jesus' sacrifice on the cross? How are each of the three divine Persons of the Trinity connected to Jesus' death, Resurrection, and Ascension?

to be there with you. It is like having a friend to listen to you—someone who has gone through the same pain and suffering as you. The good news is that God is all of these!

One God, Three Persons

"In the name of the Father, and of the Son, and of the Holy Spirit." How many times have you said or heard these words? Have you ever really thought about what the phrase means? During Mass on Sundays, Catholics stand to say the Creed. Together we state, "We believe in one God . . . " But if someone thinks the Father, Son, and Holy Spirit are three separate individuals, he or she would be misunderstanding the central aspect of our faith.

The earliest Christians were Jewish followers of Jesus. Because they were Jewish, they knew there could be only one God. One of the most basic prayers of the Jewish faith is taken from the Book of Deuteronomy, as follows: "Hear, O Israel: The LORD is our God, the LORD alone. You shall love the LORD your God with all your heart, and with all your soul, and with all your might" (6:4–5, NRSV). Yet these Jewish Christians knew that Jesus was the Son of God and was one with the Father. They were also aware that the Hebrew Scriptures—our Old Testament—spoke of the Spirit of God. Through these experiences, they realized that the one true God revealed himself as three Persons: the Trinity.

> In the beginning the Word already existed; the Word was with God, and the Word was God. From the very beginning the Word was with God. Through him God made all things. (John 1:1–3)

The central mystery of our Christian life and faith is the Trinity. God has made himself known to us in the three divine Persons of the **Trinity:** the Father, the Son, and the Holy Spirit. Yet these three Persons are all one God. The Father, Son, and Holy Spirit cannot be separated from one another. If this seems confusing, do not worry! This belief is a mystery—something beyond the ability of human beings to understand completely.

The Trinity is not divided into three parts. For example, a baseball team is made up of a pitcher, catcher, first baseman, and so on. When all nine players are assembled, you have a complete baseball team. This is not so for the Trinity.

PRAY IT!

In the name of the Father, who created everyone I love and all I know; and of the Son, who became a human being like me, and showed me the right way to live; and of the Holy Spirit, who inspires me with courage and creativity; you are my one God. In you I place my trust.

Amen

Each Person of the Trinity does not make up one-third of the whole God. Instead, the complete presence of God can be found in each of them. The Father, Son, and Holy Spirit cannot be separated from one another.

If you have ever watched a pair of truly great dancers in action, it almost seems as if you are watching just one dancer. They move in complete harmony together. When one dancer lifts the other, it seems as if there is no effort. Each move flows naturally into the next. It seems as though the two blend into one single dancer.

In a similar, but far more real, way, the three Persons of the Trinity live in complete harmony. They are distinct Persons, yet they are completely united. Unlike the dancers, they are not united just by their actions. They are also united by what they are: one divine being.

FUN FACT

The Bible often refers to God as the Father, the Son, and the Holy Spirit, but it never uses the word Trinity to describe them. Instead, this word comes from Sacred Tradition. All the major Christian traditions believe in the Trinity.

KEY WORDS

Trinity
God the Father
Son of God
Holy Spirit

The Work of the Trinity

The Father, Son, and Holy Spirit are one God. Therefore all the works of God are done by all three Persons. However, some of God's works are more strongly associated with either the Father, the Son, or the Holy Spirit.

God the Father is the first Person of the Blessed Trinity. When we say God created the earth, we tend to think of God the Father as the Creator. This is true, but remember, it is also true that the Son and the Holy Spirit created the world. Like a parent, the Father is the source from which life comes. It is natural to think of God the Father when we think of the Creator.

God the Son is the second person of the Blessed Trinity, Jesus Christ. The **Son of God** is the title often given to Jesus Christ. We also call Jesus Christ the "Savior" to recognize his saving actions on our behalf. But we cannot forget that the Father and the Holy Spirit also save us.

Did You Know?
The Sign of the Cross

Christians have been making the Sign of the Cross for almost two thousand years. In the early days of Christianity, Christians moved their thumbs across their foreheads in the shape of a cross. It was a reminder to carry the cross of Christ in their lives. In other words, we are called to sacrifice ourselves to help others. During the times and in the places Christianity was illegal, making the Sign of the Cross became a secret way for Christians to recognize one another. Today, we Catholics often make the Sign of the Cross when we enter the Church. We dip our fingers into the holy water to make the Sign of the Cross. It reminds us of our Baptisms.

There are different kinds of spiritual gifts, but the same Spirit gives them. . . . The Spirit's presence is shown in some way in each person for the good of all. (1 Corinthians 12:4,7)

The Trinity is a never-ending circle of love. Family members mirror the love of the Trinity when they share love with one another. What if the whole world knew about this circle of love?

© Richard Hutchings/CORBIS

God the **Holy Spirit** is the third Person of the Blessed Trinity, who inspires, guides, and makes the lives of the believers holy. The Gifts of the Holy Spirit are truly given by the Father and the Son too. Yet it is proper to recognize the gifts as being from the Holy Spirit.

The Trinity is a Communion

Because God is three divine Persons in one, the Trinity is the communion of those three persons. Another way of saying this is that the Father, Son, and Holy Spirit are completely in union with each other. They communicate perfectly and are in perfect harmony.

Because the Trinity is a perfect communion of the three divine Persons, we can see how the Trinity is the perfect community. The love and unity that the Father, Son, and Holy Spirit share are so perfect that they flow out to us. Our families share in this love and community. The love of a mother and father extends past themselves to the children they share. When they do this, that love can extend even past the family. The love in our families should flow out in service to the rest of the community and the entire world.

Live It!

The Trinity is a community that lives in complete harmony, unity, and love. Unlike the Trinity, human families are not perfect communities. But you can work toward creating a home of harmony, unity, and love by doing some simple things. For example, you might do your chores without being asked. This might seem like a typical corny response an adult would give. But what would happen if you did? Your parents would quit riding your back about taking out the trash. You wouldn't have to listen to them complain. The house would smell a lot better too! Doesn't that sound like a more harmonious community to you? This is only one way of making a home of unity, harmony, and love. However you do it, it will take some work, but the payoff is divine!

"Go then, to all peoples everywhere and make them my disciples: baptize them in the name of the Father, the Son, and the Holy Spirit, and teach them to obey everything I have commanded you. And I will be with you always, to the end of the age."

(Matthew 28:19–20)

PEOPLE OF FAITH
Saint Patrick

© 2009 Saint Mary's Press/Illustration by Vicki Shuck

Saint Patrick was born in the fourth century AD in what later became Britain. As a youth Patrick was kidnapped and taken to Ireland, where he became the slave of a warlord for several years. At that time Ireland was a rough place to live. The Irish tribes were often at war, slavery was common, and human sacrifice was practiced. After several years, Patrick either escaped or was released. He returned home,

Stockphoto

Saint Patrick used a shamrock to teach people about the Trinity. What does a shamrock have in common with the Trinity?

where he soon became a Christian priest. Later Patrick returned to Ireland, the land of his former captors, to preach the Gospel. This was an extremely brave step. Ireland certainly had been a difficult place for him earlier, and at that time, few people had traveled to such a foreign place to convert others to Christianity. He bravely went and later was appointed the Bishop of Ireland.

Patrick planted the seeds of Christianity in Ireland. Over the next few decades, the practices of both slavery and human sacrifice ended in Ireland. Legends say Patrick used a shamrock to explain the Trinity to the Irish people. Like the three Persons united in one God, the shamrock is made up of three leaves united to make this single, unique plant. Today Patrick is remembered for his courage, his strong faith, and of course, the shamrock—the symbol he used to teach about the one true God.

4 CREATION

A falling star in the night sky away from city lights. A beaver building a dam. People doing good things for others. Friends having fun together. A family gathering to celebrate a special occasion. Have these or any other things ever made you recognize God's goodness? Have you ever wondered where everything that exists has come from? Have you wondered why you exist or where you came from? Do you sometimes question where the world is headed or where life is taking you?

Beautiful scenes of nature are like billboards from God: See how much I love you! I created a world this awesome for you!

iStockphoto

In the beginning, when God created the heavens and the earth, the earth was a formless void and darkness covered the face of the deep, while a wind from God swept over the face of the waters. Then God said, "Let there be light"; and there was light. (Genesis 1:1–3, NRSV)

The first line of the Bible is a good place to begin looking for some answers. Genesis 1:1 proclaims that God created the heavens and the earth. **"Heaven and earth"** is a way of referring to the entire universe. This passage from Genesis says God is the creator of all that exists. Everything depends on God. He created out of nothing and without help. The universe is not the result of fate or blind chance.

Scientists work on figuring out the physical nature of the universe. This includes trying to determine how big it is, how old it is, and what chemicals make it up. Why did God create the universe, the earth, and all living things? Why did God create us? Science can't answer these questions. The good news is that God can answer them. He has revealed to us that he created everything because of love.

God didn't have to create the world. It was a free choice motivated by love. He wanted to share his love with his creatures. That includes you. **Creation** is a gift, and all creation is

Pray It!

Lord,
God of all creation,
thank you for everything you have created and everything you have given me. Help me recognize my own goodness. Continue to bless me and everyone else as we strive to understand your will for our lives and as we care for all creation.
Amen

good. God wants everyone to share in his wisdom, beauty, and goodness and to live in union with him. He desires a personal, loving relationship with everyone. He created the world and all of us so we might share in his glory.

THiNk About It!

Catholics are called to be "co-workers" with God in the work of creation. What does this mean? Identify some examples of things people your age can do that help make the world around us what God wants it to be.

Why Does Evil Exist?

The things that help us recognize the goodness of God's creation are only part of the reality we know. Our world includes evil too. We see signs of this in such things as war and violence, people doing selfish and hateful things, nature spoiled by pollution, and people in many parts of the world suffering because they lack food, shelter, and other necessities. Why does evil exist when God created everything to be good? If you have ever wondered about this question, you are not alone.

Part of the mystery of creation is that God makes good things happen, even in evil situations. This doesn't turn evil into goodness. It does, however, give us confidence that God would not allow an evil to happen if it were not possible for something good to come of it. Even though we can expect to continue to struggle to understand why evil exists, we trust that we will fully understand God's plan after we die. We'll see God face to face and come to understand his ways of guiding the world.

Our trust and hope are rooted in Jesus Christ. His suffering and death on a cross—his execution—were great evils, but that was not the end of the story. An amazing good followed. Jesus was raised from the dead. He invites us to share in his new life.

We know that the final end to evil has not yet happened, but we live with the faith that it will. At that time God's plan for the world and for us will be fully realized.

Sin

One reason helps explain why some evil exists, and that reason is human sin. God created all people, "making them to be like himself" (Genesis 1:26). Another way to say this is we are created in God's image. This means we were created for love. For our love to be genuine, it must be something we freely choose to do. Think about it. If loving behavior is simply programmed into us, it isn't really love, is it?

Most of us are not major polluters. But any sin is like poisoning the delicate balance in the environment of love God created. Even a small sin has a ripple effect. Can you think of an example?

iStockphoto

Because we have the freedom to choose to love, we also have the freedom to choose the opposite. We can choose to do things that are unloving. These choices separate us from God and from one another.

Another word for this type of action is *sin*. Sins also include things we should do but choose not to. Our sins can lead to results that harm other people and God's creation. Unfortunately, sin is a reality that affects us all.

Adam and Eve, our first parents, whom we hear about in the Book of Genesis, rejected God's love in the Garden of Eden. By doing this they disrupted God's plan for creation. The good news, however, is that God did not abandon us as a result. His plan for creation continues to unfold in history. God's creation is not finished yet. He continues to work to bring about the loving relationships he desires.

The high point of God's plan for creation is Jesus Christ. God became man to save us. Christ is sometimes called the "new creation," because he came to give us new life. He came to restore and deepen our union with God.

PRAY IT!
Liturgy Connection

Notice the bread and wine as they are carried to the altar during the Presentation of the Gifts next time you are at Mass. These are God's gifts to us more than our gifts to God. We are simply giving back to God the things he has already given us. The gifts are from the earth (the grain for the bread) and the vine (the grapes for the wine). They are also the work of human hands, because we work to make bread from grain and wine from grapes. These gifts are signs of the goodness of God and of our cooperation with God. They are signs of our dependence on God's creation for our physical lives—just as we depend on God for our spiritual lives.

The Journey of Creation

It is helpful to keep in mind that creation is not simply one event that happened a long time ago. God's love and presence are never-ending, and his work of creation keeps going. One way to imagine this is to think of the universe on a journey. God has a map for the journey and is guiding creation to a final end. Can you imagine all things being perfect and everyone being completely happy? This is the destiny of the human race. Everything has been created for us. This means that among all creatures, human beings are most valuable in God's eyes. This special place in creation comes with a responsibility.

Did You Know?
The Role of the Trinity in Creation

When Catholics talk about God as Creator, we are referring to all three Persons of the Trinity—Father, Son, and Holy Spirit. We associate Creation most closely with God the Father, but it is important to remember that the Father, Son, and Holy Spirit together are one God. If we think of the Father creating alone, we can make the mistake of thinking Jesus Christ and the Holy Spirit came into being after the Father and are not one with him, even today. Saint Irenaeus offers a helpful image. He emphasizes that creation is the work of all three Persons of the Trinity by referring to the Son and the Spirit as the hands of the Father. God the Father keeps the universe going through his Word, Jesus Christ, and through the creative power of the Holy Spirit, the Giver of Life.

An equilateral triangle is sometimes used as a symbol for the Trinity. The three sides are the same length. They indicate that all three Persons—Father, Son and Holy Spirit—are equal. The one triangle emphasizes that the Persons are unified and that they are one God.

We trust in God's plan, but that doesn't mean we go about our lives just waiting for it to unfold. We have a part to play. We have a special role on this journey. We must keep our eyes open so we recognize God's presence in our lives and the world around us. What's more, we are called to cooperate with God and be his coworkers. This means we share in the responsibility of helping the world around us be what God wants it to be—a place where love rules. Our challenge is to think about God's desires for the world and all his creatures. We must make choices about our relationships and our care of the earth that are in line with God's will. We don't do this on our own, however, apart from God. Through the Holy Spirit, God is always at work in our actions.

"I am putting you in charge of the fish, the birds, and all the wild animals."
(Genesis 1:28)

God created the world, and it was good. How do we help one another to restore the world to a place of peace and harmony where love rules? Why is care of the earth so important to peace among all God's people?

© Images.com/Corbis

The Seen and the Unseen

When we say the Nicene Creed, we describe God as the maker of both what we see and what we can't see. We recognize there is more to creation than the material things we can see and touch. Knowing of an unseen part of reality opens us up to the miraculous. It helps us understand that God is present and at work, even if we do not see any signs. Although we must be careful about making too many assumptions about the unseen aspects of creation, we know about one thing for certain: the existence of **angels.**

Did You Know?

Creation and Creationism

Perhaps you have heard the word *creationism* in news stories about how the creation of the world is covered in public school classrooms. Creationists read the Bible like a science textbook and believe that the accounts of the Creation in Genesis are scientifically accurate. Creationists believe God created everything in a matter of days. This leads them to completely discount evolution, the scientific theory that life has changed over time from earlier forms of life. Catholic teaching about Creation is different from creationism. Catholics don't read Genesis like a science textbook. The biblical authors didn't write scientific reports. If we read them that way, we miss the main points and set up unintended conflicts between faith and science.

Angels are as real as you and me, but they are beings of spirit, not matter. They have intelligence, will, and individuality, and they are immortal. The word *angel* comes from a Greek word that means "messenger." Angels are God's servants and messengers. They glorify God without ceasing and watch over each of us every moment of our lives.

PEOPLE OF FAITH
Saint Francis of Assisi

© 2009 Saint Mary's Press/Illustration by Vicki Shuck

Can you imagine giving away your possessions and choosing to live in poverty? That's just what Saint Francis did. He was born into a wealthy family in Italy in the twelfth century AD. Early in his life, Francis wanted to be popular and wealthy. In his twenties he spent time as a prisoner of war and then had a serious illness. While he was recovering, he had a dream that urged him to follow Jesus.

Live It!

Keep a camera with you for a few days and snap photos of things that offer glimpses of the goodness of creation. Create a slide show or photo collage and share it with friends or family.

Francis felt called to live more as Jesus had lived. His values changed, and he started to live in a simpler way. He began to spend more of his time praying, preaching, and giving to the poor. Francis's father, a successful cloth merchant, wasn't happy with his son's new way of life. After Francis sold some expensive cloth from the family business to raise funds to rebuild a chapel, his father took him to court. Francis repaid the money, gave back his fine clothes, and gave up his share of his family's wealth. Many people were attracted to Francis's preaching and his simple manner of living and began to follow him. This community evolved into the religious order known today as the Franciscans.

Francis is known also for his love of creation, including animals. He is the patron saint of environmentalists. We celebrate his feast day on October 4.

THE HUMAN PERSON

Steven was a seven-year-old boy much like most other kids his age. There was one big difference, though. Most days after school, when his friends went home to play, Steven went to the hospital for regular medical treatments. Steven had leukemia, a type of cancer that lived in his blood.

When they first found out about his illness, Steven and his family were angry. They wondered why God would let this happen to him. The young boy did not

Have you ever considered why bad things, like the serious illness of a child, often bring out the best in families and communities?

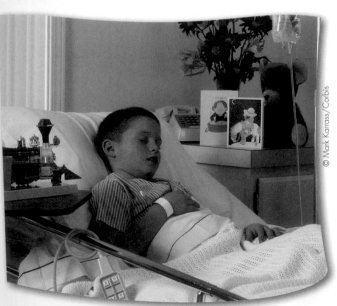

© Mark Karrass/Corbis

do anything to deserve it. But as time moved along, Steven and his family became amazed by all the help they received. They no longer thought much about why it had happened. Family members, friends, classmates, teachers, church members, doctors, nurses, and many other people helped him and his family. Even people whom Steven had never met played a big role in helping him regain his health.

After a while, Steven and his family were no longer angry with God. They no longer spent their time wondering why this had happened to Steven. They were just grateful to God for the help that came from so many good peple.

Being Human

Being human is a confusing, joyful, exciting, and painful experience. There is so much to experience in a single lifetime. We are so busy doing things, we often forget to stop and look at the meaning of the events that occur.

Being human means a number of things. First of all, it means we are not God. We are limited to our own experiences and cannot see things from God's perspective. We do not always understand why things happen the way they do, especially the difficult or painful times. Being human also means we are not perfect. We all make bad decisions sometimes.

FUN FACT

In the Book of Genesis, the name that God gives the first human being is Adam. This is an appropriate name because *Adam* comes from the Hebrew word for "man." Eve's name is just as appropriate, because it comes from a Hebrew word that means "life."

Pray It!

God,
Everything you have
created is good.
Every human
being is your child,
including me.
Like all human
beings, I am good
because I am made to
be like you.
Even when I do
something wrong, you
love me.
Please give me the cour-
age to do what you have
created me to do.
Help me see others as
you see them.
Help me forgive others as
you forgive them.
Help me love others as
you love me.
Amen

Being human is not all dark and dreary. It means we are not alone. More than six billion of us live here on earth. We have one another to be our friends, families, and companions. Being human also means we are made in God's image. We all have the ability to love and care for one another. For the most part, that is what we do.

We Are Both, Not Just One

The **human person** is a living being made up of both a physical body and an immortal, spiritual soul. A **soul** is the spiritual element that gives humans life and survives after death. Our soul is created by God at the moment of conception. After our death our soul will be reunited with our resurrected body at the final Resurrection. It is important to remember that humans are not just physical bodies. God created us to be both body and soul, existing together in perfect unity.

Having fun with friends gives us a sign of how God made us—to be in relationship with one another.

iStockphoto

You may notice that many young people look like their parents in some way. They might have similar-sounding voices or similar facial features. Sometimes they have the same color eyes or hair. That is because physical bodies are determined to a great extent by the parents' genes. When God made Adam, he formed the soil into his body and then breathed life into him (see Genesis 2:7). Like Adam, we also have God's breath or spirit within us. Each of us has a soul that comes from God and that is united with our bodies when we are conceived in our mothers' wombs. Although our bodies will one day get old and die, our souls never will.

When God created Adam, he did not want Adam to be alone, so God created a companion for him. God does not want us to be alone, either. Just as the Trinity is a communion of Persons in loving relationship with each

Did You Know?

Not Just Our Souls

The Catholic Church is concerned not only with things like praying and going to church. The Church cares about all different parts of human life. For example, in 1891, Pope Leo XIII demanded that working people be paid appropriately and treated with dignity by their employers. In 1963, Pope John XXIII wrote a letter that addressed human rights, freedom, and world peace. In 1995, Pope John Paul II addressed a number of human life issues, such as abortion and the death penalty. In 2007, the Vatican (the Church's headquarters) even gave us ten commandments for driving to encourage us to be safe and responsible when we are in our cars. Because human beings are both physical and spiritual, the Church cares about all parts of human life, not just our souls.

So God created human beings, making them to be like himself. . . . God looked at everything he had made, and he was very pleased. (Genesis 1:27,31)

other, we are created to be in loving relationships with other people. The biggest evidence of this is that God created human beings to be male and female. Men and women are created to be equal but still different. Men are particularly good at some things. Women are especially good at others. God created us so men and women would need each other and bond together in close relationships. The Bible's story of Creation explains why human beings need communities, especially families.

THINK ABOUT IT!

God is not male or female. God is not a human being. God does not even have the same kind of physical presence humans have. But you are made in the image of God. There is something special about you that is like God. What makes you like God? What can you do that is similar to what God does?

Original Sin

The story of Adam and Eve explains how human beings were meant to live and how we fell away from God's plan. Adam and Eve represent the first human beings. At first, Adam and Eve were at peace with God and every living thing on the earth. They were happy and free. There was no pain or suffering.

Adam and Eve had only one rule to follow. God said, "You may eat the fruit of any tree in the garden, except the tree that gives knowledge of what is good and what is bad" (Genesis 2:16–17). Tempted by the serpent, they thought that by eating from this tree, they could know what God knows. Adam and Eve chose to disobey God. The first parents of the human race wrongly decided they could be happy without God and his guidance.

Key Words

human person

soul

Original Sin

temptation

As a result, human beings were banished from the Garden of Eden. We separated ourselves from God. Because of Adam and Eve's choice, they and every human being since then—except Jesus and Mary—no longer has had that same perfect relationship with God. We have lost the freedom and the holiness human beings were meant to have.

This condition is called **Original Sin.** Original Sin means two things. First of all, it is the sin that Adam and Eve committed. Second, it is the sinful condition that all human beings have from birth. The first human beings' own wrongdoing wounded them. Now no one is able to enjoy that perfect relationship with God that Adam and Eve once had. This wound, or the sinful condition of Original Sin, has now been passed on to every human being.

A **temptation** is something that makes sinful things seem fun, exciting, or even good to do. Original Sin makes it hard for human beings to say no to temptation. For example, have you ever seen someone drop money from a pocket while walking away? If no one was nearby, you might have felt the temptation to pick up the money and keep it. Original

Sin is what makes us want to be selfish rather than do what is good. It makes us think of our own pleasure instead of doing what is right.

You might think that having Original Sin is not fair. Since the time of Adam and Eve, not one person has done anything to deserve Original Sin. It is much like the sick boy in the introduction to this chapter. He did not do anything to deserve the disease he had. He didn't learn how or decide to be sick. We sometimes do not know why some people get illnesses. Similarly, how Original Sin is transmitted is a mystery we do not fully understand. But we do know that it is passed on from one generation to the next. Except for Jesus and his mother, Mary, it is a sin that affects every person, not a sin that we have committed.

Even though we all have the wound of Original Sin, we are not born evil. We are still created in God's image and have the desire to be united with God and to be good. Even though Original Sin affects us all, it does not stop us from returning to God.

"Everybody does it." The temptation to cheat is an example of how Original Sin affects all of us. But the truth is we were born to be good. As Jesus said, "The truth will set you free."

iStockphoto

Coming from God, Heading Toward God

Have you have ever been away from home for a long time? Then you might know what it feels like to be homesick and want to return to the place where you are loved and things are familiar. This is also true in people's spiritual lives. Being with God is our true home. Returning to God is what will make us happy. Our worries and spiritual restlessness are kinds of spiritual homesickness.

This is why we have the Church. Human beings are all religious in the sense that we are all trying to find our spiritual homes. It is our job to help ourselves and others realize that being with God is our true home. This does not mean God has left us. Even though we cannot physically see him, God is still with us.

Christ is the model of the perfect human being. It is our destiny to live as he did. Christ may be invisible to us, but we can see Christ at work when people do his will.

PRAY IT!
Liturgy Connection

During Mass comes a moment when the priest pours a little bit of water into the wine. As he does this, he whispers something that usually the people in the church cannot hear. He says, "By the mystery of this water and wine, may we come to share in the divinity of Christ, who humbled himself to share in our humanity." This mixing of the water and wine is a gesture that reminds us that the Son of God, the second person of the Trinity, became one of us. The priest is also saying humans are supposed to share in the divinity of Christ. We do that by receiving the Eucharist and also by living our faith so one day we will once again be in union with God.

There is one God and Father of all people, who is Lord of all, works through all, and is in all. (Ephesians 4:6)

The doctors and nurses who help people battle illnesses are examples of how we can see the work of our invisible God. By doing God's will, we can become the way others are able to see God's work. The following prayer, thought to be written by Saint Teresa of Ávila, says it best:

LIVE IT!

Every human being is made in the image of God. This is one of the most important things to remember when dealing with other people, especially people you do not like. It is easy to see the good in your friends and in those who do nice things for you. But God asks us to be good even to those whom we do not like. For example, when people insult you, it hurts. You might want to strike back in the same way they hurt you. But when you do this, you have sunk to their level. You have done the same thing they did. If you were to respond with understanding and kindness, though, you would acknowledge that these people are worthy of the same respect you deserve. When you do this, you allow them to see the image of God within you.

An act of kindness is one way of being Christ's Body here on earth. When we help others, we are being the people God created us to be.

© Anna Peisl/zefa/Corbis

Christ has no body now but yours,
    no hands but yours,
    no feet but yours.
Yours are the eyes through which
    Christ's compassion must look out on the world;
Yours are the feet with which
    He is to go about doing good.
Yours are the hands with which
    He is to bless us now.

Looking Back

Created from Love, for Love

The Book of Genesis has two different Creation stories. The first story is about the seven days of Creation. It was written around the sixth century B.C. At that time the Israelites had been captured and were being held in Babylonia. There they learned about the Babylonian creation story. It is a fierce tale where many gods battle one another to create the universe. The Babylonians believed that one of their gods, Marduk, made human beings from the blood vessels of a demon. Their creation story teaches that humans were made simply to be slaves to the gods. Guided by the Holy Spirit, the Israelites responded by writing the beautiful Creation stories that reveal what the true God is like. The world and human beings were created out of love, not from violence and bloodshed. We are created in God's image, not as slaves but rather to be God's partners in caring for creation.

6 GOD'S PLAN FOR SALVATION

Trust is an extremely important part of life. We trust people so often that we often do not even think about it. We trust that our parents will have food for us to eat. We trust that our teachers will tell us the correct information. We trust that other drivers will obey the traffic laws. We trust that our friends will keep our private talks a secret. To ensure this trust, we sometimes make promises to each other.

Imagine what life would be like if you could trust no one. What would be different about getting in a

Trust is one of the most important qualities in a friendship. Our relationship with God is one friendship we can always trust. He always keeps his promises.

© Comstock/Corbis

car? How would your friendships change if you could not trust anyone with your secrets? What would it be like if you could not count on your parents to provide for you? Sooner or later, you would probably become isolated and lonely. You would travel less. talk less. rely on others less.

Fortunately, God is not like that. God is someone we can trust. Trusting God brings us closer to him. Throughout history he has made promises that he keeps. On the other hand, we human beings have not always kept our part of the bargains. That is when things fall apart. Despite our sins and weaknesses, God is always faithful in his promise to save us from sin and death. We can trust God, because he has always been faithful to his promises.

Salvation History

PRAY IT!

God,

People are not perfect.

My parents make mistakes.

My friends do not always do what they promise.

Teachers tell us to act one way, but even they sometimes act differently.

I am glad I have you to trust.

Even though I do not always understand your ways, I know you keep your promises.

Thank you.

Amen

Salvation history is the pattern of events in human history through which God makes his presence and saving actions known to us. If you think about it, that includes all of history—everything that's already happened and everything that will happen in the future. The Bible reveals God's plan for salvation by focusing on his Chosen People in the Old Testament and on Jesus Christ in the New Testament.

When God makes a covenant with someone, the person's name is often changed. The new name symbolizes the new relationship with God. For example, Abram became Abraham and his wife, Sarai, became Sarah. Jacob took on the name Israel.

Imagine a timeline where we could see the ups and downs of salvation history as told in the Bible. It would probably look like a roller coaster. Though God is always faithful to his promises, his Chosen People were not always faithful to their promises. There were the times when they followed God's will. When this happened, things tended to work out better. When they did not follow God's will, life got pretty difficult.

"When the rainbow appears in the clouds, I will see it and remember the everlasting covenant between me and all living beings on earth." (Genesis 9:16)

We human beings today still are not always faithful to our covenant with God. We are still on this roller coaster ride. We can count on one thing. Although human beings do not always hold up their end of the bargain, God keeps his promises.

God chose a rainbow as a sign of the promise he made with all living things that he would never again destroy the earth.

Shutterstock

God Gives Second Chances

In the Old Testament, we can read about the first promises and covenants God made with people. When God created Adam and Eve, he made them a promise. They would live in happiness with him forever, as long as they obeyed him. Sadly, Adam and Eve disobeyed God by eating from the forbidden tree. Then they were driven out of the Garden of Eden. Humans had separated themselves from God.

This does not mean God abandoned them. He still loved Adam and Eve. But as time passed, God became more and more unhappy with human conduct. He was angry at everyone except for a man named Noah. With a flood God wiped out all the human wickedness

Did You Know?

Jesus Christ Saves All

Did you know the Catholic Church does not condemn the people of non-Christian religions? Salvation is possible for anyone, whether they are Catholic or not. Christ is the savior of all people. The Church has stated that non-Christians who "sincerely seek God and moved by grace strive by their deeds to do his will" may achieve eternal salvation (*Dogmatic Constitution on the Church [Lumen Gentium]*, number 16). This does not mean every religion is equal. The full truth and grace needed for salvation can be found only in the Catholic Church. It does mean no one is out of reach for God in his plan of salvation.

Key Words

salvation history

covenant

Ten Commandments

from the earth. Afterward, only Noah and his family remained.

God then made a covenant with Noah. A **covenant** is a sacred agreement between people, or between God and a human being, where everyone vows to keep a promise forever. God promised Noah never to destroy the human race with a flood again. The Bible identifies the rainbow as the symbol of that covenant.

Despite their sins, God still promised salvation to his people. Like a good parent, he cares for his children. He gives them a second chance. Even when we do something wrong, God still loves us. He continues to give all of us second chances when we do something wrong.

THiNk AbouT It!

When God appears, it can be scary. When God makes his covenant with Abraham, the Bible says "fear and terror came over him" (Genesis 15:12). When Jonah hears God, he runs the other way (See Jonah 1:3). When Jesus' disciples hear God on the mountaintop, they "were so terrified" (Matthew 17:6). God speaks because he wants us to know something new or act differently. That can be scary. What do you think God wants you to do differently? Why might that be scary?

God's Covenant with Abraham

Throughout history God has called certain individuals to lead his people back to him. The first of these is Abraham, the father of our faith, from whom God established his people. When God calls Abraham, both he and his wife, Sarah, are already old. They never were able to have children.

God makes a covenant with Abraham. He promises to give him land and many descendants, who will be a blessing to all people. In return, Abraham promises to be faithful to God. Abraham's many descendants became God's people, the Israelites.

One of the most important Israelites was Moses. Moses led the Israelites out of slavery in Egypt. After the Israelites escaped into the desert, Moses received the laws from God. Through Moses, God told the Israelites how he wanted them to live. These laws guided all parts of the Israelites' daily lives and were their part of the Covenant promise they made with God. The **Ten Commandments** are the summary of these laws that guide people on how God wants us to live.

And the LORD said to himself, "I will not hide from Abraham what I am going to do. His descendants will become a great and mighty nation, and through him I will bless all the nations." (Genesis 18:17–18)

PRAY IT!
Liturgy Connection

Every year the Easter Vigil is celebrated on the Saturday evening before Easter Sunday. It begins the Church's remembrance of Jesus' Resurrection. It is also special for two other reasons. First, we welcome new members into the Church on this night. Second, during the Easter Vigil, we also recall God's saving actions throughout history. There are as many as seven readings from the Bible. They recall the seven days of Creation, the Israelites crossing the Red Sea, the prophets pointing the way toward the Messiah, and Christ's Passion, death, and Resurrection.

In this liturgy we get an overview of God's plan of salvation. The Easter Vigil is a dramatic thanksgiving for all God has done for us. Next Easter ask your parents to take you.

Bill Wittman

The Ten Commandments are as important today as they were in the time of Moses. They are like a Top Ten list for living in good relationship with God and with each other.

God Fulfills His Promise

All through history, God has been faithful to his promise of salvation. When we human beings have gone astray, he has sent his prophets to guide us. In his greatest act of salvation, God became one of us. In the New Testament, we can read how he fully revealed himself by sending his only Son. Through his Son, Jesus Christ, he established the covenant forever. This is sometimes called the New Covenant, but it is really the fulfillment of the covenant God made with Noah, Abraham, and the Chosen People. You will read much more about Jesus in later chapters.

The Good News that God's promise of salvation was now fulfilled in Jesus Christ was preached to everyone. Jesus gave his Apostles the power to carry on his mission. They passed on their work to others. They passed it down too. This continued down through the centuries all the way to us today. The Holy Spirit continues to guide the Church and will do so until Christ returns. When Christ returns, God's promise of salvation will be complete.

LiVe It!

There are no excuses when it comes to doing God's work. Some of the greatest figures in the Bible seem at first like they aren't well suited to what God asks of them. Abraham and Sarah are too old to have children. Yet God chooses them to be the parents of a new nation. Moses is a poor speaker. God still makes him God's spokesman. The prophet Jeremiah says he is too young. Yet God knows he will become a great leader.

You are also a part of God's plan of salvation. You have a special task to do. Each morning think of one thing you can do to help another person. You could make sure your car is always stocked with bottled water ready to hand out to someone in need. You could help a friend prepare for a test. There are countless possibilities, even if at first you don't think you're the right person for the job.

FAITH: RESPONDING TO GOD

Often people say you need to have faith. They tell each other, "Keep the faith" or "Have faith in God." Has anyone ever asked you the question "Do you have faith in God?" Have you ever considered what your response would be? Maybe your first thought was, "Yes. Of course I do!" If so, that is a fine answer. Maybe this is the first time you have ever thought about it, and you do not have a quick answer. That is okay too. Having faith does not mean you have all the answers. In fact, just considering the question is one of the first steps of faith. This chapter will look into what having faith means. Afterward, you may realize you have more faith than you thought you did.

Some of life's most difficult questions are matters of faith. God does not expect us to have all the answers.

Shutterstock

What Is Faith?

Throughout history God has called upon people to follow his will. **Faith** is the way people respond to God's call. On a simple level, faith means a belief in God. For Christians it means more than that. Faith is believing and accepting that God made himself known to us through his words and actions, especially through Jesus Christ. It is accepting God's truth with our minds, but more than that. Faith is something that guides our entire lives. It is the way we live in harmony with what God has taught us.

In a way it would be simple to say, "I believe that Jesus Christ is the Son of God, who is our Savior." It would be easy if that was all that was required for salvation. But having faith also requires us to live our lives based on this belief. Following is a short story that makes this point.

A two-year-old boy is playing on a wooden playground structure that has all sorts of slides, swings, and ropes to climb. He runs toward a ledge near where his father is standing. As he gets closer to the ledge, his father smiles and moves closer, because he knows exactly what is going to happen. The little boy stops at the edge of the five-foot drop and starts to laugh. Then he throws his arms up over his head and flings his body into the air toward his father. As

FUN FACT

Laughter is a sign of great faith. God promises Abraham and Sarah they are going to be the parents of many descendants. But they are so old that Sarah laughs at the thought. Abraham and Sarah keep their faith in God. So when their son is born, they name him Isaac, a Hebrew name that means "laughter."

PRAY IT!

Jesus, I am like the man who cried out to you, "I do have faith, but not enough. Help me have more!" (Mark 9:24). Sometimes it seems like my faith is as small as a mustard seed. But with even that much faith, you said I could do anything.

It does not seem possible, but with you nothing is impossible. I place my trust in you, knowing you will not disappoint me. Amen.

he has done a hundred times before, his dad reaches out and catches the boy. The boy is not even finished with his laughing before he runs back around to make the jump again.

To leap into his father's arms, the boy has to have faith in his father. He has to believe his father can catch him. He also has to trust that his father will catch him. Leaping is just the final step in his act of faith. Because he believes and trusts his father, it is the natural thing to do. A person with faith in God is like the child who leaps into the hands of his father. Our salvation depends upon our faithfully placing ourselves into the hands of God.

A leap of faith is like jumping into the arms of God. We trust that he will always be there for us.

iStockphoto

72

Faith Is a Gift Freely Chosen

Faith is first of all a gift from God. Someone cannot have faith without the Holy Spirit, who helps us see our need for God. Before a person can have this gift of faith, he or she must first have the freedom to choose it. Being faithful can be done only by someone who understands and freely chooses to believe in God and his Church.

You might think, "My parents force me to go to church, so how can I ever freely choose it?" Think of it this way. What would you do if someone offered you a box and said that if you accepted it, you would carry it around for the rest of your life? You would want to know what was in the box before you made a decision, right? Without looking inside it, you cannot really make a choice. The box is like the faith God wants to give you. It often comes to you through the words and examples of your parents. If you are ever going to choose to accept the faith God offers, you must look into it. You have to learn about it before you

Did You Know?

The "Heart" of Our Beliefs

The word *belief* can be traced back to Old English and Old High German words that mean "to hold dear and to love." The word *creed* can be traced back to two Latin words, *cor* and *do*. Cor means "heart" and *do* means "I give." So when we say our creed, or our beliefs, we are doing more than just saying the things that we think. We are stating what is in our hearts. A creed is the set of beliefs to which our hearts are devoted.

KEY WORDS

faith
belief
creed
monotheistic

accept it. Only then can you really make a free and informed decision.

Faith Is Believing

Having faith means you believe. A **belief** is something people consider to be true. For Christians, this belief is found in the life, death, and Resurrection of Jesus Christ. At Mass, we declare our core beliefs when we pray the Nicene Creed. A **creed** is an official statement of one's faith, or what one believes.

Believing is also an act of the entire Church. Don't confuse Church—with a capital C—with a building. The Church is the community of faithful people who put their faith in Jesus Christ. In a way your first Church is your family. It is the Church that teaches you. It is the Church that is a role model for you. It is the Church that supports and nourishes your own faith. Without your family and the Church, there is no one to pass on the faith.

The words from the beginning of the Nicene Creed are probably familiar to you. Check out the rest of the Creed in appendix A, Catholic Prayers.

Nicene Creed

We believe in one God, the Father Almighty,

maker of heaven and earth,

of all that is, seen and unseen...

We believe in one Lord, Jesus Christ...

Belief is not the end of the road when it comes to having faith. In fact, believing is only the beginning. Belief is the foundation on which the rest of our faith is built.

Faith Is Trusting

Having faith also means you trust. Trust is when you confidently turn control of your life (or part of your life) over to someone or something else with hope. If you have ever worked on a school project with others, you know what it is like to trust. Working hard on your part of the project, you trust that your partners will complete their parts. You have given some of the control over your grade to your partners with hope that they will do their jobs.

When we trust God, we acknowledge that we cannot ever be truly happy without him. We can do our part, but without God, our "project," which is our lives,

THiNK ABouT IT!

Being a faith-filled person does not mean all your questions will be answered. It also does not mean you will never have another doubt. God is mysterious, and it is part of your human nature to try to understand him. Your questions can even bring you closer to God. How could bringing your doubts and questions to God in prayer be helpful in your spiritual life? What questions do you have for God?

"I assure you that if you have faith as big as a mustard seed, you can say to this hill, 'Go from here to there!' and it will go. You could do anything!" (Matthew 17:20)

will never be complete. So having faith means we trust God—we put God in control of our lives.

Trusting God is a required ingredient of faith. Trusting him does not mean things will always go the way we want them to go. Human beings are not perfect. We often bring much misery and pain upon ourselves. By trusting God and allowing him to lead our lives, we will give and receive more joy and happiness in this world and in the next.

Faith Is Doing

Finally, having faith means you do something about it. Doing means you act upon what you believe.

In fact without the doing, someone could argue that you don't have faith at all. You may have heard the phrase "The proof is in the pudding." This means we see the true significance of ideas or beliefs when they are put into action. This applies to faith too. Your

Mother Teresa used the words "Jesus in disguise" to describe those who are in most need of our help. Like Mother Teresa, when we reach out to others, we are putting our faith into action.

© Gideon Mendel/CORBIS

actions make real your belief and trust in God. The Letter of James says it best, as follows:

> My friends, what good is it for one of you to say that you have faith if your actions do not prove it? Can that faith save you? Suppose there are brothers or sisters who need clothes and don't have enough to eat. What good is there in your saying to them, "God bless you! Keep warm and eat well!"—if you don't give them the necessities of life? So it is with faith: if it is alone and includes no actions, then it is dead. (2:14–17)

Faith in God Alone

Christianity is **monotheistic,** a word that describes the belief that there is only one God. Yet even we who call ourselves Christians do not always completely place

> "Israel, remember this! The LORD— and the LORD alone—is our God." (Deuteronomy 6:4)

PRAY IT!
Liturgy Connection

Every time we celebrate Mass, we offer our petitions, or requests, in what is called the Prayers of the Faithful. Here we ask God to fulfill our needs. This does not mean God will grant every wish we ask. It just means we trustfully place our needs into God's hands. Imagine if you were babysitting a two-year-old, would you give him everything he asked for? Sometimes the most loving thing a person can do is say no.

In a similar way, God does not grant our every wish. We do not always understand why. Nonetheless, we trust that he will provide what is best for us. Next time during the Prayers of the Faithful, offer your own needs to God and trust that he will provide what is best for you.

our trust in God alone. Instead we sometimes look to money or worldly power for our protection. We can also spend too much time and attention trying to get lots of stuff. We begin to think we can be happy only when we have the best sports equipment, the newest video games, or whatever new catches our eyes. Those things become like false gods when we forget that our true happiness can be found only in God. None of us is perfect, but as our faith in God grows, we will not allow anyone or anything to be substituted for him. God is our true home, and we will be truly satisfied only by doing his will and being with him.

Some Christians have chosen to give up all they have to place their faith in God alone. For example, those who join the Maryknoll Missionaries leave their homes to work in the poorest areas of the world. They choose to abandon the comfort and security of their homes. Led by their belief in the Good News of Jesus Christ, they trust God's call and act upon it.

Even Jesus was tempted to rely on something other than God. When he was in the desert, the devil tried to convince Jesus to look for material things and worldly power to save himself. Jesus replied, "Go away, Satan! The scripture says, 'Worship the Lord your God and serve only him!'" (Matthew 4:10).

Live It!

Mother Teresa is a wonderful inspiration for those who want to be faithful to God. But the stories about saintly people like her overwhelm many people. Many might think, "I could never be as great as she was," and then decide to do nothing. Mother Teresa did not see herself as someone great. She saw her work as simple—not easy, just simple. She read the Gospels. She believed in Jesus' call to serve those who are the neediest in our world. She trusted that God would help her. Then she went out and did it. When asked about her work, she emphasized that faithful people did not have to help the entire world. They just needed to help one person. She said, "We do no great things, only small things with great love" (Rai and Chawla, *Faith and Compassion*, page 158). What is a small thing you can do with great love?

You are like light for the whole world. A city built on a hill cannot be hid. No one lights a lamp and puts it under a bowl; instead it is put on the lampstand, where it gives light for everyone in the house. In the same way your light must shine before people, so that they will see the good things you do and praise your Father in heaven. (Matthew 5:14–16)

PEOPLE OF FAITH
Blessed Mother Teresa

© 2009 Saint Mary's Press/Illustration by Vicki Shuck

Mother Teresa was a woman of great faith. She was born Gonxha Agnes Bojaxhiu in 1910 in Skopje, Macedonia. At age eighteen, she joined the Sisters of Loreto and took the name Teresa after Saint Thérèse of Lisieux. She became a missionary in Calcutta, India, where she was a schoolteacher and principal. After living there for almost twenty years, Teresa had an encounter with God in which she heard Christ tell her, "Come be my light."

Teresa was inspired to help those who suffered from the most extreme poverty. In 1948, after a few years of prayer and determination, Mother Teresa received permission to leave her convent to work with the poorest of the poor in the streets of Calcutta. She soon formed the Missionaries of Charity, who set up hospitals and homes for the dying. In 1979, after years of dedication to her mission, this "saint of the gutters" was awarded the Nobel Peace Prize for her work. By the 1990s the Missionaries of Charity could be found all over the world, helping homeless people, abused women, and orphans, as well as those suffering from AIDS, drug addiction, and other illnesses.

Mother Teresa died in 1997. She left behind a thriving order of priests, nuns, and laypersons devoted to the service of the neediest people in our world. Pope John Paul II beatified Mother Teresa in 2002. After she died, her private letters revealed that she had overcome many years of spiritual doubt and anguish. Considering the extreme poverty she faced in Calcutta, it is no surprise she questioned why God would remain silent and allow such things to happen. In spite of these feelings, she trusted God and kept hard at work at her mission. Because of God's silence, her work demanded an even greater faith from her. Her belief and trust in God showed in all her wonderful work.

PART 2

JESUS THE CHRIST

I believe in Jesus Christ, his only Son, our Lord.
He was conceived by the power of the Holy Spirit
and born of the Virgin Mary.
He suffered under Pontius Pilate, was crucified, died,
and was buried. He descended into hell.
On the third day he rose again.
He ascended into heaven and is seated at the right hand
of the Father. He will come again to judge
the living and the dead.

8

THE GOSPELS

Almost everyone likes books about heroes. These books can encourage and inspire us. They can help us have bigger dreams for our lives and become better people.

The Gospels are books about the greatest, most inspiring hero of all time. Jesus Christ is a man who is also our Lord and Savior—the Son of God. He reveals the truth about God and about our lives. He tells stories that force us to stop and think about what we are doing and why. He shows us that our lives have a meaning and purpose. He assures us we are loved and are able to love God and others in return.

> This is the Good News about Jesus Christ, the Son of God. (Mark 1:1)

Jesus has inspired millions down through the ages to follow him. Now he invites us to get to know him. We sometimes hold back. We think we know him already.

KEY WORDS

Gospels

inspiration

synoptic

© Brooklyn Museum/Corbis

Where would you be in this picture? Sitting close to Jesus, wanting to know and follow him? Standing outside the circle, afraid to change your life?

We think we are too busy or too young. Down deep we may fear—and it might be true—that we will need to change some things in our lives if we get to know Jesus well. But we cannot be afraid to let into our lives the person who best knows and loves us. Jesus will show us how we can become truly great.

Jesus and the Scriptures

How can we get to know Jesus Christ and the fullness of truth he brings? To answer this, think about how we get to know people in our families who lived before us. Sometimes our still-living older relatives tell all kinds of stories about family

THINK ABOUT IT!

"Go throughout the whole world and preach the gospel to all people" (Mark 16:15). Imagine that Christ has just given this mission to you and your friends. You don't have a lot of money. Probably you don't have many friends in important places. You don't have much experience in speaking to other people. But you know you need to, want to, and can do it. How would you go about spreading his teachings? We have means of communication that were not available to the Apostles. What means would you use most? Why?

FUN FACT

Have you ever had to copy some writing by hand? Now we have machines that can copy anything written or printed. But before the 1500s, even printing presses didn't exist. Trained people had to copy by hand writings like the Gospels. They must have been patient and careful to be as accurate as they were.

members who have already died. Maybe the people who have died— or the people who lived with them— left written records like diaries or memoirs.

This is the way it happened with Jesus. The men he was closest to, the Apostles, were the chief witnesses of his public life. After Jesus rose from the dead and ascended into Heaven, they told others about Jesus' life and teachings. They did this through their preaching and by their examples. The Holy Spirit guided them to remember everything we need to know for our salvation.

The Holy Spirit also led some of the Apostles or their helpers to write down their teachings about Jesus' life and message. These writings became the four **Gospels** of Matthew, Mark, Luke, and John. The word *gospel* means "good news."

For we did not follow cleverly devised myths when we made known to you the power and coming of our Lord Jesus Christ, but we were eyewitnesses of his majesty.
(2 Peter 1:16)

We learn about Jesus' life and teachings chiefly from the four Gospels. They are at the heart of the whole Bible. The Old Testament prepares the way for Christ, the promised Savior. The New Testament centers on him and on following him with the help of the Holy Spirit.

Other written reports of Christ's life appeared in early Christianity. But the Gospels of Matthew, Mark, Luke, and John are special. They are the only Gospels included among the inspired books of the Bible.

Inspiration means God is the ultimate author of these books. He wanted them written, and he wanted certain points to be made. The Holy Spirit led the human writers to say without error the truths God wants told for our salvation.

The human writers were not just puppets. They had to do their own research and may have written with certain questions or problems in mind. Each had his own style of writing. Each may have omitted details or combined different sermons of Jesus into one. But the Holy Spirit made sure they gave

Did You Know?

Reading the Scriptures

Many people living during Jesus' earthly lifetime could not read. So the Jewish Scriptures (our Old Testament) were read out loud in the Jewish places of worship, called synagogues. Luke's Gospel, for example, shows Jesus returning to Nazareth, his hometown. In the synagogue he reads out loud a passage from the Book of Isaiah. In the passage is a promise of a savior coming to bring Good News to the poor. Jesus says that promise has come true in him (see Luke 4:14–21).

Christians have kept the practice of reading and explaining the Scriptures during worship services. Especially in Catholic worship, we read from both the Old and New Testaments. This helps us see how they relate to each other.

Pray It!

Dear God,
Thank you for telling me about yourself in the Scriptures. Thank you for showing me yourself most fully in the Gospels. May the Holy Spirit help me understand Jesus' life and teachings. Let them inspire me to grow in friendship with you. Help me serve you and others as the Gospels teach us to do. May I become more and more like Christ, so that others can see him in me.

Amen

honest reports of all the important points of Jesus' life and teachings. They passed on the truths God wants us to know to follow Jesus and be saved.

Writing the Gospels

Have you ever done one of those oral history reports that are popular assignments at some schools? They can be fun. You talk to people who lived through some big historical event. You may look at written records they have. Then you write a summary.

Other students may do a report on the same historical event. They may talk to different eyewitnesses. They may include other facts or order them differently. Their reports will end up slightly different from yours.

The Gospel writers did something similar. Each one chose facts about Christ's life and teachings that had been passed on by word of mouth. They may have used earlier writings about Jesus' life and teachings. For example, Luke's Gospel explains his approach and purpose clearly.

Many people have done their best to write a report of the things that have taken place among us. They wrote what we have been told by those who saw these things from the beginning and who proclaimed the message. And so, Your Excellency, because I have carefully studied all these matters from their beginning, I thought it would be good to write an orderly account for you. I do this so that you will know the full truth about everything which you have been taught. (1:1–4)

The four Gospels all portray Jesus Christ, and so they do share many of the same stories about his life and teachings. In particular, the Gospels of Matthew, Mark, and Luke often record the same events in about the same order. They are called the **synoptic** Gospels, because these similarities are clear when their contents are "seen together" or listed side by side. The Greek word from which synoptic comes means "seen together."

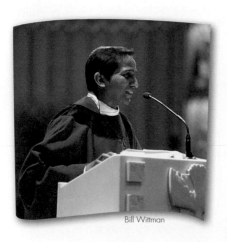

Bill Wittman

At Mass we stand for the Gospel and listen carefully, because what is proclaimed is truly Good News! Just as we stand to hear the Gospels, it is important to take a stand for what the Gospels teach us about Jesus.

PRAY IT!
Liturgy Connection

The Liturgy of the Word is the first major part of the Eucharist. A reading from the Gospels is always included. The order of readings for Sunday Masses follows a three-year rotation. Each year in the cycle is referred to by letter: A, B, or C.

Many of the Sunday Gospels during the seasons of Advent, Christmas, Lent, and Easter come from John's Gospel. A reading from the other three Gospels is usually read on the remaining Sundays. (We call these weeks outside special liturgical seasons "ordinary time.") Readings from Matthew are proclaimed in Year A, readings from Mark in Year B, and readings from Luke in Year C. So, the Church helps us think about the whole Gospel message over time.

But each is slightly different, because the sources and readers of each were different. Matthew, for example, writes mostly for Jewish people. He often shows how Jesus' life fulfills the promises and prophecies of the Old Testament. Mark writes more for Gentiles, that is, people who are not Jewish. So he explains Jewish customs and words. Early Christian writers say Mark gives us Peter's teachings.

The Gospel of Luke often reminds us that Jesus came to save all people. It records some unique stories and teachings that stress this point. For example, the story of the prodigal son shows that God's mercy can forgive the worst sinners (see Luke 15:11–32). The story of Lazarus and the rich man teaches that we should love people who are poor as God does (see Luke 16:19–31). Luke also tells more about Jesus' childhood. Even when he is a child, some people see that Jesus comes to fulfill God's promise to send a savior (see Luke 2:22–50).

John wrote his Gospel some years after the others were finished. His organization and focus are different from those of the synoptic Gospels. He also reflects more deeply on Jesus' teachings.

His readers were mostly Greek-speaking and not Jewish. He wants to make clear right from the beginning of the Gospel that Christ is truly divine, the Son of God. John's Gospel doesn't start with the earthly life of Jesus as the others do. Instead, he shows that the second Person of the Trinity exists always with God and is God. He is the Word by which God expresses himself in Creation and the Old Testament. Finally, God shows himself fully by having the Word become someone like us.

© Brooklyn Museum/Corbis

Mark writes his Gospel. Mark's Gospel is the earliest of the four Gospels. It is also the shortest. Find out more about this Gospel and the other Gospels written by Matthew, Luke, and John.

Getting to Know Christ

A few key ideas can help us get the most out of reading or hearing the Scriptures, as follows:

First, the writers' different audiences and purposes help explain what each author includes and stresses. Matthew, for example, is not trying to bore us with his lists of Jesus' ancestors. He's showing his

Jewish readers that Jesus really is from the line of the Messiah (see Matthew 1:1-17).

> I passed on to you what I received, which is of the greatest importance: that Christ died for our sins, as written in the Scriptures. (1 Corinthians 15:3)

Second, we do not have to understand every word to get the basic idea. But knowing the literal meanings of words can deepen our appreciation. At the same time, the Gospels often use physical things to stand for spiritual things. For example, Jesus says his disciples will fish for men. Jesus means by this that his disciples will work to bring others to his Kingdom.

Third, events in the Gospels often complete or make perfect events that happened earlier in the

Have you ever participated in a Bible study group? Reading and discussing the Bible with others can be a great way to grow in faith and knowledge of God's Word and how it applies to your life.

Shutterstock

Old Testament. In chapter 6 of John's Gospel, for instance, Jesus recalls how God provided a kind of bread for his people in the desert so they wouldn't die (see Exodus, chapter 16). Then Jesus reveals that he is the perfect bread from heaven that gives eternal life to everyone who believes in him.

Fourth, we do not have to figure out everything ourselves. Many Bibles have helpful notes and comments. Thoughtful Christians have written many commentaries on the Gospels.

Live It!

God speaks to us personally in the Scriptures. We read them to understand. We also want to apply God's word to our daily lives. So, we need more of a plan for reading the Gospels than for reading other books.

First, we can ask the Holy Spirit to help us understand and live the Gospel message.

Second, we can read carefully. We can imagine the people and events and even "make a movie" of them in our minds.

Third, we can pause to think about what we have read and apply it to our own lives. How does the Spirit encourage, teach, correct, challenge, comfort, or inspire us in this passage?

Sometimes this practice will give us big insights. Other times, we seem to see nothing. But if we keep trying with faith, the fruits will be great.

Finally, we are not alone. The Spirit especially guides the bishops who have succeeded, or followed, the Apostles. They have the full power and responsibility to explain the Scriptures and Tradition rightly. But the Church also urges us to study and think about Jesus. If we ask in prayer, the Holy Spirit will guide us in our reading.

Reading the Gospels has changed lives. Missionaries have risked their own safety to bring the Good News to those who have not heard. Others have

Looking Back

Copies of the Gospels

Did you know that the original copies of the four Gospels from the early centuries have fallen apart or been destroyed? So how do we know our Gospels are the same as what the authors wrote?

This is a question experts ask about all old books. They study and compare the oldest whole and partial copies of those books to determine their accuracy.

Bible experts have found hundreds of early copies of the Gospels. We have more and older copies of them than of any other ancient book. Experts say that the copies from different places and times are basically the same. So our versions of the four Gospels are extremely reliable, more so than any other ancient book. We can thank the early Christians who treasured these books and accurately copied and preserved them.

made the lives of those around their homes much better by their Gospel-inspired words and deeds.

If you want to make a difference in the world, try reading the Gospels. You will meet unforgettable, real people like Mary, Joseph, Peter, James, and John. Above all, you will get to know Jesus, the most unforgettable and real person of all. He will enlighten, challenge, encourage, comfort, and amaze you. He will become your hero and ideal. He will make you truly happy in this life and the next. He will enable you to inspire others.

© Jim Hollander/epa/Corbis

In 1947 herders discovered old manuscripts in a cave near where Jesus lived. They are called the Dead Sea Scrolls. They include some of the oldest biblical manuscripts ever found.

JESUS CHRIST, TRUE GOD AND TRUE MAN

Imagine getting some really unbelievable good news. Pretend you've tried out for the basketball team or school play but figured you had no chance of starting or getting a big part. Or imagine you'd love to have another child in the family, but your parents have said it wasn't possible. Then suddenly you learn your dream has come true. You're named a starter. You're chosen to play the part. You're going to have a little brother or sister.

Can you think of some great news you have received? Think about all the people you wanted to tell. For the past 2,000 years, the Church has been telling the best news ever.

Jose Luis Pelaez, Inc./Blend Images/Corbis

As good as news like this is, the Church has even better news for the whole human race. The Gospel of John tells it as follows: "The Word became a human being, and full of grace and truth, lived among us. We saw his glory, the glory which he received as the Father's only Son" (John 1:14). This incredible Good News of the Gospels is called the mystery of the **Incarnation,** the truth that Jesus Christ, the Son of God and the second Person of the Trinity, is both fully God and fully man. He took on our human nature, which means that the Son of God became one with us. By doing this Jesus makes it possible for us to get to know him, trust him, love him, follow him, and show him to others. He wants us to join freely with him in the great adventure of spreading his Kingdom. He wants to teach us what human and divine life are all about. He wants to give us the power to imitate him, to become like him, so he lives through us. He wants us and those around us to be happy now and forever.

Pray It!

Jesus,
Thank you for your great gift of love in becoming human for us. Help me to honor and love you as my Savior, Lord, and God in all my thoughts, words, and actions. Teach me through your holy life to live a holy life too. Through the Holy Spirit, give me the grace to know and follow your teachings with humility, generosity, and persistence. May others see your goodness in me. Amen.

He always had the nature of God, but . . . of his own free will he gave up all he had, and took the nature of a servant. He became like a human being and appeared in human likeness. (Philippians 2:6–7)

Who Is Jesus Christ?

How do we get to know who Jesus Christ is? We might start by thinking about how we get to know and understand people in general. We spend time working, playing, and relaxing with them. We think about what they say and do. We get to know them as persons. Someone is kind and caring. Someone else is determined and stubborn. We get to know their talents and abilities. One is great in math. Another is a terrific storyteller.

We get to know Jesus Christ in a similar way. Only, because his earthly life is long in the past, we have to rely on the reports of others who were with him at the time. Those reports are part of God's Revelation, which is passed on to us through the Scriptures and Tradition. What do the Scriptures and Tradition tell us about Jesus?

They show us that Jesus is a divine person with two natures. He keeps the divine nature that he has had for eternity. He also takes on our human nature. He is not just God or just man or some sort of half-and-

Jesus wept when his friend died. He must have laughed sometimes too, because he was one of us. He was like us in all things except sin and experienced the same emotions we do.

© Brooklyn Museum/Corbis

Live It!

How can we get to know Jesus better?

We can pay attention to the Good News of his life and lessons. We can read the Scriptures on our own or listen to them at Mass. We can read writings or listen to talks by people who have thought about Jesus Christ.

We can speak with Jesus. We can pray to him in a group or on our own. The Spirit will use our openness to Jesus to help us grasp his life and message.

We can be touched by Christ in the sacraments, especially the Eucharist. Jesus works through them to help us know and follow him better.

We can see Christ shine through the witness of faithful people. We can study the lives of saints and learn to see goodness in people we know. Jesus gives us many ways to build our relationships with him.

half mix of the two. He is truly and fully divine and truly and fully human, but without sin of any kind.

Jesus Christ is truly human, like us. He grows, walks, talks, works, has friends, and jokes around. He enjoys meeting and talking with people of all kinds. When Jesus' friend Lazarus dies and when he thinks about how his own people will reject him, he cries. He enjoys a good meal, good talk, the beauty of flowers, and the innocence of children. He gets hungry, tired, and angry. When people ignore him or are ungrateful, his feelings are hurt.

"The Son of God . . . worked with human hands; he thought with a human mind. He acted with a hu-

Did You Know?

Jesus Talks About His Divinity

Jesus is slow to reveal he is God. In the Gospels he sometimes refuses to answer questions about his godhood (see, for example, Matthew 16:20, Mark 8:11–12, and Luke 20:1–8). Why? If you look closely, you will see it depends on when and to whom he is talking.

God had taught the Jewish people that he was the only God. If Jesus had claimed to be God right from the beginning, the other Jews would have killed him for blasphemy—which eventually happened, anyway (see John 8:59, 10:31). Blasphemy is an action regarded as an insult to God. Jesus needed time to show by words and deeds that divine power worked through him. Then his followers could accept his word that he was one with God. Jesus often would not answer questions about his divine nature from those who ignored the proof of his words and deeds. They wished only to trap him, not know him.

Miracles, like Jesus' walking on water, are signs of Jesus' divinity. He truly is God.

© Brooklyn Museum/Corbis

man will, and with a human heart he loved. Born of the Virgin Mary, he has truly been made one of us, like to us in all things except sin"[1] CCC, number 470).

Jesus Christ is truly God. He does things only God can do. He performs miracles of healing and raising the dead. He forgives sins and foretells the future. He dares to explain and add to God's teachings from the Old Testament. Simon Peter calls him "the Son of the living God," and Jesus agrees. "For this truth did not come to you from any human being, but it was given to you directly by my Father in heaven" (Matthew 16:16–17).

Although Jesus is only thirty years old in human age, he claims to have existed before the founder of the Jewish people. "Before Abraham was born, 'I Am'" (John 8:58). "I AM" is the name God gives himself when Moses asks on Mount Sinai (see Exodus 3:14). Jesus says he is the real and natural Son of God, not an adopted son or just someone close to God. "Whoever sees me sees also him who sent me" (John 12:45). "The Father and I are one" (John 10:30). Jesus is God himself. In fact, his accusers charge that he breaks Jewish law "because he claimed to be the Son of God" (John 19:7). He does not deny it.

Jesus also allows others to call him "Lord." We might think this is just an older way of showing respect for people. It might be like saying "sir" or "ma'am." But in the Greek Bible, LORD is the word used in place of the Hebrew word *Yahweh*, which is a special name for God. So to call Jesus Lord is like calling him God. It expresses our belief in Jesus' divinity. That is especially clear in the reaction of Thomas to the risen Jesus: "My Lord and my God" (John 20:28).

PRAY IT!
Liturgy Connection

Jesus is at the center of every liturgy and especially the Eucharist. We address our praise, needs, thanks, and sorrow for sin to him as our Lord. We end our prayers with "through Christ, our Lord." It is only through him, with him, and in him that we can approach the Father.

We know Jesus will understand us in our weaknesses. He can and will present our needs to the Father and respond to them. "On the contrary, we have a High Priest who was tempted in every way that we are, but did not sin. Let us have confidence, then, and approach God's throne, where there is grace" (Hebrews 4:15–16).

"This is my own dear Son—
listen to him!" (Mark 9:7)

What the Incarnation Means for Us

The Catechism of the Catholic Church (CCC) gives the following summary of who Jesus is. "At the time appointed by God, the only Son of the Father, the eternal Word, that is, the Word and substantial Image of the Father, became incarnate; without losing his divine nature he has assumed human nature" (CCC, number 479).

It is important that Jesus is really both God and man for several reasons. First, Jesus is called the *Christ*, the Greek word for the Hebrew word **Messiah,** or "anointed one." In the Old Testament, priests, kings, and sometimes prophets were anointed. That is, they had precious olive oil poured over them to show that God had chosen them for a special purpose. The Messiah promised by God was expected to be a priest, prophet, and king who would save the people of Israel. In fact, the name **Jesus** means "God saves." That is the prime goal of his mission to us. He comes to save us from the Original Sin that we all inherit and that infects human nature. He also can save us from our personal sins that hurt us and our relationships with God and others. Christ comes to give us the grace—that is, a share in God's own divine life and love—to save us from sin and death.

"Lean on me." Imagine Jesus saying that to you, especially in tough times when you need a friend the most.

Illustration by Elizabeth Wang, 'Jesus' love is personal, tender, and unchanging; he is present with us always, especially in the Blessed Sacrament', copyright © Radiant Light 2008, www.radiantlight.org.uk

Looking Back

Mistakes About Christ

The Church has always affirmed Jesus Christ's divinity and humanity in response to people who have said he was either only God or only human. While the New Testament was still being written, some people claimed Christ was only divine. So John, for example, insists on the physical presence of "the Word of life." "We have heard it, and we have seen it . . . and our hands have touched it" (1 John 1:1).

Others in the early Church argued that Christ was not divine or not equal to the Father. The Council of Nicaea (AD 325) responded by affirming Jesus' full divinity. You may come across people today who believe that Jesus was only human. We can try to help people who believe this to see Christ's full picture in the Scriptures. We can pray that God will help them understand and believe the truth.

Second, because Jesus is both God and man, he is the one and perfect **mediator** between us and God. You know how sometimes when two friends fight, a third friend will talk with each of them and get them to be friends again? That is part of what a mediator does; a mediator helps restore broken relationships.

Key Words

Incarnation
Messiah
Jesus
mediator

For God loved the world so much that he gave his only
Son, so that everyone who believes in him may not die
but have eternal life. (John 3:16)

As our mediator, Christ offers himself in
sacrifice on the cross and in Mass to restore
our relationships with his loving Father. He
goes to the Father on our behalf and comes
to us on behalf of the Father to reveal the love of the Father for us.

Third, by becoming truly
man, Jesus shows he wants to
and can be our friend. Good
friends understand us well and
stick by us. They are there for us,
stubbornly loyal, sometimes bru-
tally honest.

As God, Jesus knows us better
than we know ourselves and has the
highest hopes for the saints we can
become. He loves us and is patient
with us beyond all human measure. As
man, Jesus understands us, our strengths
and weaknesses, joys and sorrows, emotional highs and lows. He sympathizes,
encourages, advises, and corrects, all
with great affection.

Fourth, Jesus offers himself as a teacher and a
model for us to imitate. You probably have heroes already whom you imitate. You may admire and try to
become like a certain athlete or performer. Christ is
our model for a holy life. "I am the way, the truth,

Think About It!

As a fully human person,
Jesus is an example for us. But
we need to think about his life
and teachings to follow him. For
example, Christ tells us we will
be happy and God's children if
we work for peace (see Matthew
5:9). How can you work for
more peace in your family? for
more peace among your friends?
What other teachings of Jesus
do you remember and how can
they guide your life?

and the life; no one goes to the Father except by me" (John 14:6). Jesus presents the Beatitudes as ideals that we should strive for, but he also lives them. If we want to follow him, he tells us that we must love one another as he loves us (see John 15:12).

But how can we possibly become like Christ? Saint Thomas Aquinas wrote, "The only-begotten Son of God, wanting to make us sharers in his divinity, assumed our nature, so that he, made man, might

PEOPLE OF FAITH
Saint Joseph

© 2009 Saint Mary's Press/Illustration by Vicki Shuck

God called Saint Joseph to be the husband of Mary and legal father of Jesus. Joseph heroically did what God wanted even when it caused him to suffer. He married his beloved, Mary, although she was mysteriously pregnant. He left his relatives, friends, job, and home to lead his family into Egypt so Jesus would be safe from King Herod's massacre of the innocent children.

make men gods."[2] (CCC, number 460). Through the grace Christ gains for us, we become children of God. Especially in Baptism and the other sacraments, the Holy Spirit helps us think, feel, and act as Jesus would. "God's divine power has given us everything we need to live a truly religious life through the knowledge of one who called us to share in his own glory and goodness" (2 Peter 1:3).

Most of Joseph's life was not that exciting. But he showed the same steady faith and obedience to God's will during his quiet years in Nazareth. He fulfilled the ordinary duties of a husband, parent, worker, and citizen well and with love. Like any good father, Joseph taught Jesus many things, including his own trade of carpentry. In her *Autobiography*, Saint Teresa of Ávila encourages praying to Joseph. Jesus, she says, who obeyed him on earth, honors Joseph in heaven by always doing what he asks.

It's easy to imagine Joseph as a reliable, upright person who does what needs to be done without a lot of talk. His commitment to doing the right thing in the Gospels inspires us to do what God wants without whining or complaining. He teaches us to look at and listen to Jesus in silent prayer. March 19 is his feast day.

10 THE BIRTH OF JESUS

Can you see signs of God's love in the faces of babies?

© moodboard/Corbis

Every baby is a miracle. A baby is the result of the love between a man and a woman. A baby is the result of God's love. God has created the physical laws that form the baby's body. God has directly given the baby a spiritual soul.

We would expect Jesus' birth to be even more miraculous. As the eternal Son of God, the second Person of the Trinity, he has always existed. But he wants to be like us, which means having a human birth.

An angel appeared to Mary to announce that she would be Jesus' mother. Her yes has made all the difference in the world.

© Brooklyn Museum/Corbis

In the Bible, God sends the angel Gabriel to ask Mary to become Jesus' mother. Gabriel explains the wonderful way it will happen. "The Holy Spirit will come on you, and God's power will rest upon you . . . For there is nothing that God cannot do" (Luke 1:35,37). According to the Nicene Creed, Jesus is "conceived by the power of the Holy Spirit and born of the Virgin Mary" (see appendix A, "Catholic Prayers"). We call Gabriel's message to Mary the **Annunciation**.

Every Christmas we remember the story of Jesus' birth. It is good to look at the Gospels closely and think about them prayerfully. The Gospels of Matthew and Luke have stories about Jesus' birth. (John starts with a hymn about the Son of God.) Only the Son of God has ever been able to choose how he will be born as a human. He seems to make his birth as humble and hard as possible.

Mothers about to give birth usually try to prepare everything perfectly for the babies. But in Luke's Gospel, Mary and Joseph have to be away from home among strangers. They cannot even get housing or a proper bed. So the Son of God is born in some kind of stable. His cradle is a manger,

PRAY IT!
Liturgy Connection

The Church's liturgy has a yearly rotation of seasons. Each stresses a different stage in the history of salvation. The liturgical year starts with Advent. For four weeks, we prepare for the Lord's coming into the world and into our hearts. The Christmas season begins with celebrating the Lord's birth on Christmas Day. It ends with the feast of his Baptism on the second Sunday in January. It includes the feasts of the Holy Family, Mary's motherhood, and the Epiphany. In this season we relive the early history of the Holy Family. We rejoice in Christ's coming.

one of those open boxes that hold food for animals. "She gave birth to her first son, wrapped him in cloths and laid him in a manger—there was no room for them to stay in the inn" (Luke 2:7). The Gospel of Luke shows us that God is one with even those who seem to be the poorest of people. It warns us from the start not to judge the true worth of others by what they have or how they appear.

"This very day in David's town your Savior was born—Christ the Lord!" (Luke 2:11)

God does reveal Jesus' true nature to some people. Angels suddenly cover the sky where shepherds are tending their flocks. "Don't be afraid! I am here with good news for you, which will bring great joy to all the people" (Luke 2:10). In the Gospel of Matthew, a strange star guides **Magi,** wise men who studied the skies, over a long trip to greet the King of the Jews. "Where is the baby born to be the king of the Jews? We saw his star when it came up in the east, and we have come to worship him" (Matthew 2:2).

Both the simple Jewish shepherds and the

Kings and shepherds come to worship Jesus. How do you worship Jesus?

© Pascal Deloche/Godong/Corbis

educated foreigners respond with faith to these heavenly signs. They adore the child who appears poor and helpless, without any important friends. Through the shepherds and Magi, God reminds us that Christ has come to all people. He shows we need faith to believe in and follow Jesus.

In the Gospel of Matthew, King Herod is not happy to get the news of Jesus' birth (see Matthew 2:1–3). Herod fears the baby will take over as king. Like the Pharaoh in the Book of Exodus, Herod doesn't care what it takes to destroy the threat to his kingdom. "He gave orders to kill all the boys in Bethlehem and its neighborhood who were two years old and younger" (Matthew 2:16). Jesus escapes from Herod just as the infant Moses escaped from the Pharaoh. In this way Matthew shows us that Jesus is like the great leaders of the Old Testament. He is the Savior promised by God. His coming proves that God loves us and wants us to be happy.

Mary, the Mother of Jesus

God chose Mary to be the Son's mother. She is a human being like us. She is also truly the Mother of God. She gives

THINK ABOUT IT!

Sometimes we lose the true spirit of the Christmas season. How can we keep Christ's spirit of self-giving? Maybe we can help with cleaning or cooking without being asked. We may visit a shelter or nursing home, where people might feel lonely, especially at Christmas. What else can you and your family do to truly remember that Christmas is about the coming of Christ into the world?

Key Words

Annunciation

Magi

Immaculate Conception

Pray It!

Dear Jesus,
Thank you for coming as a small child who is easy to love. Teach me to be simple and humble too. Help me rely on God more than on human strength. Show me how to serve God and others in little ways each day. Amen.

birth to the second Person of the Trinity when he becomes man. In this way, she is the Mother of God, because Jesus is God. She also becomes the Mother of the Church, which is the Body of Christ. She is our spiritual mother, and she leads us to her son, Jesus.

But when the right time finally came, God sent his own Son. He came as the son of a human mother and lived under the Jewish Law, to redeem those who were under the Law, so that we might become God's children.
(Galatians 4:4–5)

In the Hail Mary, we echo the angel Gabriel by calling Mary "full of grace." She is the first and best fruit of Jesus' coming to redeem us. God keeps her from the stain of Original Sin. We call this fact her **Immaculate Conception.** From the first moment she comes into being (her conception), she is immaculate, without a spot of sin. God also gives her the strength to remain pure from all personal sin.

Mary makes it clear to Gabriel that she is wholly the servant, or handmaid, of the Lord. (See Luke 1:38.) Jesus needs a human mother to become fully human himself. Mary cooperates by giving herself completely to God's plan, body and soul. Saint Augustine says she "'remained a virgin in conceiving her Son, a virgin in giving birth to him, a virgin in carrying him, a virgin in nursing him at her breast, always a virgin' (St. Augustine, Serm. 186, 1: J. P. Migne, ed., Patrologia Latina [Paris: 1841-1855] 38,999)" (CCC, number 510).

Mary's Example

Because Mary is both a married person and a virgin, she is an example for all the ways God calls people to follow him. She inspires those whose calling is to marriage and those whose calling is to follow God along other paths. She is a model for the Church, which has children and yet remains wholly God's. She is especially an example to us of faith and charity.

Mary is the one most closely united with her son's redeeming act. She freely obeys God's desire. "May it happen to me as you have said" (Luke 1:38). We do not hear her complain about the difficulties she must face. Following God's plan, she helps reverse the effects of the first

Did You Know?

Jesus' Birth and the Old Testament

The Old Testament foretells some details of the Messiah's birth. Matthew's Gospel refers to some of them. For example, the Gospel begins with "the list of the ancestors of Jesus Christ" to show that he is "a descendant of David," as Isaiah had said (see Matthew 1:1, Isaiah 11:1). Matthew says the Lord also spoke of the Incarnation through Isaiah. "A virgin will become pregnant and have a son, and he will be called 'God is with us'" (Matthew 1:22–23, Isaiah 7:14). The priests quote the prophet Micah to Herod to prove that the Messiah will be born in "Bethlehem in the land of Judah" (Matthew 2:4–6, Micah 5:2).

Imagine taking your troubles to Mary, the Mother of God. Do you think Jesus ever did that when he was your age? If so, how do you think she responded?

Illustration by Elizabeth Wang, 'The Virgin Mary is a tender mother to all who love her Son: we can turn to her and rest in her love at any time', copyright © Radiant Light 2008, www.radiantlight.org.uk

sin and disobedience to God. If Jesus is the new Adam, Mary is the new Eve. She teaches us to freely and faithfully bring Jesus' Spirit to others and into the world.

Mary teaches us humility, which is to admit the whole truth about ourselves. She knows that many people over the years will call her blessed. But she insists that she is great only because of God's love and gifts (see Luke 1:46–49). She serves others humbly. She

PEOPLE OF FAITH
Saint Nicholas of Myra

© 2009 Saint Mary's Press/Illustration by Vicki Shuck

Sometimes Santa Claus is called Saint Nick. Why? Saint Nicholas, sometimes known as Saint Nick, was a fourth-century bishop of Myra, in Asia Minor. He was holy and lived simply. He used his family's wealth for the needs of others. When invaders captured Myra in the eleventh century, his remains were moved to Bari, which today is located in southern Italy. These are the facts we know for sure about his life.

Many stories of his generosity have come down to us. One story tells of the daughters of a poor

hurries to help her older cousin Elizabeth, who, the angel says, is expecting (see Luke 1:36–40). She encourages us both to pray and to act in faithfulness to God.

Mary was just a young teenager when she became the Mother of God. Now, one of the most famous women in history, she is recognized for her holiness and her inner beauty.

Live It!

"Mary remembered all these things and thought deeply about them" (Luke 2:19). Mary prays about the events in her life. She tries to see God's will and hand in all of them. We may tend to drift from day to day without thinking about what we are doing or why. We need some regular quiet time to think in God's presence about our lives. We can ask God what he may be telling us or asking of us through the things that happen and the people we see each day.

family who needed money to get married. He left a purse of gold for each of them. A legend says he brought three children back to life after an evil butcher had murdered them. He gathered food for children and adults who were starving.

Such stories led to the custom of giving gifts in the name of Nicholas. We do it at Christmas. Some people do it on December 6, Nicholas's feast day. Still others do it on the Epiphany, when the Magi brought gifts to Jesus. Nicholas reminds us to use our talents and wealth to help those in need.

JESUS TEACHES

Some fairy tales tell how bad rulers take over a good king's rightful realm. The king comes back in disguise and throws out the evildoers. He loves his people and shows them how to be good and happy.

Jesus Christ is that good king. God never forgets the world. He is always active in reaching out to his people, for example, by sending the prophets. The Son of God came in person to reclaim God's Kingdom and break the devil's power.

The Kingdom of God

Some travelers tell stories about distant places. They show maps and slides. They inspire you to want to go there also.

Jesus tells us about the **Kingdom of God.** It's not a specific place, but it starts in our hearts. John the Baptist declares, "The right time has come and the Kingdom of God is near! Turn away from your sins and believe the Good News!" (Mark 1:15). John makes it clear that the Kingdom is made real when we live God's rule of love and goodness. It's what Heaven is like. It's what the earth could become if we all followed Jesus. The Kingdom of God is present wherever the children of God are.

Good teachers show us how to do things. They lead us through math problems. They walk us through basketball plays. Jesus does not just tell us about the Kingdom of God. He is "the way, the truth, and the life" (John 14:6). He shows us how we should live to be a seed of the Kingdom. He promises the power of the Holy Spirit to help us live in the Kingdom.

All of Jesus' life teaches us. He teaches by what he says and by his silence. He teaches by his big miracles, his smaller acts, and his prayers. He teaches by his love for people, especially people who are poor or in need. He teaches by his willing sacrifice on the cross and his rising from the dead.

Illustration by Elizabeth Wang, 'The Proclamation of the Kingdom of God and the Call to Conversion'; copyright © Radiant Light 2008, www.radiantlight.org.uk

Jesus was not the kind of king Israel was expecting. How was Jesus different from their expectations?

In the past God spoke to our ancestors many times and in many ways through the prophets, but in these last days he has spoken to us through his Son. (Hebrews 1:1–2)

Did You Know?

John the Baptist's Mission

As the last prophet before the coming of Jesus Christ, John the Baptist's mission is to "prepare a road for the Lord" (Matthew 3:3). John calls people to repent and reform. For their own good, he corrects those who have done wrong. He practices the self-control he preaches by living in the desert on "locusts and wild honey" (Matthew 3:4).

John also puts the Messiah's role above his own ego. "I am not good enough even to carry his sandals" (Matthew 3:11). He sends his own disciples to follow Jesus (see John 1:35–36). "He must become more important while I become less important" (John 3:30). Herod finally beheads John for correcting him (see Mark 5:17–29).

Jesus praises John's firmness and humility in leading others to Christ. "John is greater than anyone who has ever lived" (Luke 7:28).

Jesus grew up in a small town. He must have been like most boys and young men of his time. What do you think it would have been like to grow up with Jesus?

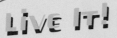

LIVE IT!

In the Bible, prophets sometimes foretell the future. Their main mission, though, is to speak for God. Jesus acts as a prophet when he teaches about the Kingdom in his Father's name.

Everyone who is baptized shares in Christ's prophetic mission. We do so in many different ways. But whenever we reveal God's Kingdom in word or action, we help pass on Jesus' teachings.

For instance, you may teach younger kids a prayer or correct their behavior. You might answer a friend's questions about your faith or give good moral advice to the friend. You may pray with friends in hard times. If you try to follow Christ daily, you will teach others by example. Sometimes you may have to stand up to others and argue for what is right. What else might you do?

Jesus Teaches in His Hidden Life

When he is about thirty years old, Jesus begins his public life as a teacher. Before that, he lives quietly in a tiny, rural town. This early period of his life is sometimes referred to as his "hidden life." The Gospels record only a few of his words during this time. How does he teach us by being so hidden and silent?

Jesus shows us that an ordinary life, lived well with love of God and others, has great worth. After all, Jesus, who is God, lived as you might have lived back then. Enjoying and helping family and friends were part of his life. So were studying, working, playing, praying, and worshiping with his community.

PRAY IT!

Jesus,
Thank you for revealing your Kingdom to us and for inviting me to be part of it. Through the Holy Spirit, lead me to learn your Kingdom's law of love. Teach me to live your Kingdom's law of love with faith and hope. Help me bring others to be part of your Kingdom through my example and words.

Amen

Jesus made all these acts holy by doing them humbly and lovingly. We can unite ourselves to our brother Christ in doing the same things well and with love.

Events in Jesus' hidden life also teach us how to live in the Kingdom. His birth shows us how to be truly humble and poor. The killing of the innocent infant boys and the Holy Family's flight into Egypt warn us that not everyone will welcome the Kingdom. We too may suffer for its sake.

When Jesus is twelve, his family travels to Jerusalem. When his parents start home, he stays behind without telling them. When they find him in the Temple in Jerusalem, he

Imagine having Jesus as a teacher. He taught small groups and large crowds without white boards, technology, or microphones. How did he keep their attention?

© Brooklyn Museum/Corbis

has an excuse. "Didn't you know that I had to be in my Father's house?" (Luke 2:49). Jesus shows we must put God first in the Kingdom. But then Jesus returns home and obeys his parents. He shows us also to respect and follow true authority. His growth in favor with God reminds us that people of all ages are called to be close to God (see Luke 2:41–52).

As he gets older, Jesus is known as "the carpenter, the son of Mary" (Mark 6:3). He shows us that using our talents of mind and body to do honest work is a noble way of praising God and serving others.

Looking Back

Your Kingdom Come

In the Gospels Jesus speaks about his Second Coming and the full Reign of his Kingdom (see Matthew 24:3–44, for instance). But despite his warning that no one knows when it will happen (see Matthew 24:36), people have always tried to guess when it will be.

Throughout the centuries, people have tried to link events in their times to Jesus' signs in the Scriptures. Some of the first Christians thought Jesus would return again during their lifetimes. Saint Augustine thought the fall of the Roman Empire might be the sign. Some people were certain that the change of the millennium in 2000 signaled the end.

Remember that Jesus says no one knows the time of his coming. We should just remain always faithful and ready to greet him (see Matthew 24:42).

Jesus Teaches in Public Life

Jesus starts his public life by having John the Baptist baptize him. Jesus' humility and respect in doing so teaches us how we should act in the Kingdom. During his public life, Jesus talks much about and ushers in the Kingdom. He gathers followers who, after him, will help plant more seeds of his Kingdom on earth. He looks forward to the Kingdom's coming through his death and rising. He teaches that all people are welcome in the family of God. "When I am lifted up from the earth, I will draw everyone to me" (John 12:32).

To enter the Kingdom, Jesus tells us, we need the faith and humility to accept his words. We need to try to admit our sins and become better. "The gate to life is narrow and the way that leads to it is hard" (Matthew 7:14). But we can rely on God's great mercy and help. "Happy are those who know they are spiritually poor; the Kingdom of heaven belongs to them!" (Matthew 5:3).

Good teachers often use something we know about to explain something new to us. For example, they might compare radio waves to the waves we have seen in water. Jesus does the same. Often he tells **parables,** or stories about situations known to his listeners that also teach surprising lessons about the Kingdom of God.

PARABLES OF JESUS

Barren fig tree, Luke 13:6–9

Canceled debts, Luke 7:41–43

Cost of discipleship, Luke 14:25–33

Dishonest manager, Luke 16:1–8

Faithful or unfaithful slave, Matthew 24:45–51; Luke 12:42–48

Fig tree, Matthew 24:32–35; Mark 13:28–31; Luke 21:29–33

Good Samaritan, Luke 10:30–37

Great dinner, Luke 14:16–24

Growing seed, Mark 4:26–29

Hidden treasure and pearl, Matthew 13:44–46

Honor at a banquet, Luke 14:7–14

Laborers in the vineyard, Matthew 20:1–16

Light of the world, Matthew 5:14–16

Lost coin, Luke 15:8–10

Lost sheep, Matthew 18:12–14; Luke 15:3–7

Mustard seed, Matthew 13:31–32; Mark 4:30–32; Luke 13:18–19

Net, Matthew 13:47–50

New wine in old wineskins, Matthew 9:16–17; Mark 2:21–22; Luke 5:36–39

Persistent friend, Luke 11:5–8

Persistent widow, Luke 18:2–8

Pharisee and the tax collector, Luke 18:10–14

Prodigal son, Luke 15:11–32

Rich fool, Luke 12:16–21

Rich man and Lazarus, Luke 16:19–31

Salt, Matthew 5:13; Mark 9:50; Luke 14:34–35

Sheep and the goats, Matthew 25:31–46

Sower, Matthew 13:3–8,18–23; Mark 4:3–9,14–20; Luke 8:5–8,11–15

Talents, Matthew 25:14–30

Ten bridesmaids, Matthew 25:1–13

Ten pounds, Luke 19:11–27

Two sons, Matthew 21:28–31

Unforgiving servant, Matthew 18:23–35

Watchful slaves, Luke 12:35–40

Wedding banquet, Matthew 22:1–14

Weeds among the wheat, Matthew 13:24–30,36–43

Wicked tenants, Matthew 21:33–44; Mark 12:1–12; Luke 20:9–18

Wise and foolish builders, Matthew 7:24–27; Luke 6:47–49

Worthless slaves, Luke 17:7–10

Yeast, Matthew 13:33; Luke 13:20–21

He says the Kingdom is like a small seed that will produce a huge tree of faith and love. But it needs to grow in the rich soil of good hearts (see Matthew 13:3–23, Mark 4:30–32). Jesus also tells a story of how the Kingdom is like a great feast or party that everyone enjoys but must be prepared for. Through his parables Jesus teaches us that we don't have to be perfect. But we must truly try to change bad attitudes and habits so we can love better. We must discover and use the talents God has given us to serve others. We show our love through our deeds, helping others because we see Christ in them (see Matthew 22:1–14, 25:1–40).

During Jesus' public ministry, the three Apostles closest to him—Peter, James, and John—witness a special view of the Kingdom of God and Jesus' divinity called the Transfiguration (see Matthew 17:1–9). At the **Transfiguration** Jesus is transformed in appearance. "His face was shining like the sun, and his clothes were dazzling white" (Matthew 17:2). A voice speaks from a cloud. "This is my own dear Son, with whom I am pleased— listen to him!" (Matthew 17:5).

At the Transfiguration, Jesus hears his Father say, "This is my own dear son—listen to him!"(Mark 9:7). What does it feel like to get your parent's approval? What do you think God was saying to and about his Son?

© Brooklyn Museum/Corbis

The vision deepens the faith and loyalty of these three leaders of the early Church. Jesus also gives Peter "the keys of the Kingdom." This means Peter is in charge of leading the Church. Jesus tells him, "You are a rock, and on this rock foundation I will build my church" (Matthew 16:18).

Simon Peter answered him, "Lord, to whom would we go? You have the words that give eternal life." (John 6:68)

Jesus and the Law

Some teachers are more believable than others. Jesus' teachings awe even his enemies. Officers sent to arrest him say they just cannot. "Nobody has ever talked the way this man does!" (John 7:46).

God first taught the Jewish people through the Law of Moses and the prophets. But only Jesus, the Son of God become man, can fully reveal the things God needs to teach us. First, Jesus affirms all the true teachings that were passed down in the past. He does not "do

PRAY IT!
Liturgy Connection

The liturgical season of Lent lasts from Ash Wednesday up to the Holy Thursday service. Lent prepares us for Easter. It reminds us that to live in the Kingdom, we need to change bad habits and express sorrow for our faults.

The Gospel readings of the first Sunday in Lent tell how Jesus prepares to announce the Kingdom. The Spirit leads him into the desert, and he fasts for forty days. Then the devil tempts him to set up a self-centered kingdom, but Jesus refuses to go against his Father's plan. The season of Lent reminds us we need to sacrifice for the Kingdom. The Spirit will give us the power to be faithful and to use our gifts to serve God and others.

FUN FACT

Some Jewish customs may sound strange to us. "Look at the straps with scripture verses on them which they wear on their foreheads and arms, and notice how large they are!" (Matthew 23:5). This custom of strapping Scripture verses to their heads and arms—which many Jews still follow today when they pray—reminds Jewish people to keep God's Law in their minds and hearts (see Deuteronomy 6:6–8). Jesus criticizes those who do it just to look holy.

away with the Law of Moses and the teachings of the prophets." As King, he comes "to make their teachings come true" (Matthew 5:17). "Whoever obeys the Law . . . will be great in the Kingdom of heaven" (Matthew 5:19). This means we must be faithful to the Ten Commandments, for example.

Second, Jesus makes clear the bigger picture of living the Law in the Kingdom. "You have heard that people were told in the past, 'You shall not commit murder . . .' But now I tell you: if you are angry with your brother you will be brought to trial" (Matthew 5:21–22). We should not just avoid doing what a commandment forbids. Our hearts and our acts should be pure in love. In fact, Jesus sums up all the laws into two. We must love God and love our neighbor truly and fully (see Matthew 22:36–40).

Third, Jesus rejects some ways the Jewish teachers live and explain the Law. For instance, they attack Jesus because he heals on the Lord's Day. They think the command to keep that day holy by avoiding extra work is more important than doing good deeds (see Luke 13:10–17). They get so caught up in rules about eating and washing that they forget that a clean heart is more important (see Mark 7:18–22).

Jesus does not just preach the true Law. His whole life shows how to live these teachings perfectly. He carries out the promises made about the Messiah. He freely offers himself on the cross to redeem us from sins against the Law. He sends the Spirit to enable us to freely live as God's children in his Kingdom.

Did You Know?

The Prodigal Son

Read and think about Jesus' parable of the prodigal, or wasteful, son (see Luke 15:11–32). What key truths does it teach about our relationships to God and others?

Here are some common ideas about it. The younger son's behavior is wrong. Egoism and disregard for others, like his, are the core of every sin. But he comes to his senses and repents. The father, who has every right to be upset, doesn't reject him. He hugs his son and throws a big party. His dead son has come back to life! That's how great God's mercy and love are. We only need to repent truly.

As long as heaven and earth last, not the least point nor the smallest detail of the Law will be done away with. (Matthew 5:18)

JESUS HEALS

We trust people who can actually do what they say they can do. They show us some signs of their ability. People who say they are good baseball players should be able to hit. People who say they can star in a musical should be able to sing.

Jesus said he was God, backing up his claim with signs of his divine power. He worked many **miracles,** special signs of God's presence and power in him and in human history. These actions went beyond our understanding of the normal laws of human or physical behavior. For example, Jesus walked on water. He ordered the wind and waves to become calm in a storm (see Matthew 14:22–33, Mark 4:35–41).

Jesus calmed the storm when his Apostles thought all was lost. Miracles like this helped them realize who Jesus is. Jesus can calm the storms of your life when you feel afraid or lost.

Jesus' miracles help people have faith in him. Most of his miracles also relieve people's suffering. The Gospels point to these as signs that Jesus is the Messiah the prophets predicted. "The blind can see, the lame can walk, those who suffer from dreaded skin diseases are made clean, the deaf can hear, the dead are raised to life, and the Good News is preached to the poor" (Luke 7:22; see Isaiah 35:5–6). Jesus' healing of people in body and soul is done out of the love and compassion that mark the Kingdom of God.

Did You Know?

Response to Christ's Miracles

Most people react with joy to Christ's miracles. "And all who heard were completely amazed. 'How well he does everything!' they exclaimed. 'He even causes the deaf to hear and the dumb to speak!'" (Mark 7:37).

Some people refuse to believe. They accuse Jesus of doing wrong. They say it's bad to heal on the Lord's Day (see Mark 3:1–12). They say the devil, not God, gives Jesus his power over demons (see Mark 3:22–23). Some, like King Herod, just want to be entertained (see Luke 23:8–11). Jesus sadly says they show their hate of God by not accepting his miracles. "They would not have been guilty of sin if I had not done among them the things that no one else ever did" (John 15:24).

We can pray that all people will be open to Christ's healing power.

All the people tried to touch him, for power was going out from him and healing them all. (Luke 6:19)

LooKiNG BacK

A History of Healing

The Church has always been faithful to Christ's concern to heal the body. Bishops have promoted care for the poor, sick, orphaned, and aged in their dioceses. Monasteries of monks and nuns have provided for the needy. Many religious orders over the years have built and staffed hospitals, nursing homes, and other places of care. Some serve people with diseases, even the most disgusting.

Through the centuries, disciples of Christ have followed him in helping heal the whole person. They see Christ in each person who suffers. The person's religion, race, and social class do not matter. Find out which Catholic organizations and places provide healing in your area. Do they allow young people to help? In what ways?

KEY WoRDS

miracle

reconciles

works of mercy

Jesus Heals the Body

Good doctors don't make people better just to show how smart they are. They are concerned with the patients as persons. They want the patients to be well and happy.

Jesus cures people's illnesses and diseases out of concern for the people. The Gospels tell us Jesus heals many people. The Gospels focus on a few stories that present common points. First, Jesus helps people of all kinds. They can be important people like Jairus, an official whose daughter is very ill (see Mark 5:21–24). Or they can be unimportant people, like the widow who suffers in poverty because her only son and support has died. Jesus feels sorry for her and tells the young man to get up. The son returns to life to take care of his mother (see Luke 7:13–15).

Second, Jesus often ties the cures to belief in him. A woman touches Jesus in a crowd. She alone is cured of her illness. Jesus says her faith has made her well (see Luke 8:43–48). When messengers tell Jairus that his daughter has died, Jesus encourages him not to be afraid and just keep believing (see Mark 5:35–36). He does not work many miracles in Nazareth. The people there have too little faith (see Matthew 13:53–58).

Third, Jesus often cures the body to improve a person's soul. The father of the boy with an evil spirit sees this need in himself. "I do have faith, but not enough. Help me have more!" (Mark 9:24). Jesus cures a man who was born blind and has not even followed Jesus before (see John 9:35–38). The man ends up adoring him. "'I believe, Lord!' the man said, and knelt down before Jesus" (John 9:38).

THiNk ABouT iT!

Jesus sometimes uses his physical miracles to make points about the life of the soul. For instance, he feeds a large crowd with five loaves of bread and two fish. He tells the crowd to work instead for "the food that lasts for eternal life" (John 6:27). Jesus makes the point that he is the Bread of Life, who heals spiritual hunger. Read about the miracles in Matthew 8:5–13 and Luke 5:1–11. What spiritual lessons can you learn from them?

MIRACLES OF JESUS

These miracle stories are listed in the order in which they first appear in the Bible.

Leper, Matthew 8:1–4; Mark 1:40–45; Luke 5:12–16
Centurion's servant, Matthew 8:5–13; Luke 7:1–10
Many at Peter's house, Matthew 8:14–17; Mark 1:29–34; Luke 4:38–41
Gadarene (Gerasene) demoniacs, Matthew 8:28–34; Mark 5:1–20; Luke 8:26–39
Paralytic, Matthew 9:1–8; Mark 2:1–12; Luke 5:17–26
Woman with bleeding, Matthew 9:20–22; Mark 5:25–34; Luke 8:43–48
Two blind men, Matthew 9:27–31
Mute man, Matthew 9:32–34
Man with a withered hand, Matthew 12:9–13; Mark 3:1–5; Luke 6:6–11
Blind, mute, and possessed man, Matthew 12:22
Canaanite woman's daughter, Matthew 15:21–28; Mark 7:24–30
Boy with a demon, Matthew 17:14–21; Mark 9:14–29; Luke 9:37–43
Blind Bartimaeus, Matthew 20:29–34; Mark 10:46–52; Luke 18:35–43
Man with an unclean spirit, Mark 1:21–28; Luke 4:31–37
Deaf man, Mark 7:31–37
Blind man at Bethsaida, Mark 8:22–26
Crippled woman, Luke 13:11–13
Man with dropsy, Luke 14:1–4
Ten lepers, Luke 17:11–19
High priest's servant, Luke 22:50–51
Official's son, John 4:46–54
Man at the pool of Bethzatha, John 5:1–9

Fourth, Jesus does not try to cure all physical evils. His main work is to cure spiritual evils. Sometimes he makes this clear even when healing the body. For instance, Jesus is in a crowded house. Some friends of a paralyzed man decide to make a hole in the roof and lower the man down. "Seeing how much faith they had, Jesus said to the paralyzed man, 'My son, your sins are forgiven'" (Mark 2:5). Some of the people who saw this complain that only God can forgive sins. Then Jesus proves he has the power to forgive sins by also healing the man's paralysis. The man picks up his mat and walks home (see Mark 2:1–12).

Jesus Heals the Soul

When we're physically sick, even with just the flu, we feel terrible. We have no strength to do anything. We ache all over. We can also become sick in our inner thoughts and desires, that spiritual part of human beings we call the soul. When our souls are sick, we are stuck in sinful actions and desires. The Gospels say this sickness of the soul is even worse than physical sickness.

Jesus can cure these ills of the soul. He is a doctor for our pride, laziness, self-seeking, and bad desires. He can also treat ills that attack both the soul and the body. He wants to help cure our worries, discouragement, and nervousness. He wants us to find peace in him. The cure can hurt because it has to change wrong acts and thoughts. But we feel better because of it.

"Peace is what I leave with you; it is my own peace that I give you. I do not give it as the world does. Do not be worried and upset; do not be afraid." (John 14:27)

FUN FACT

Luke may have been a doctor (see Colossians 4:14). Maybe that's one reason the Gospel of Luke and the Acts of the Apostles recall so many cures. Luke's Gospel tells of about fifteen healings, more than any of the other Gospels. A doctor would know how truly impossible some of the cures were. He would be especially amazed.

Zacchaeus was up a tree without Jesus. But Jesus turned the tax collector's life around, healing his soul just as he had cured the physical ailments of others.

© Gunnar Bach Pedersen

Like Bartimaeus, we may just need to keep calling to Jesus to help us. He is a blind man sitting by the road as Jesus passes. He starts shouting for Jesus to have mercy on him and ignores others who tell him to be quiet. Jesus cures him, and he can follow Jesus along the road (see Mark 10:46–52).

In the Gospels Jesus always seeks out people whose souls need healing. One of the stories is about Zacchaeus, who is a tax collector living in Jericho. He has become rich by working for the occupying Romans. When he collects the taxes, he also takes extra money for himself. When Jesus invites himself to this sinner's home, the people of Jericho are upset. But Jesus' words and kindness move Zacchaeus to change his ways. "Listen, sir! I will give half my belongings to the poor, and if I have cheated anyone, I will pay back four times as much" (Luke 19:8). Jesus rejoices that salvation has come to that home (see Luke 19:1–10).

Healing the body sometimes means closing a cut. Jesus' healing of the soul also closes wounds. It **reconciles** sinners, that is, it gives us peace within us and restores our relationships with God and other people. Zacchaeus's change of heart sets him right with God and his fellow Jews. He is also at peace with himself. The greatest sinners know Jesus has forgiven them the most. They may become the best models of Christ's healing love.

Jesus also keeps healing the souls of those who are already close to him. When the guards come for Jesus, the Apostles break their promises to stay with him, and they flee. Peter, who boasts the most of his loyalty, is afraid even to admit he knows Jesus. Peter is sorry for his betrayal of Jesus. Jesus forgives him and reminds Peter to take care of the others now that he has reconciled himself with the Lord (see John 21:15–19).

We all need this healing of the soul. Jesus is the doctor always ready and able to heal us. He just needs us to desire to be sorry for our sins and to be reconciled with God, the

PRAY IT!
Liturgy Connection

The liturgy of the Mass often talks about the healing power of God. For example, just before Communion the priest says of the Eucharist, "This is the Lamb of God who takes away the sins of the world. Happy are those who are called to his supper." We respond, "Lord, I am not worthy to receive you, but only say the word and I shall be healed." Our words echo those of a Roman officer in the Gospels who is confident that Jesus can heal his sick servant even from a distance (see Matthew 8:5–10). Like him, we ask God's mercy. We humbly admit we are not worthy. We have faith that Jesus can and will heal us spiritually. The Eucharist can strengthen us to follow our good impulses and cure us of giving in to our bad ones.

Did You Know?
The Early Christians Heal

The Acts of the Apostles tells stories about the first Christians healing people physically just as Jesus did. They do it in Jesus Christ's name, so it is clear that it is his power doing the healing, not theirs. Peter orders a lame man to walk "in the name of Jesus Christ of Nazareth" (Acts 3:6). Later, he tells a paralyzed man that "Jesus Christ makes you well" (Acts 9:34). When the people see the man walk, they become Christians.

Paul's cures make the people of Lystra think he is a Greek god. Paul has to explain. "We ourselves are only human beings like you! We are here to announce the Good News, to turn you to the living God" (Acts 14:15). Paul lists "the power to heal" as one way the Holy Spirit might be present in a person "for the good of all" (1 Corinthians 12:7,9).

Church, others, and ourselves. We show our desire and are healed by Jesus through prayer, the Eucharist, and acts that show our sorrow. We are healed in a special way through the two Sacraments of Healing: the Sacrament of Penance and Reconciliation and the Sacrament of the Anointing of the Sick (see chapter 30).

© Gabe Palmer/CORBIS

Playing bingo may not seem like a work of mercy, but anytime we lift the spirits of others, we help heal their souls. Works of mercy are good for our souls too.

Jesus Sends Us to Heal

Jesus passes on to his followers his mission to heal the body and soul. At one point, he gives the power to expel demons and cure sickness to the Twelve, another name for the Apostles. They go throughout the region, teaching and healing (see Luke 9:1,6). Through the Holy Spirit, Jesus keeps this power to heal always alive and active in his Church.

> "The Son of Man came to seek and to save the lost." (Luke 19:10)

God calls all Christians to help in this healing mission. The **works of mercy** sum up some of the ways we can help heal others. They are acts of charity by which we help others meet their basic needs. By the corporal works of mercy, we help others in their physical needs. We can live out our concern for the needs of the body, for example, by getting money, food, housing, and clothes for and to people who are poor. We can visit the sick, the aged, and those in prison.

We should be just as concerned with the needs of the soul. Those who are sick, for example, need our encouragement to keep their spirits up. We can help them unite their sufferings with those of Christ.

PRAY IT!

Jesus,
Divine doctor, heal
our bodies and souls.
Bring relief to those
who suffer from sick-
nesses and diseases.
Clean the minds of
those who suffer
from bitter and lonely
thoughts. Cure the hard
hearts of those who suf-
fer from sin of any kind.
Make us healers. Help us
sow joy and love among
our friends. Inspire in us
deeds of reconciliation.
Give us words of comfort
and advice for those who
hurt. Work through us to
make others healers too.
Amen.

The spiritual works of mercy include generously sharing our knowledge, advice, and sympathy with those who need it. We do works of mercy when out of love we correct, forgive, and are patient with others' mistakes. We live these works whenever we model

Corporal and Spiritual Works of Mercy

Corporal

Feed the hungry.

Give drink to the thirsty.

Shelter the homeless.

Clothe the naked.

Care for the sick.

Help the imprisoned.

Bury the dead.

Spiritual

Share knowledge.

Give advice to those who need it.

Comfort those who suffer.

Be patient with others.

Forgive those who hurt you.

Give correction to those who need it.

Pray for the living and the dead.

and explain the faith to others or give them good Christian guidance. We live them whenever we comfort those who are sad or discouraged and when we are patient and forgiving toward those who annoy or hurt us. (See appendix B, "Catholic Beliefs and Practices.")

We must work to heal the wounds in those around us. Mostly we do this through our friendship. We listen to them. We show them respect, care, and concern. Sometimes we can help both sides in a quarrel reconcile and forgive one another. We may be able to help some people get to Church and encourage them to receive the sacraments as they are able. We can always pray and offer sacrifices for them.

Live It!

We are called to heal people in our daily lives. How can we do this better? Do we look down on certain people or even groups of people whom we don't try to get along with? Could we be more open and understanding with these people? Could we help friends be the same?

Simple friendliness can be a way to heal. Sometimes people feel alone and unloved. Often they hide their hurt by acting as if they don't care. But they do. We can show we care about them by being nice to them even when they seem to ignore us.

Can you think of other ways you can help heal others in ordinary life?

THE DEATH OF JESUS

Maybe you've helped clean the house because friends were coming over. Perhaps you've made a gift for someone's birthday. Perhaps you've shared a talent or helped a young child learn how to do something. Maybe you've done a work of mercy to help someone. (See appendix B, "Catholic Beliefs and Practices.")

People often give of their time and talents to make others happy. They could be doing something just for themselves. Instead they work hard to please someone they like.

"The greatest love you can have for your friends is to give your life for them." (John 15:13)

God is the origin of such selfless acts. "This is what love is: it is not that we have loved God, but that he loved us and sent his Son to be the means by which our sins are forgiven" (1 John 4:10). In previous chapters we have already seen that Jesus freely comes to save us from our sins, heal us, and make us friends of God and one another. But it is in Christ's Passion and his suffering and death on the cross that his saving work for us is completed. The **Passion** is the extreme sufferings of Jesus' last hours—the whipping, the crown of thorns, the carrying of the cross, and his agony while nailed on the cross—and his death. Through his suffering and death, Jesus frees us from death, which came with sin. Through Christ, we can live with God after death and forever.

Jesus is aware throughout his whole public life of this future final act of love for us. Several times he foretells that he will undergo suffering and death in Jerusalem but also that he will be resurrected after three days (see, for example, Matthew 16:21). He freely gives himself up for each of us. His whole life is given to doing the will of the Father, which is to save us. "No one takes my life away from me. I give it up of my own free will. I have the right to give it up, and I have the right to take it back. This is what my Father has commanded me to do" (John 10:18).

I live by faith in the Son of God, who loved me and gave his life for me. (Galatians 2:20)

THINK ABOUT IT!

Taking up Christ's cross means growing in habits of love. It means accepting the suffering in our lives without becoming bitter. It means giving up some of our comforts and leisure time to help others. What are some ways young people can take up the cross? What people in your family, parish, and community seem to be taking up Christ's cross?

Looking Back

The Stations of the Cross

Most Catholic churches have the **stations of the cross,** images of fourteen scenes from Jesus' sorrowful path to his Crucifixion. They start with Pilate's judgment and end with Jesus' burial. Most of the fourteen traditional stations come from events in the Gospels. Pope John Paul II also created a stations of the cross that is completely based on the Gospel events.

How did the stations become so popular in Catholic churches? Christians have always visited Jerusalem and prayed along the traditional path Jesus took to his Crucifixion. But not everyone could make the trip. By the fifth century, some churches had images of these holy places. Eventually they became so popular that all churches had them.

You can make good use of this devotion by pausing at each of the stations in turn. Imagine each scene and think prayerfully about it. Reading a book of reflections on the stations may also help.

Jesus' Passion

At Mass throughout the year, but most especially during Holy Week and the Easter season, we hear the story of Christ's final sacrifice. We can meditate and pray about Jesus' suffering and death at any time to recall how much God loves us. These stories encourage us to love Christ well and to avoid sin. They teach us to bear our own sufferings with patience. They give us more pity for other people's suffering and pain.

In chapters 22 and 23 of the Gospel of Luke, the story of the events leading to Jesus' Crucifixion goes as follows: some of the Jewish leaders decide Jesus must die, because his teachings challenge their authority and because he claims to be the Messiah. Judas, one of Jesus' Apostles, betrays him for money. Judas leads Jesus' enemies to a garden where Jesus is praying on the Passover evening. Peter and the other disciples desert Jesus. The Jewish council's guards mock and beat him. Unfairly, the council judges him a liar because he claims to be the Messiah.

They bring Jesus before Pilate, the Roman governor, who has Jesus whipped and finally allows him to be crucified as a threat to the Roman Empire. Jesus

THE STATIONS OF THE CROSS

1. Jesus is condemned to death.
2. Jesus takes up his cross.
3. Jesus falls the first time.
4. Jesus meets his mother.
5. Simon helps Jesus carry the cross.
6. Veronica wipes the face of Jesus.
7. Jesus falls the second time.
8. Jesus meets the women of Jerusalem.
9. Jesus falls the third time.
10. Jesus is stripped of his garments.
11. Jesus is nailed to the cross.
12. Jesus dies on the cross.
13. Jesus is taken down from the cross.
14. Jesus is laid in the tomb.

carries his cross through the streets like a common criminal to a place outside the city. There the Roman soldiers strip Jesus of his clothes, nail his hands and feet to the wood, and raise up the cross. Jesus feels lonely and deserted even by the Father. He bleeds and chokes to death.

Even while undergoing this suffering, Jesus shows us an example that teaches us not to judge our enemies. He forgives his torturers. "Forgive them, Father! They don't know what they are doing" (Luke 23:34). He prays the same for all sinners. He suffers and dies to free each of us from our sins so we may truly live.

Images of Jesus' Suffering and Death

The New Testament compares Christ in his suffering and death to several images that Jewish readers would recognize. For instance, John the Baptist calls Jesus "the Lamb of God, who takes away the sin of the world!" (John 1:29). The name recalls the time when God had to force the stubborn Egyptian Pha-

"Lamb of God, you take away the sins of the world." We pray these words at Mass to remember that Jesus is the Passover lamb who is sacrificed to free the people from the slavery of sin.

Shutterstock

Illustration by Elizabeth Wang, 'At the Last Supper, Jesus instituted the Holy Eucharist, which makes present the one sacrifice he offered for our salvation', copyright © Radiant Light 2008, www.radiantlight.org.uk

When Jesus told the Apostles that he would give them his Body and Blood, they must have been very puzzled. When you participate in Mass, what connection do you see between the Last Supper and Jesus' death on the cross?

raoh to free the Jewish people from slavery. The Angel of Death took the oldest male child and animal in each home. But the angel passed over the Jewish homes that had the blood of a lamb sprinkled on the door (see Exodus 12:1–14). The Jews remember this event during the **Passover** festival each year.

Jesus celebrates the Passover with his disciples at the Last Supper, which we recall on Holy Thursday. He himself becomes the Passover lamb who sacrifices himself so his people may escape their slavery to sin and death (see 1 Corinthians 5:7–8). "Then he took a piece of bread, gave thanks to God, broke it, and gave it to them, saying, 'This is my body, which is given for you. Do this in memory of me.' In the same way, he gave them the cup after the supper, saying, 'This cup is God's new covenant sealed with my blood, which is poured out for you'" (Luke 22:19–20). The Last Supper was the first Eucharist. The bread that was broken

PRAY IT!
Liturgy Connection

The Liturgy of the Eucharist begins with the Preparation of the Altar and the Gifts. The bread and wine, which will become Christ's Body and Blood, are presented for the sacrifice. We are also invited to add our own offerings.

Usually a few people attending the Mass bring the bread and wine to the altar. They might also bring money or other goods that have been collected. The priest blesses God, through whose goodness we have the bread and wine. God has also willed that human hands have helped to make them. We respond by praying that God accept our sacrifice "for the praise and glory of his name, for our good, and the good of all his Church."

became Jesus' Body broken for us, and the wine poured out became Jesus' Blood shed for us.

In the Gospel of John, Jesus is both shepherd and sacrificed lamb. Jesus calls himself the Good Shepherd, who cares for his sheep and is willing to die to save them when wolves attack (see John 10:11–13). Jesus too gives up his life for us. Because *paschal* is another word that means "Passover," Jesus is sometimes called the Paschal Lamb. The mystery of how his Passion, death, Resurrection, and Ascension saves us from sin and death is called the **Paschal Mystery.**

Jesus suffered torture, humiliation, and severe pain on the cross. As he died, he spoke words of forgiveness and love to those around him. He even forgave his executioners!

© Brooklyn Museum/Corbis

The Gospel of Matthew quotes from chapter 53 of the Book of Isaiah, which describes the Messiah as the Suffering Servant (see Matthew 8:17). Read the following verse from Isaiah: "My devoted servant, with whom I am pleased, will bear the punishment of many and for his sake I will forgive them" (53:11). Doesn't it sound as if it is talking about Jesus? Many of Isaiah's details of the Messiah's suffering actually happen to Christ.

Think of all the things Jesus allows others to do to him from Holy Thursday evening through Good Friday. He endures physical tortures and emotional turmoil. He experiences rejection, betrayal, desertion, and loneliness. He suffers terrible humiliations and a slow, painful death. He deserves none of these sorrows.

Sometimes we wonder why innocent people suffer. Why does God allow children to die in war or of awful diseases? Why do bad things happen to good people? We know God

Did You Know?
Jesus' Death and the Old Testament

The Old Testament foretells many details of Christ's Passion. For example, Isaiah, chapter 53, says he will be looked down on, rejected, wounded, beaten, arrested, and sentenced. "He took the place of many sinners and prayed that they might be forgiven" (53:12).

In Matthew and Mark's Gospels, Jesus on the cross begins praying Psalm 22: "My God, my God, why have you abandoned me?" (22:1). Other parts of that psalm fit Christ's death. "I am no longer a human being; I am a worm, despised and scorned by everyone! All who see me make fun of me; they stick out their tongues and shake their heads" (22:6–7).

Amazingly, Psalm 22 also refers to Christ's weakness, stretched bones, thirst, and torn hands and feet. People even gamble for his clothes in the psalm. All these things happen at the Crucifixion.

FUN FACT

It is interesting to try to imagine the stories of people who appear only briefly in the Bible. Remember Simon of Cyrene, who was forced to carry the cross (see Mark 15:21)? Simon must have been upset. He was just walking by. This criminal, Jesus, was none of his business. Ever wonder how this meeting with Jesus affected Simon and his family? Our tradition tells us that Simon's sons, Alexander and Rufus, were faithful Christians later.

leaves us free to love. We also can misuse freedom to hurt others. We sometimes see how God brings good results from evil deeds. Pains can bring people closer to God and make them more understanding of others. But innocent suffering is still hard to accept.

Jesus shows us through his totally underserved suffering that God understands and feels our pain. He teaches us that our pain can be offered to God as a pleasing sacrifice and prayer. We can unite our sufferings and all our efforts to do good with the sufferings and good deeds of Christ. In a way we cannot fully understand, they will help Christ's saving and healing action in the world.

Jesus Frees Us from Death

Jesus was without sin. Unlike other human beings, he did not have to die. He chose to die to save us from spiritual death.

Still, no normal person likes to suffer or die. In the Garden of Gethsemane, Jesus prays that he might avoid suffering and death. But he only wants to if it is the Father's will (see Matthew 26:39). Jesus teaches us to overcome our fear of sacrificing ourselves for God and others. He masters his fear of death so we will no longer fear it as our final state.

Jesus Christ has tasted death so we can live forever with God after our earthly lives have ended. He

Live It!

All baptized Christians can unite their efforts to be holy with Christ's sacrifice on the cross. We all can "offer spiritual and acceptable sacrifices to God through Jesus Christ" (1 Peter 2:5). But what exactly can we offer?

A good, basic rule of thumb comes from Paul's First Letter to the Corinthians, as follows: "Whatever you do . . . do it all for God's glory" (10:31). You can offer family time, classes, fun things, and chores. You can offer your efforts to be friendly, patient, and kind. You can offer all your joys and pains. You can offer your attempts to bring others to Christ and to be Christ to them.

Trying to follow the hints of the Holy Spirit from within us, we can offer everything, big or small, that happens in our daily lives. At Mass we can unite our offerings with Jesus' sacrifice. Through them, we can praise and thank God. We can ask for help and show our sorrow for our sins.

"Where, Death, is your victory? Where, Death, is your power to hurt?" Death gets its power to hurt from sin. . . . But thanks be to God who gives us the victory through our Lord Jesus Christ! (1 Corinthians 15:55–57)

This icon shows Jesus descending into hell to free the souls of those who had died before him.

© The State Russian Museum/CORBIS

can accomplish this because he is the Son of God made man, who died and was buried. But can God die? Of course, as the second Person of the Trinity, Christ is eternal and cannot cease to exist. But for a human being, death means the body is so damaged that it can no longer support earthly life. The soul and body separate. Earthly life ends. Jesus freely accepted death in this sense for our sake.

From Good Friday until Easter Sunday, Jesus' body was in the tomb. It did not decay, because his physical body was still united to the divine Person of Christ. But the human soul did not give it life.

PEOPLE OF FAITH
Saint Dismas

© 2009 Saint Mary's Press/Illustration by Vicki Shuck

Do you know the story of Saint Dismas, the Good Thief? You can read it in Luke 23:32–43. One of the two criminals crucified with Christ insults him. The other, known to us as Dismas, defends Jesus as an innocent man. "And he said to Jesus, 'Remember me, Jesus, when you come as King!' Jesus said to him, 'I promise you that today you will be in Paradise with me'" (Luke 23:42–43). Jesus sees that Dismas has a good

Where was Jesus' human soul? The Apostles' Creed tells us that after death, Jesus "descended into hell." Hell here means the place where the souls of all the people who had died before Christ's coming, good and bad, had gone after death. None of them could go to Heaven until Christ reconciled them with God. Now "in his human soul united to his divine person, the dead Christ went down to the realm of the dead. He opened heaven's gates for the just who had gone before him." Christ led their way to Heaven when he was raised from the dead on Easter Sunday.

PRAY IT!

Jesus,
Thank you for your generous love in sacrificing yourself for me and all people. Help me forget about myself and give my life for others. Show me how I can take up your cross by serving people in little ways. Remind me to offer everything I do in union with you in joy and hope. Teach me to bear pains well and to comfort others who are in pain.

Amen

heart and is sorry for his sins. Jesus promises him a place in Heaven.

Dismas is the patron saint of criminals and condemned prisoners. We might see him as the saint of so-called hopeless cases. His story reminds us not to give up on anyone. Even very bad people can turn to God's mercy while they live. Many great sinners have become great saints. We celebrate the Feast of Saint Dismas on March 25.

14 THE RESURRECTION OF JESUS

In any class or activity, some basic facts are especially important. In math, you need to grasp what the different math signs mean. In soccer, you need to learn what you're expected to do in playing your position. In chess, you need to know how the different pieces can move.

Jesus' **Resurrection,** the fact that on the Sunday after Good Friday, he rose from the dead, is a key fact of our faith that enables us to understand and live it rightly. It is God's greatest miracle. It proves beyond doubt the truth of Jesus' claims, teachings, and mission. It completes our reunion with God. It promises our own resurrection and eternal life with God.

Christ's first followers clearly saw the importance of the Resurrection. They either saw the risen Jesus with their own eyes or knew honest people who had seen him. What if Jesus hadn't risen, asked Paul? "Then we have nothing to preach and you have nothing to believe" (1 Corinthians 15:14). Some people made fun of Paul for preaching that

Key Words

Resurrection
Ascension
judgment

Christ was raised from the dead, but others were curious and wanted to know more (see Acts 17:32). Let's take a closer look at why it is so important for us to believe in Jesus' Resurrection.

Jesus said to her, "I am the resurrection and the life. Those who believe in me will live, even though they die." (John 11:25)

Did You Know?

Views on Resurrection

Some Jews in Jesus' time had strong views about the rising of the dead. The Pharisees taught that the soul would join its body when the Messiah's reign ended. On the other hand, the Sadducees believed there was no life after death, that not even the soul lived after death.

Once, Paul was arrested but not getting a fair trial. He delayed it by getting the two groups to argue over whether there was a resurrection (see Acts 23:6–11).

When Jesus rose from the dead, it was great news for his followers. Why does the Resurrection continue to be good news for Christians today?

Illustration by Elizabeth Wang, "The Resurrection," copyright © Radiant Light 2008, www.radiantlight.org.uk

Imagine the great joy Mary Magdalene felt when she recognized Jesus in the Garden! She was the first witness to the Resurrection. How would you have reacted if you had seen Jesus alive after he was crucified? Whom would you have told? Whom will you tell about Jesus?

© Alinari Archives/CORBIS

The Risen Christ

Jesus had told the disciples he would rise again. Still, most of them were not expecting that Jesus would actually die, especially in such a horrible way. Why? The disciples had often seen Jesus brush aside his enemies. They saw the people of Jerusalem hail him as a hero a few days before his arrest. He was their superstar who would triumph against the opposing team—who in this case was the Jewish and Roman leaders.

Then suddenly something completely unexpected happened. Their hero, who seemed so strong and in control, now seemed weak and powerless. After his arrest Jesus seemed totally defeated. Within one day he was put to a horrible death. The disciples were in shock.

They didn't believe it when the women reported the empty tomb and the angel's message. They thought it was nonsense (see Luke 24:1–12). They believed only after Jesus had appeared several times to a variety of people. Even after he appeared to Simon and the others, John's Gospel says that the absent Thomas refused to believe (see John 20:24–28). Jesus even scolded the disciples because "they did not have faith and because they were too stubborn to believe those who had seen him alive" (Mark 16:14).

God gives us faith to believe in the Resurrection. "How happy are those who believe without seeing me!" (John 20:29). But for the first disciples it was an unexpected and wonderful reality that they believed, because they saw the risen Jesus with their own eyes. They really saw and spoke with the risen Christ.

Jesus raised others from the dead. His own return is different. His body and soul are reunited through God's power. His body is still human. It has the scars of his suffering and death. Jesus can build fires, eat, and be touched. But his body is now glorified.

Think About It!

People recognize the risen Christ in different ways. Mary Magdalene knows him by his voice. The disciples of Emmaus know him by the way he breaks the bread at table. Thomas says he actually has to touch Jesus' wounds. Do people see Jesus in us? Can they see him in the way we behave toward others? in the way we talk about them? in our attitudes toward people and things? How else can others see Jesus in us?

PRAY IT!
Liturgy Connection

Funerals are sad events. We will miss our friend or relative who has died. Especially when he or she is someone close to us, our loss can be painful. We know we will not be able to see him or her in this life again.

But the funeral liturgies remind us of our hope in the resurrection. For example, in Masses for the dead, we pray that the dead person may share in the final resurrection. We also pray that "Christ will raise our mortal bodies and make them like his own in glory." We ask Jesus to welcome his friends into his Kingdom. "There . . . every tear will be wiped away . . . We shall see you, our God, as you are. We shall become like you and praise you for ever."

Jesus' humanity has entered a new realm beyond earthly time and space. He can pass through walls, appear and disappear at will, and change how he looks. His humanity has entered the divine life of God's Kingdom.

May you always be joyful in your union with the Lord. I say it again: rejoice! (Philippians 4:4)

Jesus' death and Resurrection free us from sin. We begin to share in his death and Resurrection when we are baptized. We become reconciled with God, his children, and brothers and sisters of Christ. Jesus is the "first-born Son, who was raised from death" (Colossians 1:18). In and through him, we too will be resurrected. Our souls and bodies will be reunited. We die because we are descendents of Adam. But "all will be raised to life because of their union with Christ" (1 Corinthians 15:22). He will make our mortal bodies become like his glorious body (see Philippians 3:21).

The Ascension

"For forty days after his death he appeared to them many times in ways that proved beyond doubt that he was alive. They saw him, and he talked with them about the Kingdom of God" (Acts 1:3–4). During this time Jesus completes his teaching. He explains what is "said about himself in all the Scriptures, beginning with the books of Moses and the writings of all the prophets" (Luke 24:27). He again says Peter must follow him as the chief shepherd of the Church (see John 21:15–19). He again gives all the Apostles the mission to teach and baptize in his name throughout the entire world (see Matthew 28:18–20).

Fun Fact

We don't know what our glorified bodies will be like. Do you think Jesus had fun walking around without being recognized after the Resurrection? He could have just shown himself to the disciples on the road to Emmaus. Instead, he hides his true identity from them when they first meet. Finally he reveals himself and gives them great hope (see Luke 24:13–35).

After the Resurrection and before Jesus ascended into Heaven, he gave his friends some final instructions. Read these pages to find out what Jesus wanted them to know.

At the Last Supper, the Gospel of John recalls, Jesus has already told them he must return to the Father. He must prepare a place for them. He must go for the Spirit to come (see John 14:2, 16:7). So "he was taken up to heaven as they watched him, and a cloud hid him from their sight" (Acts 1:9). By his **Ascension** Jesus returns to the Father. His humanity enters God's heavenly realm completely. The glory of his resurrected body, veiled on earth so it would not overwhelm his disciples, shines forth fully. Jesus opens the way for us. He gives us the power to enter into God's life and eternal joy.

The Creed says Jesus "is seated at the right hand of the Father." This shows the honor given Jesus' humanity. It also means he is the true ruler of the world. Now that he has ascended into Heaven, we his followers continue Jesus' mission of announcing his endless Kingdom of love and hastening its coming on earth.

Live It!

All baptized people share in Christ's kingly mission. God calls us to help make his Kingdom spread more throughout the world.

First, we have to let God's Kingdom reign more in us. We need to overcome the reign of sin within us and let the Holy Spirit guide our minds, hearts, and wills. For example, we may need to control our tempers, unkind talk, or impatience more.

We also need to make Christ's Kingdom more present around us. Our good examples can help others live in the Kingdom more. If they see we treat people well, they are more likely to do the same.

Our good leadership can also help others. As team captains or class officers, for instance, we might help the rest understand and respect one another better.

Enemies attack the Kingdom often. The Church and God's people must suffer many trials. The Scriptures even refer to the Antichrist, a wicked person or persons who put themselves in the place of God. They will try to make people think that the world's problems can be solved without God's truth and help.

Jesus tells us to watch but not to worry. He is always with us, and he gives us the Holy Spirit to guide and strengthen us. He urges us to remain loyal, no matter what happens. Christ will come again in glory at the end of time to reveal himself to the entire world.

PRAY IT!

Jesus,
  Help us recall your
    Resurrection often.
  May its hope be
    with us always.
  May we desire, pray,
    and work to hasten
    your Kingdom's coming on earth. May we
    enjoy its glory with
    you forever.
        Amen

All who follow Christ, both the living and the dead, share community. We live and pray with hope for the day when we will all be united in love with God in Heaven.

Illustration by Elizabeth Wang, 'The Glory and the Gathering', copyright © Radiant Light 2008, www.radiantlight.org.uk

Then Christ will judge the living and the dead. In this last **judgment,** he will reveal our inner thoughts and desires, good and bad. He will know if we have accepted or refused the spiritual helps he gives us. He will judge whether we have known how to see and serve him in the needs of other people. He will give to each of us fairly according to our deeds.

In fact, Jesus' primary mission is not to judge us. His primary purpose is rather to save us so we can enjoy eternal life with God. In a sense, we

PEOPLE OF FAITH
Saint Mary Magdalene

© 2009 Saint Mary's Press/Illustration by Vicki Shuck

The first person to see the risen Christ is Saint Mary Magdalene. She goes with others on Easter Sunday to prepare Jesus' body for burial. They find the tomb empty (see Luke 24:1–11). She is upset. She thinks Jesus' enemies have taken away the body. In the Gospel of John, Jesus appears at first to her alone, and she gladly goes to report the event to the others (see John 20:11–18).

really judge ourselves when we reject Jesus and the salvation he offers us. But God wants everyone to be saved (see 1 Timothy 2:3–4). We have to keep trying to grow in the Spirit, whom Jesus sends to us. Then we will live in the kingdom of love forever.

> My dear friends, we are now God's children, but it is not yet clear what we shall become. But we know that when Christ appears, we shall be like him.
> (1 John 3:2)

Jesus drove seven demons out of Mary (see Mark 16:9). She is grateful and close to him. She helps Jesus and the Apostles when they travel to preach the Good News. When almost everyone else deserts Jesus, she remains loyal. She overcomes her fear. "Standing close to Jesus' cross were his mother, his mother's sister, Mary the wife of Clopas, and Mary Magdalene" (John 19:25).

The Lord has healed us too. Mary Magdalene should inspire us to be loyal and grateful to him. Her bravery should give us the heart to stay close to Jesus when it is tough to do so. We celebrate her feast day on July 22.

PART 3

The Holy Spirit and the Church

I believe in the Holy Spirit, the holy catholic Church, the communion of saints, the forgiveness of sins, the resurrection of the body, and the life everlasting.

15 The Holy Spirit

"Let's see who can hold their breath the longest!" You and your friends have probably challenged each other to this contest at some time. You know how it goes: you watch each other take a deep breath and hold it until you both begin to turn red (or blue!). Your eyes start to bulge. Then one of you gasps for air. Have you gone under water to see if you can reach the other side of a pool without taking a breath? Have you run a 100-meter dash and thought, "I could have done better if I hadn't run out of breath"?

Actually, most of us don't think about our breathing often, maybe not at all (that is, until we're out of breath and gasping for air). At their children's birth, parents wait to hear the cry that tells them their babies are breathing. Why? A newborn who breathes is alive. The phrase breath of life definitely has meaning in human biology, even if we do take breathing for granted.

What if we let our experiences of breathing lead us to a deeper reflection? What (or who) is the breath of life for the universe? What is the life

force that makes it all hang together? Who brings us together, energizes us, gives us life, and helps us live fully—not just in a I'm-a-human-who-breathes sort of way—but also in a spiritual, holy way? These questions lead us straight to the **Holy Spirit,** the third Person of the Trinity.

The Breath of God

The Holy Spirit might not be as familiar to you as the Father and the Son, the two other Persons of the Holy Trinity. People don't talk about the Holy Spirit as much as they do the Father and the Son. He's more often behind the scenes rather than on center stage. We might not be aware of his activity, much as we don't notice our own breathing. Yet a truth of our faith is that the Father, Son, and Holy Spirit are one God, and together they are responsible for creation. In fact, together they are responsible for everything. Jesus Christ and the Holy Spirit, the Word and Breath

Live It!

God's gift of love is his first gift to us. He wants us to share in his life: "This hope does not disappoint us, for God has poured out his love into our hearts by means of the Holy Spirit, who is God's gift to us" (Romans 5:5). People who are filled with God's Spirit show their love for God through their attitudes and actions. They are loving, joyful, peaceful, and patient. The Holy Spirit helps people be kind and faithful, full of goodness, gentleness, and self-control (see Galatians 5:22). Whom do you know who shows God's love by doing kind things for others? For example, do you know someone who expresses love by his patience with others or her faithfulness to friends and family? Write that person a thank-you note for being a witness of God's gift of love.

THiNK About It!

We believe the Holy Spirit is the breath of God. What does this image tell you about the Holy Spirit? What does this image tell you about the Holy Spirit's role in your life?

of God, are inseparable from each other and from the Father. Whenever the Father sends his Son on a mission, he always sends his Spirit.

One way to understand the Holy Spirit is with the image of breath. Think of it in the following way: God's Spirit breathes God's life into us. Much as our own breath, which keeps our bodies alive, the breath of the Spirit gives us God's life. Through the Spirit we experience God's gift of love. We might not always be aware of the Holy Spirit's presence, but through him we come to know who God is. Through him we can know Jesus.

One artist pictures the Holy Spirit's power to transform us. Take a deep breath and imagine this transforming power within you and around you.

Illustration by Elizabeth Wang, 'If we allow Him, the Holy Spirit will transform us and make us holy', copyright © Radiant Light 2008, www.radiantlight.org.uk

God's Spirit Prepares the Way

Let's take a minute to look at the movement of the Holy Spirit throughout time. The Spirit of God first appears in the Book of Genesis as the wind that moves over the water: "In the beginning when God created the heavens and the earth, the earth was a formless void and darkness covered the face of the deep, while a wind from God swept over the face of the waters" (Genesis 1:1–2, NRSV). Here we focus on the word *wind*. In Hebrew, wind is *ruah*, which can also mean "breath" or "spirit." Substitute those words for wind, and we can read the verse the following way: "a Spirit of God, or Breath of God, swept over the face of the waters." We see that the Spirit of God was present in the beginning, bringing life out of nothingness.

Did You Know?

Symbols of the Holy Spirit

The Catholic Church uses visual symbols to help us understand the Holy Spirit. The following are three of them:

+ **Water** symbolizes the Holy Spirit's actions in Baptism. Jesus tells us that the Spirit is the "living water" that quenches our thirst for God (see John 7:37–39).

+ **Fire** transforms. It is vibrant and full of energy. The Holy Spirit appears to the Apostles as tongues of fire at Pentecost (see Acts 2:1–4). The Holy Spirit energizes and transforms us.

+ **A cloud and light** hide and reveal. In the Old Testament, God often appeared as a fire or light within a cloud (see Exodus 40:38, Ezekiel 1:4). The Holy Spirit hides and reveals God's glory. Clouds play a role in Jesus' Baptism (see Matthew 3:13–17), Transfiguration (see Matthew 17:1–8), and Ascension (see Acts 1:6–11).

PRAY IT!
Liturgy Connection

The next time you are at Mass, notice how, during the Eucharistic Prayer, the priest joins his hands and then holds them outstretched over the altar and makes the Sign of the Cross. He prays as follows: "Let your Spirit come upon these gifts to make them holy, so that they may become for us the Body and Blood of our Lord, Jesus Christ."

At this moment, the priest asks the Holy Spirit to make holy the bread and wine so Christ will be truly present. The gift of Communion, made possible by the Spirit, is the food that nourishes us to bear fruit in the Church as disciples of Jesus.

Throughout the Old Testament, the Spirit of God works quietly behind the scenes, preparing God's people for the coming of the Messiah. The Spirit does amazing work to prepare a people for the Lord. God speaks through the prophets about what the Messiah will be like. "The spirit of the Lord will give him wisdom, and the knowledge and skill to rule his people" (Isaiah 11:2). Isaiah also announces that the Messiah to come is filled with God's Spirit and that "he will bring justice to every nation" (Isaiah 42:1). Through the Holy Spirit, people will come to know Jesus Christ.

The spirit of the Lord will give him wisdom, and the knowledge and skill to rule his people. (Isaiah 11:2)

Read the "Liturgy Connection" article above to find out what the priest is doing when he makes the sign of the cross over the bread and wine at Mass.

© Design Pics/Corbis

In the Fullness of Time

One of the Holy Spirit's greatest success stories is Mary, the teenager from Nazareth who became the Mother of God. The *Catechism of the Catholic Church* calls her "the masterwork of the mission of the Son and the Spirit in the fullness of time" (CCC, number 721). Imagine being God's masterwork. This is what the Spirit can do. The Holy Spirit prepared Mary to give birth to **Emmanuel,** which means "God with us." Through her, God's plan of bringing Jesus into the world would happen.

How did the Holy Spirit prepare Mary to welcome Jesus? By his power and love, Mary was "full of grace," full of God's life and love. Filled with the Holy Spirit, she conceived and gave birth to the Son of God. Watch what happened next. Thanks to Mary's cooperation, the Holy Spirit brought people together into relationship with her Son, Jesus Christ. The first of these people were the poor and humble like the shepherds, Simeon, and Anna.

Jesus and the Spirit

Nearly two thousand years ago, Jesus began his earthly ministry with the following words:

> "The Spirit of the Lord is upon me, because he has chosen me to bring good news to the poor. He has sent me to proclaim liberty to the captives and recovery of sight to the blind, to set free

the oppressed and announce that the time has come when the Lord will save his people" (Luke 4:18–19).

By reading this Scripture passage to those gathered in the synagogue, Jesus tells them that his mission and the Spirit's mission are the same. In fact, Jesus' whole work is a joint mission with the Holy Spirit. Jesus reveals this close connection with the Holy Spirit before his death when he makes the following promise to the disciples: "I will ask the Father, and he will give you another Helper, who will stay with you forever. He is the Spirit, who reveals the truth about God" (John 14:16–17).

On a Mission

After Jesus is crucified and raised from the dead, he visits the Apostles. Remember that he has promised to send the Holy Spirit. But the disciples are afraid. They have just watched Jesus die on the cross. They are huddled behind locked doors when, suddenly, Jesus appears in the middle of the room. He says to them, "'Peace be with you. As the Father sent me, so I send you.' Then he breathed on them and said, 'Receive the Holy Spirit. If you forgive people's sins, they are forgiven; if you do not forgive them, they are not forgiven'" (John 20:21–22).

Pray It!

Holy God, our Father,
We praise and thank you for the gift of love that your Holy Spirit poured out on us. May your Spirit breathe on us and fill us with your grace. Help us recognize that the Holy Spirit is bringing us closer to your Son and that with the help of the Holy Spirit, we can live as Jesus' disciples. Amen.

© Laura Dwight/CORBIS

Simple acts of kindness may not seem like a big deal. But they are actually signs of the Holy Spirit's life within us.

"Peace be with you. As the Father sent me, so I send you." Then he breathed on them and said, "Receive the Holy Spirit. If you forgive people's sins, they are forgiven; if you do not forgive them, they are not forgiven." (John 20:21–22)

Fifty days after Jesus rises from the dead, on the Feast of Pentecost, the Holy Spirit descends on the disciples. The breath of God fills them in a new way. It gives them the courage to go out and preach the message of Jesus Christ. Think of it in the following way: through Christ and the Holy Spirit, God the Father gives the Church her job description: go to the ends of the earth. Spread the Good News of salvation. This job description is the Church's mission. "The mission of Christ and the Spirit becomes the mission of the Church" (CCC, number 730). Sometimes you might hear

FUN FACT

Since that day when the Holy Spirit descended upon the small group of Apostles and empowered them to make disciples of all nations, the number of people who believe in Jesus Christ has grown to more than two billion people. This is 33 percent of the world's population. More than one billion of them are Catholic. In the United States, 23 percent of the population, more than 69 million people, are Catholic (Bunson, 2007 Catholic Almanac, page 333).

people say Pentecost was the birthday of the Church. This is because in a certain sense, the Church's mission began in a new way at Pentecost. Strengthened by the Holy Spirit and under the guidance of the Spirit, the Church continues the mission of Christ in the world.

How does the Holy Spirit act in the Church? He prepares God's people and goes out to them with his

PEOPLE OF FAITH
Saint John the Evangelist

© 2009 Saint Mary's Press/Illustration by Vicki Shuck

Saint John, a fisherman, was one of the first Apostles. Jesus chose him and his brother, James. Jesus "saw two other brothers . . . in their boat with their father Zebedee, getting their nets ready. Jesus called them, and at once they left the boat and their father, and went with him" (Matthew 4:21–22). John witnessed and participated in Jesus' ministry. He may also have been the beloved disciple in St. John's Gospel but this is unclear. If so, he was also at the foot of the cross with Mary,

love, to bring them to Christ. The Holy Spirit shows us who Christ is. He opens our minds to understand the mystery of Jesus' death and Resurrection. He makes present today the mystery of Christ through the sacraments of the Church—mainly the Eucharist, so that we will be one with God—in communion with him. The Holy Spirit, the Breath of God, works in the Church to build her up, to bring her life, and to make her holy.

when Jesus told his mother that John would take care of her from now on. "Jesus saw his mother and the disciple he loved standing there; so he said to his mother, 'He is your son'" (John 19:26).

Tradition tells us that John's teachings about the Good News to the early Church are the source of the Gospel of John. John is called the Evangelist because to evangelize means to "spread the Good News." An important part of John's message is Jesus' promise to send the Holy Spirit. John calls the Spirit an **Advocate,** a helper and supporter who "will teach you everything and make you remember all that I have told you" (John 14:26, NRSV). You will notice that John's Gospel spends more time reflecting on the meaning of Jesus' words and actions rather than describing them. You may recognize the following Scripture passage: "For God loved the world so much that he gave his only Son, so that everyone who believes in him may not die but have eternal life" (John 3:16). John the Evangelist's message is that we love God and love one another. We celebrate his feast on December 27.

16 GRACE AND THE GIFTS OF THE HOLY SPIRIT

FUN FACT

One of the most common forms of prayer is meal prayers, or grace. Prayers of thanksgiving for food are found in religious texts and cultures all over the world. Grace is the thanks-to-God acknowledgment for our food, which is a gift from God. When we say grace at mealtimes, we acknowledge God's presence among us.

Have you ever received a gift that was really amazing and unexpected? Maybe it wasn't a material thing that cost a lot of money. Maybe instead it was a kind gesture, help with a difficult task, or a thoughtful compliment from a friend. When you received this gift, maybe you thought to yourself, "Wow! That's really cool. I don't deserve it."

We actually could say the same thing about the gift of God's grace. We can't do anything by ourselves to deserve or earn this amazing gift. What is grace? **Grace** is the gift of God's loving presence in our lives. It is the help he gives us through the Holy Spirit to participate in God's life. God wants us to be with him. At Baptism, we receive the life of the Holy Spirit. The Spirit breathes love into us. This gift of grace draws us into close relationship with God the Father and Jesus Christ and gives us the help we need to become God's adopted sons and daughters.

God Takes the First Step

God made us to be with him. Every human heart longs for truth and goodness. This longing comes from God, and only he can satisfy it. God's gift of grace responds to the deepest yearnings of our hearts. One way to think about this is to imagine that there is a God-shaped vacuum or hole in every heart. Only God can fill it. We are made to be with God. God takes the first step with grace, his life. God does not force his gift of love on us. How we respond to it is up to us. God has created us in his image and given us the freedom and ability to know him and love him. God is going to love us, regardless. Nothing forces us to love God in return.

Key Words

grace

sanctifying grace

Gifts of the Holy Spirit

Live It!

Every day this week, look at your life in a new way. Look around you to see what God makes possible in your life. Perhaps God's grace makes possible the random acts of kindness you witness and the loving forgiveness family members offer each other. Maybe you will find God's grace in the gesture of a consoling hug or the words of a grateful friend. Do you see that God's life in you gives you the courage to say no to choices that will hurt you or others? Do you recognize that through God's presence, you can say words like "I am sorry" and "I forgive you" and really mean them? God's grace makes it possible for us to live healthy and holy lives. Choose to be with God every day.

Let God's Grace In

What happens when we let God's grace in? Grace achieves real change in us. When a person is filled with God's life, it shows. In the Gospels Jesus used the metaphor of good fruit to explain what happens when a person says yes to God. "You will know them by what they do. Thorn bushes do not bear grapes, and briers do not bear figs. A healthy tree bears good fruit" (Matthew 7:16–17).

> "Those who love me will obey my teaching. My Father will love them, and my Father and I will come to them and live with them." (John 14:23)

A person who says yes to God's invitation to participate in his life acts in a way that reflects the values of Jesus. We don't do this because we want to carn a merit badge or to get something in return. We do good works out of love for God. It's not only what we do on the outside that matters. What is on the inside matters too. Look for the following in-

Think About It!

We are sharers in God's life. This means we can be with God every minute of every day. How is your life different because God is a part of it?

Compassion is evidence that grace, God's love, is at work. Can you think of times, both happy and sad, when you were aware of grace in your life?

© Creasource/Corbis

dicators that God's grace is working in you and others: friendliness, willingness to forgive, respect for others, peacefulness, compassion, humility, thankfulness, and a helping spirit, just to name a few. All our actions that point others and ourselves to God are because of God's grace working in us.

Give Love Away

When we participate in God's life, we give love away. We have to. Why? Because God made us in his image and likeness, and that is what God does. He gives his love away. All the good we do and all the love we have belongs to God. It is for God. Grace is never something we earn. But something amazing happens when we choose to love. We open ourselves more and more to the gifts God constantly offers us. The love and the grace just keep coming. We keep giving it away to others because God's love has transformed us from the inside out.

Did You Know?

Sanctifying Grace

God loves us. He wants to be part of our lives. He wants to be involved. God freely offers us the gift of his life. We call this gift **sanctifying grace.** We need God's help to be holy, to be right with God. The sin of turning away from God, which is what Adam and Eve chose to do, damages the relationship God wants to have with us, his creatures. The gift of his sanctifying grace repairs the damage of sin and enables us to experience God's love. Through the Holy Spirit, we are united to Christ's dying and rising. We die to sin and are given new life. Sanctifying grace heals our sins and makes us holy. God wants our relationship with him to be put right again.

Jesus was filled with God's love and gave it away to others. Jesus made God's life real for us; he was incarnate grace, that is, in-the-flesh grace. We can be in-the-flesh grace too. We can bring God to others.

Reference: 443-MW

JOB DESCRIPTION

Job Title: Being Christian

Reports To: God and the community

Job Summary: Living as disciples of Jesus Christ

Responsibilities: Loving God, loving others, loving ourselves

Job Requirements: Willingness to let God's grace work in you!

Everything Is Possible with God's Grace

Grace definitely has an eternal effect on our relationship with God. Exactly what the effect is depends on how well we accept the gift. Think about what you do when you receive a gift. You don't leave it wrapped and put it high on the shelf in your closet, do you? You open it. This is what we need to do with the gift of God's grace in our lives.

People who accept the gift of God's grace open the gift and use it. We fulfill our job descriptions as Catholics. We can reach out to the new person at school and offer our friendship. We can forgive the person who hurt us, even when it is difficult. We can clean out our closets and give our extra clothes to someone who needs them. We can pitch in at home to help with the chores and resist the urge to fight with our brothers or sisters. We can thank God, every day, for

Did You Know?

Everything Is Possible

There are times you might think, "Doing what God wants me to do is hard work." The fact is, we cannot, by ourselves, keep the Commandments. We cannot, on our own power, love as God calls us to love. We need the grace of God. Jesus tells us, "I am the vine, and you are the branches. Those who remain in me, and I in them, will bear much fruit; for you can do nothing without me" (John 15:5). Even the very beginnings of our relationship with God are a result of his initial love for us. The good news is, everything is possible with God in our lives. He wants us to be happy and to have the things we need for this life and eternal life. He makes all this possible because he loves us so much.

his blessings. We can love God and love our neighbors as ourselves.

"As I have loved you, so you must love one another. If you have love for one another, then everyone will know you are my disciples." (John 13:34–35)

The Gifts of the Holy Spirit

God gives us the **Gifts of the Holy Spirit** to help us love him. These are special graces that help us respond to God's call to live holy lives. The Seven Gifts of the Holy Spirit are wisdom, understanding, right judgment (or counsel), courage (or fortitude), knowledge, reverence (or piety), and wonder and awe (or fear of the Lord). These gifts help us follow Jesus Christ and live as his disciples. Let's take a closer look, as follows:

- **Wisdom.** Wisdom is to see as God sees. Imagine that. A person with the gift of wisdom looks at life through God's eyes, assesses the things going on in his or her life and in the world from God's point of view. A wise person recognizes where the Holy Spirit is at work in the world.

PRAY IT!

God of all grace, I praise you and thank you for sharing your life with me. Through Jesus, your Son, I see how your grace can change the world. Help me accept your invitation to participate in your life. May the grace you offer me through your Holy Spirit put things right between you and me. Heal me and make me holy in your sight. Amen

- **Understanding.**
  Understanding is an important gift for finding the meaning of God's truths and their significance for our lives. Understanding helps us recognize how God wants us to live.

- **Right judgment (Counsel).** This gift helps us make choices that will lead us closer to God rather than away from God. The gift of right judgment, also called counsel, helps us figure out what God wants. It helps us know the difference between right and wrong when we make decisions.

- **Courage (Fortitude).**
  Life can be difficult. The gift of courage, also called fortitude, is the special help we need when faced with challenges or struggles. Those who have the gift of courage don't let life's obstacles pull them away from God.

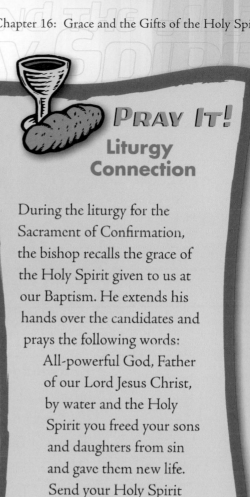

PRAY IT!
Liturgy Connection

During the liturgy for the Sacrament of Confirmation, the bishop recalls the grace of the Holy Spirit given to us at our Baptism. He extends his hands over the candidates and prays the following words:

All-powerful God, Father of our Lord Jesus Christ, by water and the Holy Spirit you freed your sons and daughters from sin and gave them new life. Send your Holy Spirit upon them to be their Helper and Guide. Give them the spirit of wisdom and understanding, the spirit of right judgment and courage, the spirit of knowledge and reverence. Fill them with the spirit of wonder and awe in your presence.

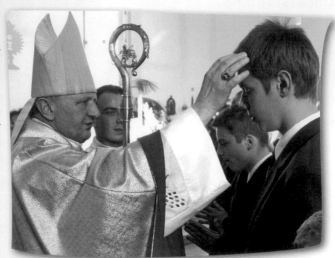

In the Sacrament of Confirmation, the bishop anoints the candidate and says, "Be sealed with the Gift of the Holy Spirit."

© Krzysztof Œwiderski/PAP/Corbis

- **Knowledge.** This gift helps us understand the meaning of what God has revealed, particularly the Good News of Jesus Christ. A person with the gift of knowledge keeps striving to learn more about God through the Scriptures and the Church's Tradition. This gift is closely related to the gifts of understanding and wisdom.

- **Reverence (Piety).** This gift, sometimes called piety, gives us a deep sense of respect for God and the Church. A reverent person honors God and approaches him with humility, trust, and love.

- **Wonder and Awe (Fear of the Lord).** The gift of wonder and awe makes us aware of God's greatness and power. This gift is also called "fear of the Lord." This is because the wonder of God's love and unlimited power can overwhelm us. It may fill us with tears of joy or bring us to our knees when we recognize that God is present in our midst.

PRAY IT!
Liturgy Connection

The Holy Spirit is a central focus of the Sacrament of Confirmation. The connection of the Holy Spirit to Confirmation can mislead us into thinking that the Holy Spirit isn't with us until we celebrate that sacrament. Yes, we receive the Seven Gifts of the Holy Spirit at Confirmation, but that doesn't mean the Holy Spirit has not already been at work in us. Each of us receives the gift of the Holy Spirit at our Baptisms. In Baptism, God brings us new life "through water and the Holy Spirit." God adopts us as his sons and daughters. We are entrusted with the mission of Jesus Christ.

17

PENTECOST AND THE EARLY CHURCH

To spread the news about Jesus Christ in the early years of the Church, there were no cable news networks, satellite TV, cell phones, Internet, e-mail, MySpace, or blogs; no IM-ing or texting; and no Fed-Ex overnight delivery. Yet, within twenty years after Jesus' death, Christianity had spread across a large

The good news about Jesus spread far and wide. Check out this map of Saint Paul's travels. Trace his journey to Rome, where he was martyred.

PAUL'S THIRD AND FOURTH JOURNEYS
(ACTS 18:23—21:16; 27—28:16)

→ Third missionary journey (c. A.D. 53–57)
- - → Fourth missionary journey (c. A.D. 59–62)

© 2001 by Thomas Nelson, Inc.

geographical area. How could Christianity have spread so quickly without modern means of communication?

Hop in a time machine. Take yourself back to the first century AD. You know when friends change—you notice something different about how they act or look. Sometimes you wonder and want to ask, "What's different about you? Something's different." Now imagine that your friend next door, back in the first century, is acting a bit differently. You can't quite pinpoint what it is. His family regularly gathers with other families in their homes. You're not sure what they do when they meet. His parents still go about their daily business of taking care of work and ordinary tasks. Even your parents comment there seems to be a certain something different that wasn't there before, like a peacefulness or joy in them. You notice this in your friend too. There's something different about how

Did You Know?

On This Rock

Jesus knew that after he was gone, his disciples would need a leader. He prepared the Apostle Peter for this role. In a conversation between Jesus and Peter, Jesus asks him, "Who do you say that I am?" Peter replies, "You are the Messiah, the Son of the living God" (Matthew 16:15–16). Peter understands who Jesus is. Jesus says to him, "And so I tell you, Peter: you are a rock, and on this rock foundation I will build my church, and not even death will ever be able to overcome it. I will give you the keys of the Kingdom of heaven" (Matthew 16:18–19). Peter would be the one to lead the Church after Jesus was gone.

THiNk About It!

The work of making the Good News of Jesus Christ known in the world today is the responsibility of every follower of Jesus. How do you participate in the call to make disciples of all nations? How does knowing that the Spirit is alive in you affect how you see the world and your place in it?

he is treating his sister (whom he's never gotten along with well), and he is actually helping out around the neighborhood.

Finally, you ask, "You've changed. Something is different. What's happened?" Your friend might say something like, "Yes. I have changed. My family is Christian now. We follow the teachings of Jesus Christ." You're curious, so you say, "Tell me more." Now remember, this is the first century. Your friend does not whip out a Bible from his pocket or pull a *Catechism* off the shelf. None of these things was in the early Church. Instead, he would rely on the spoken word and the modeling of a new way of life. With the help of the Holy Spirit, he would share this new faith with you.

The Spirit at Work

Hop back into your time machine. Come back to the present. Imaginative scenes like the one just described can't capture the reality of life during the early years of the Church. While some families like the one mentioned above may have kept their faith fairly quiet, other Christians were open and vocal. They actively recruited followers and preached the Gospel, even when this meant risking persecution.

The Acts of the Apostles gives us the earliest written accounts of the Church. Acts describes what we call the Apostolic Church—the Church of the Apostles and their first followers. It describes the travels of Peter and Paul spreading the Word of God from Jerusalem to the far reaches of the Roman Empire. A main theme in Acts is how the Holy Spirit worked to guide the community so the Word of God could spread.

Let's recall how it all started. Jesus does not leave his Apostles, not even Peter, with a "getting started" guide. There are no step-by-step instructions for what to do next. Jesus doesn't map out an organizational plan for the Church. He doesn't give them a practice schedule or leave them with a week-at-a-glance

Fun Fact

Rome was the most important city in the Roman Empire at the time of Jesus' earthly ministry. Thanks to the work of people like Peter and Paul, the Church in Rome became the most important in the Church, and the bishop of Rome became the most important Church leader, known as the Pope. Pope Benedict XVI is the current bishop of Rome and the Pope.

Live It!

After they received the Holy Spirit, the Apostles could speak to total strangers and spread the Good News to people with whom they shared nothing in common, not even their languages. You might experience a world of difference between you and another person such as culture, interests, friends, race, ages, and religion. Sometimes it is difficult to overcome those differences.

Get to know someone who is different than you are. Take the time to find out about the beliefs you share and the beliefs that are different for each of you. Discover that people who are different from you can be a gift. They help you be more accepting and respectful. They can help you become a better person. Maybe you will even have a chance to share why Jesus is important to you, as the early Christians did.

planner, homework assignments, or agenda items for meetings. Instead, what he leaves them with is the promise that he will send his Spirit to guide them. "The Helper, the Holy Spirit, whom the Father will send in my name, will teach you everything and make you remember all that I have told you" (John 14:26).

In the first chapter of Acts, we read about how Jesus stays on earth for forty days after the Resurrection. He appears to the Apostles and instructs them by the power of the Holy Spirit. He talks with them about the Kingdom of God. He tells them to stay in Jerusalem and that "in a few days you will be baptized with the Holy Spirit" (Acts 1:5). He even gives them the following hint as to what the Spirit will help them do: "When the Holy Spirit comes upon you, you will be filled with power, and you will be witnesses for me in Jerusalem, in all of Judea, and

Tongues of fire. This is what the disciples saw on the great feast of Pentecost. Filled with the power of the Holy Spirit, they went out to transform the world. When we are on fire with the Spirit, we can do the same.

Illustration by Elizabeth Wang, 'The Descent of the Holy Spirit at Pentecost', copyright © Radiant Light 2008, www.radiantlight.org.uk

Samaria, and to the ends of the earth" (Acts 1:8). Jesus tells the Apostles what they are to do and what their mission will be: to **evangelize.** This means to continue the mission of Jesus Christ by spreading the Good News to the ends of the earth.

Come, Holy Spirit

Jesus' promise about the coming of the Holy Spirit came true a short while later. We call this event **Pentecost.** "When the day of Pentecost came, all the believers were gathered together in one place. Suddenly there was a noise from the sky which sounded like a strong wind blowing, and it filled the whole house where they were sitting. Then they saw what looked like tongues of fire, which spread out and touched each person there. They were all filled with the

Did You Know?

Bishops and Priests

The Apostles formed new Christian communities when traveling to preach the Good News. Before leaving these places, they would designate leaders for the communities by laying their hands on them. These leaders were called bishops, or *episkopos* in Greek. Christianity spread quickly, and soon the Church communities were too large to be cared for by one bishop. The bishop ordained priests to help him in his ministry. By the end of the first century, the Church had defined the roles of bishops, priests, and deacons. You can read more about the ordained ministry of bishops, priests, and deacons in chapter 31 of this handbook.

Peter was the first bishop of Rome and the head of the Church. To this day, the bishop of the Church of Rome is the Pope. He is the successor of Peter and is the head of the universal Church on earth.

Holy Spirit and began to talk in other languages, as the Spirit enabled them to speak" (Acts 2:1-4).

> Suddenly there was a noise from the sky which sounded like a strong wind blowing. (Acts 2:2)

Holy God,
  Send your Holy Spirit
to fill my heart with
your love. Help me
live in harmony with
others as the first
Christians did. Help
me resolve differences
and forgive. May the
power of your Spirit
help me teach others
about your Son by the
way I live. Come, Holy
Spirit! Fill my heart and
kindle in me the fire of your
love. I pray this in the name
of Jesus, your Son. Amen

What Does This Mean?

Before Pentecost, Peter emerged as the leader of this Christian community struggling to find its way. One of the first things Peter does after Jesus ascends to heaven is guide the Apostles in choosing a successor to Judas (see Acts 1:12–26). On Pentecost, Peter, along with the other Apostles takes on a more visible and brave role in spreading the news about God's Kingdom.

Imagine the scene after the Holy Spirit has come. The Apostles are speaking in different languages. There is noise and confusion. People are wondering, "What does this mean?" (see Acts 2:12).

When we open ourselves to the energy of God's love, great things happen.

Illustration by Elizabeth Wang, 'Through the Touch of the Holy Spirit', copyright © Radiant Light 2008, www.radiantlight.org.uk

Things are so wild and crazy that "others made fun of the believers, saying, 'These people are drunk!'" (Acts 2:13).

What is Peter to do? He gets up in front of the crowd with the other Apostles gathered around him and speaks. First, he tells the crowd: "These people are not drunk, as you suppose; it is only nine o'clock in the morning" (Acts 2:15). Then he reminds everyone that God has promised he will pour out his Spirit (see Acts 2:18). He also reminds them about Jesus of Nazareth and the meaning of the Resurrection. He makes a stunning announcement to the crowd: Jesus is the one whom God has made Lord and Messiah! (see Acts 2:36).

> "God has raised this very Jesus from death, and we are all witnesses to this fact. He has been raised to the right side of God, his Father, and has received from him the Holy Spirit, as he had promised. What you now see and hear is his gift that he has poured out on us." (Acts 2:32–33)

Pray It!
Liturgy Connection

Every year, the Church celebrates the feast of Pentecost during the Easter season. When you go to Church on Pentecost Sunday, you will see red vestments (the special religious clothing worn by priests) and red decorations. One of the things the color red symbolizes when you see it at church is the Holy Spirit. The red tongues of fire descended on the Apostles at Pentecost.

If you go to the vigil Mass on the Saturday evening before Pentecost, you will hear John 7:37–39 proclaimed. In this passage, Jesus refers to the Holy Spirit as living water. What does this tell you about how the Holy Spirit works in your life?

Troubled by this, the people ask the Apostles, "What shall we do, brothers?" (Acts 2:37). Peter answers them: "Each one of you must turn away from your sins and be baptized in the name of Jesus Christ, so that your sins will be forgiven; and you will receive God's gift, the Holy Spirit. For God's promise was made to you and your children, and to all who are far away—all whom the Lord our God calls to himself" (Acts 2:38–39).

Know, Love, and Serve the Lord

From this moment forward, the job is clear: spread the Good News. Baptize in the name of the Father, Son, and Spirit. From this moment forward, the Holy Spirit takes charge. Believers gather in community as followers of Jesus Christ. These believers come together to know, love, and serve the Lord. They are

Saints Peter and Paul (center, in front of tapestry) took seriously the mission Jesus gave us to go out and make disciples. How do young people contribute to this mission?

Bill Wittman

called **Christians** because, like Christ, they have been anointed by the Holy Spirit in Baptism. *Christos* is Greek for "anointed one." From this moment forward, followers of Jesus Christ, on fire with the Spirit, will take his message to the ends of the earth.

Looking Back

The Epistles

The Acts of the Apostles gives us a wonderful sense of the early Church communities and the spread of the Gospel of Jesus Christ. The New Testament also includes letters, called epistles, that tell the story of the early Church. The epistles include thirteen Pauline letters written to various communities to help them with particular issues. (The letters are called "Pauline" because either Paul wrote them or someone else wrote them and they were attributed to Paul.). The epistles contain songs of praise, advice for family life, and instructions on how to live and how to run the Church. To see an example, open your Bible and read 1 Corinthians 13:4–7. In this passage, Paul teaches the people of Corinth about a special kind of love called "agape." This is love that is offered without any conditions. It is love that is constant, no matter who you are or what you do. How can you live the kind of agape love Paul talks about?

18 THE MISSION OF THE CHURCH

Think about a group to which you belong. What is the purpose of the group? An example is an orchestra or a school band. One of the main purposes of these groups is to produce good music. The bands want to sound good at the Christmas concert. So a group of people comes together with their instruments to practice. It takes the commitment of each individual musician and the ability to work together as a team. Each instrument has something special to offer.

Groups of people joining to contribute their gifts to a larger goal can give us some idea about what the Church is like. The Church, however, is a type of community with characteristics that make it different from other groups. The word *church* means "convocation."

Illustration by Elizabeth Wang, 'With Jesus, in the Holy Sacrifice of the Mass, the whole Church is united in offering praise and thanks to the Father', copyright © Radiant Light 2008, www.radiantlight.org.uk

One artist imagines the Church. What is the image saying about our relationship with one another and with God?

To *convoke* means to "call together." A convocation is a community of people who gather in response to a call. What makes the Church unique is that it is an assembly of people who come together in response to God's call. God calls everyone, everywhere. No auditions. No tryouts. No age requirements. All are welcome. The people who respond to God's call are one family through faith and Baptism. They are united in love by the Holy Spirit. They are the Body of Christ in the world.

God has a plan for the world, and the goal of the plan is the Church. This doesn't mean the visible Church as we see it today is the goal. It means that the goal of God's plan is for all people to come together in unity with one another and with God.

Jesus founded the Church during his earthly ministry more than two thousand years ago. Since then the Church has been on a journey toward the full unity that God intends. Since the life, death, and Resurrection of Jesus, Christians from all over the world have been inspired by God's love to spread the Gospel and bring to people everywhere the truth about God's love.

LiVE iT!

Find out more about how your parish accomplishes the mission of the Church. What gifts do members of the parish bring to help spread the Good News of Jesus Christ? How do members of your parish help each other know, love, and serve God more completely? What things are going on that bring people closer to God and support and nurture their faith? Think about how you are a part of the Body of Christ in your parish. Join several of your peers to discuss a way you can contribute your gifts to the parish. Then do it.

KEY WORDS

People of God
marks of the Church
catholic
apostolic

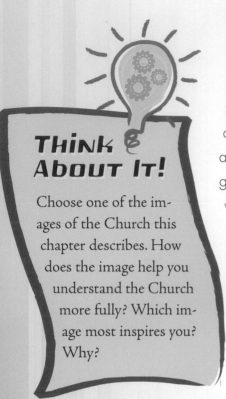

THiNK About It!

Choose one of the images of the Church this chapter describes. How does the image help you understand the Church more fully? Which image most inspires you? Why?

How do people do this? With the help of the Holy Spirit, they strive to live like Jesus and love others without requiring anything in return. They are selfless instead of selfish. They forgive friends and even enemies. They pray and worship. They serve those in need. They act with justice. The Church is more than just a group or an organization. It is a way of life. A way of summarizing this is to say the Church is the goal of God's plan and also the means. The Church is God's way of carrying out his plan until the end of time, when all people will be united with him.

"I pray that they may all be one, Father! May they be in us, just as you are in me and I am in you. May they be one, so that the world will believe that you sent me . . . and that you love them as you love me." (John 17:21,23)

Images of Church

From the beginning of Christianity, leaders in the Church looked for ways to describe the who, what, and why about the Church. To help people understand the mystery of the Church, Peter and Paul used the images of the People of God, the Body of Christ, and the Temple of the Holy Spirit. These images help us understand that unity in the Church is rooted in the unity of the Father, Son, and Holy Spirit.

People of God

Long before Jesus' birth, the people of Israel understood themselves to be the **People of God,** the chosen ones through whom God would save the world (see Exodus 6:7). The first Christians, who were Jews, came to see that they were God's chosen ones through Christ and the Spirit. Peter wrote the following in a letter to first-century Christians:

Did You Know?
The Church Is a Sacrament

Sacraments are encounters with Jesus Christ that help us see that God is with us. The first, or primary, sacrament is Jesus Christ. He, more than anyone or anything else, helps us see God's presence in the world. The Church is also a sacrament. She makes visible the communion we share with God—Father, Son, and Holy Spirit. The Church is sometimes referred to as a "sacrament of salvation." This phrase emphasizes that through the Church, we can come to know God and be saved. The Church shows us God's love for all people, everywhere. That is why we can add universal to our description and call the Church the "universal sacrament of salvation." God wants all people to be saved and to know he loves them. Jesus Christ gave to the Apostles the mission to preach the Gospel message to the whole world (see Matthew 28:18–20) and the Church continues to carry out this mission today. Through the Church, God spreads the message far and wide about the truth of his love for us.

Did You Know?

The Church Is Human and Divine

The Church is visible and spiritual. . She is one, but is made up of two components, human and divine. We see the visible reality of the Church in such things as people gathered for the Eucharist; the church buildings; the Pope, bishops, and priests; young people praying on retreats and serving others; the Bible; and so on. But the Church is more than what we can see. The Church is also a spiritual reality. This is a mystery we see only with the eyes of faith. It builds on the visible reality. Through the constant action and presence of the Holy Spirit, the aspects of the Church that we can see communicate and put us in touch with the divine component of the Church. The Holy Spirit assures us that the Church is carrying out Christ's mission despite the occasional sins and failures of the members. Through us God is doing what we could never do on our own. Our work is a participation in the real, but unseen, divine life of the Trinity.

"You are . . . God's own people, chosen to proclaim the wonderful acts of God, who called you out of darkness into his own marvelous light" (1 Peter 2:9).

The people are "of God," because they do not belong to any one nationality, race, or region. Everyone is welcome. They don't inherit or earn membership. People become members through Baptism and faith in Jesus Christ.

The Body of Christ

The Church is also the Body of Christ. Paul describes the Church as follows: "Christ is like a single body, which has many parts; it is still one body, even though it is made up of different parts. . . . All of us. . . . have been baptized into the one body by the same Spirit. . . . All of you are Christ's body, and each one is a part of it" (1 Corinthians 12:12,13,27).

In the Church, where there are many members and functions, every person's gifts are important for the Church to carry out her mission. The Church is the whole body, the members united to the head, Jesus Christ. Our salvation comes through the Church, because salvation comes first through Christ. Christ lives with and in the Church. The Church gets its life from Christ.

The Body of Christ that we receive in the Eucharist reminds us that we are the Body of Christ. When we receive the Eucharist, the Body of Christ nourishes us so we become the Body of Christ to the world.

The Church is also called the Bride of Christ. This is an image of the Church presented in the Scriptures: "Husbands, love your wives, just as Christ loved the church and gave himself up for her" (Ephesians 5:25). Christ's relationship with the Church is compared with the relationship between husbands and wives.

Pray It!
Liturgy Connection

All baptized believers participate in the Church's mission of fulfilling the commission of Jesus to "go, and make disciples of all nations" (Matthew 28:19). Next time you pray the Nicene Creed at Mass, think about how believers have been witnesses of the Gospel over the centuries. Think about what it means to be a part of a Church that is one, holy, catholic, and apostolic. Think about the gifts you have to offer the Church. Pray about what it means to be a part of the Body of Christ and a Temple of the Holy Spirit. Then go, be a believer.

Holy God,
 I praise and thank
 you for your good-
 ness. Thank you
 for the new life you
 have given me in the
 waters of Baptism.
 I share in your life,
 through Christ, your
 Son, who died and
 rose for me. Help me
 be a good disciple of Jesus. Help me spread the
 Good News in my family
 and my community.
                    Amen

Temple of the Holy Spirit

Paul also explains the mystery of the Church as follows: "Surely you know that you are God's temple
and that God's Spirit lives in you!" (1 Corinthians
3:16). In the Old Testament, the Temple in Jerusalem was the place where God dwelled. Paul
tells us that God dwells in us, in the Church.
Jesus Christ has poured out his Spirit onto all
the members of the Church. The Spirit is
the center or soul of the Church's life. The
Spirit gives the Church unity, even when
all her members are so different from
one another. The Spirit is the source of
the Church's gifts.

"Surely you know that you are God's
temple and that God's Spirit lives in
you!" (1 Corinthians 3:16)

The Marks
of the Church

In the Nicene Creed, we express belief in "one,
holy, catholic and apostolic Church." These four
characteristics, or **marks of the Church,** are essential features of the Church. As we look at what
these marks tell us about the Church, it is important to
keep in mind that the fullness of Jesus Christ's Church
is found only in the Catholic Church. This means the
Catholic Church, led by the Pope and the bishops in

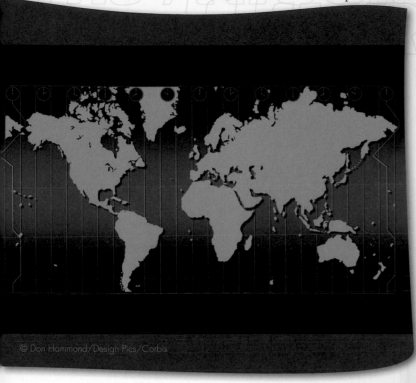

The Church has been practicing globalization for a very long time. Catholics live on every continent in the world. There are more than a billion of us.

© Don Hammond/Design Pics/Corbis

communion with him, is the only Church with the fullness of the four marks. However, when we express our belief that the Church is one, holy, catholic, and apostolic, we do so with humble hearts. We pray knowing the members of the Church struggle with sin. We pray also with the knowledge that holiness and truth can be found outside the visible organization of the Catholic Church.

One

When we say the Church is one, we profess one Lord, one faith, one Baptism, one Body, and one Spirit who gives us life and unites all the members of the Church. The Church,

FUN FACT

There are almost three million Catholic catechists in the world, sharing their gift of teaching the faith. (Bunson, 2007 Catholic Almanac, page 333)

A Nigerian woman receives communion. Using a map, locate the countries represented by the Eucharistic celebrations pictured on pages 202–205.

whose foundation is the Holy Trinity, reflects the unity of the Trinity—the loving communion of God the Father, Jesus Christ, and the Holy Spirit. We believe we are children of God the Father, saved by Jesus Christ, and made one by the Holy Spirit. Unfortunately, divisions have developed among Christians. The many different Christian denominations that people belong to today reflect this lack of unity. We share in the hope that one day, through the power of the Holy Spirit, unity among all Christians will be restored.

Young people in Mexico celebrate their First Communion.

Holy

The Church is also holy. This means she is blessed with the presence and love of God and is united with him. The Church's holiness is real but not yet perfect. We fall short of the holiness God wants for us, but the Holy Spirit is constantly guiding the Church in her efforts to overcome sin and grow in holiness.

Catholic

To say that the Church is **catholic** is to say that she is comprehensive and universal. (Notice the lowercase *c*. The term *catholic* here is

A young woman attends Christmas Mass in Pakistan.

an adjective describing the Church rather than a part of a name, in which case the *C* would be capitalized, as in Catholic Church.) The Church is comprehensive, because she proclaims the fullness of faith to us. The Catholic Church contains everything we need to be saved: God's complete Revelation, the Seven Sacraments, and the ministry of ordained men whose authority comes directly from the Apostles. The Catholic Church is universal, because she is out in the world, spreading the Word of God to all people, everywhere.

Midnight Mass is celebrated on Christmas in Israel 2,000 years after the birth of Christ.

© Jeffrey L. Rotman/CORBIS

Apostolic

The Church is **apostolic,** because she was founded on Jesus' Twelve Apostles. The Holy Spirit empowered them to spread Christ's message to the world. Christ leads the Church through the Apostles even today. They are present through their successors, the Pope and the College of Bishops. Authority is passed from generation to generation, from bishop to

PEOPLE OF FAITH
Saint Josephine Bakhita

© 2009 Saint Mary's Press/Illustration by Vicki Shuck

In 1869, in a small village in the Sudan, in Africa, Bakhita (the "fortunate one" in a Sudanese language) was born. At the age of nine, she was kidnapped and sold into slavery. During her teenage years, she experienced unspeakable brutalities. In 1883, she was sold to an Italian family living in Africa and became the caretaker for a young girl. Bakhita traveled with the child to boarding school in Italy. The Catholic sisters at the school

bishop, through the laying on of hands in the Sacrament of Holy Orders (see chapter 31). This is called apostolic succession. This process assures that future generations can know the truth of God's Revelation in Christ.

Catholics in the Communist country of Vietnam celebrate Christmas Mass.

introduced her to the Gospel. She knew in her heart that God wanted her to be free. But the owners wanted her, their "property," to return to the Sudan. Bakhita prayed to the Lord for strength. She heard God's call, and she knew he wanted her for the Church's work and nothing else. She was going to stay in Italy, no matter what. Soon after, she discovered that slavery was illegal in Italy. This meant that she could not be forced to return to the Sudan. On January 9, 1890, she was baptized and took the name Josephine Bakhita. She then began to hear God's voice calling her to dedicate her life to him more fully. She responded by joining the community of sisters, serving God, whom she called the Master. Her holiness was known all around her town. She died in 1947 and was canonized a saint in 2000. She was the first native Sudanese to become a saint. We celebrate her feast on May 17.

THE STRUCTURE OF THE CHURCH

Have you ever been entrusted with an important job? a job where you needed to come through? a job where other people were counting on you? Maybe it was completing a task for a group assignment at school. Perhaps it was babysitting your younger sister and helping her with her homework. Maybe it was showing up for your team's practices or doing a service project at the church. Maybe it was relaying an important telephone message to your mom or dad. At one time or another, we all have people counting on us to come through for them.

Spreading the Gospel is the work of everyone in the Church, including young people like you. You are part of the laity, aka (also known as) lay faithful.

iStockphoto

To the Ends of the Earth

Before Jesus returns to his Father in heaven, he gathers his Apostles together. He tells them he is entrusting them with an important job. This job is to carry to the ends of the earth the message of God's love and humans' salvation through Christ. At the end of the Gospel of Matthew, we read the Great Commissioning. This is when Jesus entrusts others with his mission, as follows: "I have been given all authority in heaven and on earth. Go, then, to all peoples everywhere and make them my disciples: baptize them in the name of the Father, the Son, and the Holy Spirit, and teach them to obey everything I have commanded you" (Matthew 28:18–20). Jesus asks his Apostles to share in the job of telling everyone about God's Kingdom. He wants his followers to share in his mission As Jesus' followers, we are called to share in his kingly role. He gives his Apostles and their successors the power to baptize in his name and act in his person.

"Go, then, to all peoples everywhere and make them my disciples: baptize them in the name of the Father, the Son, and the Holy Spirit, and teach them to obey everything I have commanded you."
(Matthew 28:18–20)

Live It!

God calls all Christians to pray for and work toward full unity. Talk to some of your friends who belong to other Christian communities. What kinds of activities, such as service projects, could you do together as Christian disciples? Every year, a Week of Prayer for Christian Unity is celebrated January 18–25. Watch for news about how it will be celebrated in your community. Check out the Web site of the United States Conference of Catholic Bishops (USCCB) for ideas and plan a celebration. Pray for the unity of believers every day.

Caretaker of Souls

Think about a community or group to which you belong. Most groups want to accomplish something. They are more successful if they have a leader to guide them. The conductor guides the orchestra. The coach guides the team. Your elected peer guides your class council. The principal guides the school. Jesus knows that his community of disciples needs a leader.

The Pope

Jesus makes Simon Peter the foundation of the Church. He calls Peter "the rock." He even entrusts the keys of the Church to him. Jesus says to Peter: "I will give you the keys to the Kingdom of heaven" (Matthew 16:19). When someone gives you a set of keys, that person is saying, "I trust you. You are in charge." Jesus doesn't literally give Peter keys, but he trusts him with leading the Church. Peter is the first bishop of

Saint Peter had a starring role in the story of the new Church. Jesus called him "the rock" and gave him the keys to the Kingdom. The Church has been headed by a Pope ever since Saint Peter.

Bill Wittman

the Church of Rome. Each person who follows Peter as the leader of the Church is called the

Pope. The Pope is the head of the College of Bishops, which is the organization of bishops from all around the world. The Pope is also called the Vicar of Christ. This means he is the chief minister for Christ. Just as many of our local parishes have a pastor, the Pope is the pastor for the whole world. The Pope has a very important job and responsibility. Think of it as follows: Jesus entrusts Peter, and all the Popes who have followed, with the job of being the caretaker of the souls of all of the members of Christ's Body.

FUN FACT

Ever wonder how many Catholics serve in various roles? Following are some approximate worldwide figures:

- 406,000 priests
- 32,000 deacons
- 55,000 religious brothers
- 767,000 religious sisters
- 3,600 bishops
- 3,000,000 catechists

(Bunson, 2007 Catholic Almanac, page 430)

The Bishops, Priests, and Deacons

The Holy Spirit is always working in the Church. He established bishops to succeed, or follow after, the Apostles. A **bishop** takes care of the Church in a particular geographical area called a diocese. He teaches the faith, celebrates the sacraments, especially the Eucharist, and guides his diocese as its pastor. The bishops help all the parishes in their dioceses work together as

The Bishops and priests celebrate Mass together during Holy Week. They bless the holy oils that each parish will use during the year for sacraments.

PRAY IT!
Liturgy Connection

When we gather to celebrate the Eucharist, we pray for each other and for the Church. During the Eucharistic Prayer, we pray with the celebrant as he says:

> Lord, remember your Church throughout the world; make us grow in love, together with Benedict our Pope, [Name], our bishop, and all the clergy.

We pray for all those whom Christ has called to be ordained leaders of the Church. We also pray for growth in love and unity for the whole Church.

a united whole. Each bishop is a sign of unity in his diocese and a member of the College of Bishops. Bishops, of course, can't do all this on their own. The priests and the deacons of the local Church are their ordained coworkers. They assist the bishop in leading the Church as it carries out its mission in the world. You can read more about the ordained ministry of bishops, priests, and deacons in chapter 31 of this handbook. Consecrated religious and laypeople also share in the responsibility for carrying out the Church's mission. Let's explore their roles.

Consecrated Religious

Some men and women dedicate their lives to Jesus by living a religious vocation in the Church. They are called consecrated religious. We also call them sisters and brothers. They make public vows or promises called evangelical counsels. The word *evangelical* pertains to living the Good News, or the Gospel. The three evangelical counsels—poverty, chastity, and obedience—help them live as Jesus lived. The vow of poverty is a promise to live simply. They own nothing of their own. The vow of chastity is a promise to remain unmarried and celibate. This keeps them free to dedicate all their efforts to bringing Christ to the world. The vow of obedience means to listen attentively to God's will. They obey the laws of God and the Church. They also follow the rules of their religious order or community.

We Share in Christ's Ministry

People in the Church who are not ordained are called laity, or lay faithful. These include men, women, children (and yes, adolescents), married people, and single people. Even people who have taken religious vows are considered laity if they have not been ordained. The lay faithful have the special job of making Christ's presence known in the world. They do this by sharing in the priestly, prophetic, and kingly work of Christ. Let's take a look at these three aspects of Christ's ministry we share in.

THINK ABOUT IT!

Reflect back on your week. Which of your attitudes and actions helped others praise God? Which taught others about what God is like? Which challenged others to act more justly or with more kindness? What acts of love and service might you do in the coming week?

PRAY IT!

Holy God,
You invite me to
share in the mission
of your Son,
Jesus, who wants
all people to be
one with you, his
Father. May the way
I live—the things
I do and the things
I say—point people
to Jesus. May I be a
signpost for others on
their journeys to find
you.
　　　　　Amen

Priest

To be priestly means to worship God by the way we live. It means striving to make our lives holy by being open to the Holy Spirit in all we do. This includes how we relate to our families and friends, our approach to schoolwork, and how we take care of ourselves and others. We also share in Christ's priestly work when we pray. This includes our prayers to God during ordinary moments of ordinary days. It also includes participation in the Church's prayers and worship, particularly going to Mass.

Be holy in all that you do, just as God who called you is holy. (1 Peter 1:15–16)

Prophet

To be a prophet is to announce the Good News of Jesus Christ. Christ wants all people everywhere to know about God. We can help contribute to this goal through our words and actions. When we point others to God, we are like signposts in the world. An effective signpost gives good directions. It helps people get where they want to go. A prophet is like a signpost that directs people to God. For us this means always learning more about our faith and being willing to share it. It means being Christ's witnesses through what we do and what we say.

King

To understand kingship, we need to clear our minds of images of rich, powerful kings and leaders who seek their positions for their own gain. Our model for kingship is Jesus, a servant-king. Jesus leads by serving others. His power is the love he shares. Through his death and Resurrection, he gives of himself to bring us close to God the Father. He invites everyone into the Kingdom of God, not just the rich and famous.

Did You Know?

Not Catholic?

The image of a family can help us understand the Catholic Church's relationship with other Christians. Christians of other denominations are our brothers and sisters. We all believe in God the Father, Jesus Christ, and the Holy Spirit. Like members of the same family, all who are baptized share a certain communion or unity with each other. We also have some points of major and minor differences that keep us from being fully unified with our Christian brothers and sisters who are not Catholic. Catholics and Christians from many other denominations engage in dialogue and prayer in an effort to restore unity. This work, carried out with the help of the Holy Spirit, is called **ecumenism.**

© SW Productions/Brand X/Corbis

Did you know that when you perform service, you are being Christ in the world?

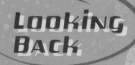

Looking Back

The Church and Other Religions

The Declaration on the Relation of the Church to Non-Christian Religions is one of the final documents the Second Vatican Council approved in the 1960s. The document marks a special moment in the Church's history with other religions, including Judaism. It rejects attitudes of contempt for Judaism and the Jewish people, and it rejects anti-Semitic (anti-Jewish) teachings. Jews are not guilty of killing Jesus. They are not cursed and rejected. The Jewish faith, unlike other non-Christian religions, is a response to God's Revelation in the Old Testament. The Church has a profound love and respect for the Jews.

Though the Church deeply respects other religions, it emphasizes that we can know the fullness of God's Revelation only through the Catholic Church. This does not mean that those who follow other religions are barred from eternal life with God. Many people are not Christian but seek God with sincere hearts. People who try to do God's will, even if they do not know Jesus Christ, may also achieve eternal friendship with God, or salvation.

During his earthly ministry, Jesus always reached out to people who were poor or outcast. He befriended people who were lonely and forgotten. As Jesus' followers, we are called to share in his kingly role. We do this whenever we lead in a genuine spirit of love and service. We take the gifts God has given us, and we follow Jesus' lead by using them to reach out to those in need.

Roles Within the Catholic Church

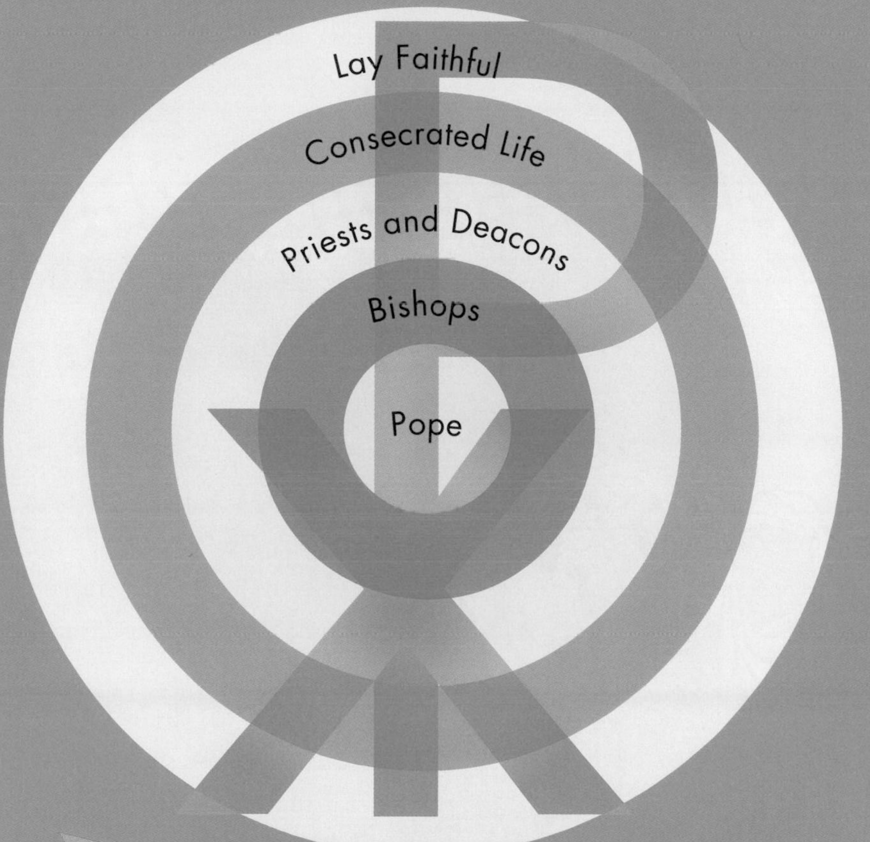

Lay Faithful

Consecrated Life

Priests and Deacons

Bishops

Pope

℞ is a symbol for Christ. By Baptism, every role is connected to Christ's ministry. As the circles get smaller, the roles are more specific.

All of you are Christ's body,
and each one is part of it.
(1 Corinthians 12:27)

PEOPLE OF FAITH
Saint Catherine of Siena

© 2009 Saint Mary's Press/Illustration by Vicki Shuck

Catherine was born in 1347, in Siena, Italy, the twenty-fourth of twenty-five children. She wanted to dedicate her life to Christ. Her family had a different idea. They wanted her to marry. The family responded to her desire by treating her as if she were a slave. She would retreat to her "secret cell." This was a place inside herself. She would pray and be with the Lord. In a vision, Christ told her that he was in her heart. He appeared to her and put a ring on her finger, as if he were promising to marry her.

216

Catherine loved the Church deeply. After several years of prayer and fasting, her dedication to the Church took on public dimension. She served people who were poor and sick. She ministered to people in prison and those suffering during the plague of 1374. During the papacy of Urban VI, the Church was in chaos and disarray. Urban was power hungry. The cardinals, recognizing their mistake in electing him, elected another pope. However, Urban refused to give up the papacy, and so the Church had two rival popes. Catherine suffered, seeing the Church suffer. She prayed she could make up for the sins of the Church.

In 1380, Catherine collapsed physically from exhaustion and a practice of extreme fasting. Within months, at the age of thirty-three, she was dead. At her death, the marks of stigmata (the wounds of Jesus) and her "wedding band" were on her body. Catherine is also known for her writings on the spiritual life. She was canonized a saint and was the first layperson named a Doctor of the Church. Saint Catherine's feast is celebrated on April 29.

20 END THINGS: HEAVEN AND HELL

The second-grade religion teacher had worked hard to prepare the youngsters for First Communion. While reviewing with the class one afternoon, she asked, "What do you have to be to get to Heaven?" Many of the children furiously waved their raised hands. The teacher called on little Susie. The teacher told the class to quiet down: "Susie is going to tell us what we have to be to get to Heaven." Without so much as a second's hesitation, Susie proudly responded, "Dead!"

Susie's answer was not what her teacher was looking for. It was the matter-of-fact answer of a child who knew that before we go to Heaven, we die—or at least our bodies do. What else, besides dead,

One artist depicts Heaven and hell. How would you draw or describe these two concepts?

Illustration by Elizabeth Wang, 'True prayer should lead us to love God and to serve our neighbor', copyright © Radiant Light 2008, www.radiantlight.org.uk

do we have to be to get to Heaven? Perhaps you wonder about this and related questions such as, What happens when we die? What is Heaven? How do we get there? What is hell? How do people end up there? What do Catholics believe about eternal matters like Heaven and hell?

The title of this chapter, End Things: Heaven and Hell, is a paradox of the Christian life. In the Nicene Creed, we profess belief "in the resurrection of the body and life everlasting." For those who believe in Christ, the "end things" are not really the end at all. They are the end of things as we know them but the beginning of our eternal life with God.

LIVE IT!

Read Matthew 25:31–46. Notice that what Jesus says isn't simply a suggestion along the lines of "You might want to do these things." Jesus demands that we do these things if we are to be counted among the righteous. God will judge us on how well we care for others, particularly people who are poor. Take a piece of paper and label three columns: "Me and My Family," "My Parish," and "My Community." Write down some ways the people listed in each column follow the demands of Jesus. Be specific. If you get the chance, discuss with a friend or family member what you discover. Choose one new thing you can do to help others. Then do it.

KEY WORDS

Heaven
hell
judgment

I Am the Resurrection

Do you know the story of Jesus' raising Lazarus from the dead? (see John, chapter 11).

Think About It!

When you think about the end of time, does it scare you or give you hope? One of the images Jesus uses to describe Heaven is a wedding feast. What does this image tell you about what Heaven will be like? What is your image of Heaven? If someone asked you what to do or what kind of person to be to get to Heaven, how would you explain the Church's teaching?

Amazing though this miracle is—that Jesus would bring a dead person to life—Lazarus will eventually die again, and that will be the end. Or will it? By raising Lazarus from the dead, Jesus gives us a preview of coming attractions. He lets us know what is in store for his disciples: resurrection to eternal life. Jesus says to Martha, the distraught sister of the dead Lazarus, "I am the resurrection and the life. Those who believe in me will live, even though they die; and those who live and believe in me will never die" (John 11:25–26). At death, our souls are separated from our bodies. But in the resurrection, God will make our bodies rise again and be transformed. We will rise, like Christ, on the last day.

> "I am the resurrection and the life. Those who believe in me will live, even though they die; and those who live and believe in me will never die." (John 11:25–26)

God never intended for us to be apart from him. After man and woman chose to turn away from him (read about Adam and Eve in the story of Creation in the Book of Genesis), God has continually been working on restoring our relationship with him. Jesus' life, death, and Resurrection are all the proof we need. God's desire is for us to be with him. But he doesn't force us. We have free will to choose to be close to him or not. How we live our

© Brooklyn Museum/Corbis

Jesus raises his friend Lazarus from the dead. Lazarus's sisters and friends must have been overjoyed. Jesus promises us eternal life. That is joyful news for us too.

lives here on earth will determine whether we are headed for Heaven or for hell.

Heaven

Imagine the perfect life. Your deepest longings are satisfied. You are completely happy. That's a glimpse of Heaven. **Heaven** is not a place. It is the state of being in perfect friendship and union with God. It lasts for eternity. If Heaven is friendship with God, being close to God, and being with God, then

Did You Know?

"Do You Believe This?"

Jesus tells Martha he has power over death. He demonstrates this by raising Lazarus. First, he asks her, "Do you believe this?" (John 11:26). Jesus asks the same question of us. After we die, it will be too late to start thinking about serious matters like Heaven and hell. It will be too late to make different choices about how to live. Jesus wants to know if we truly believe what he can do for us. He wants to know if we truly believe that, as Martha declared, he is "the Messiah, the Son of God, who was to come into the world" (John 11:27). Why? Because our belief in Jesus as our Savior makes all the difference in how we will choose to live our lives today.

certainly Heaven begins here on earth. It begins in the loving attitudes and actions we choose and in how we let Jesus be the guide for all we do and say. If Heaven is the grand party, or "heavenly banquet," that never ends, then certainly Heaven begins here on earth in our relationships. It begins in the kindness we offer one another, our parents, our siblings, our friends—even strangers and enemies.

Did You Know?

Purgatory

Many people die in God's grace and friendship, but their lives were not quite on target with the Gospel. Although these people have a place in Heaven, they will spend time becoming more holy before entering into eternity with God. This period is commonly called Purgatory, because during it people's souls are purged from sin.

Hell

The opposite, of course, would be to turn away from God, to refuse to love, to refuse to care or forgive, to think only about ourselves. The choice is ours, but if we make this choice, then we risk the reality of hell, or eternal death. **Hell** is separation from God forever. Like Heaven, hell is not a place. It is a permanent state of being. Since we all want to be happy (a longing God created within us in the first place), then not being happy, and not being with God for eternity, is the ultimate punishment for choosing not to love.

Thoughts of hell can be scary. We need to resist the urge to focus on how we're not good enough. We need to resist the urge to focus on our human weaknesses, thoughts such as "I just can't be good" or "I blew it, there's no hope." When you think about it, there is nothing we could ever do to earn Heaven. We need to remember we are sons and daughters of a God who is all loving and all forgiving. God's greatest desire is for us to be with him forever. God doesn't condemn anyone to hell. He gives us the choice either to respond to his love or not. We respond to God's love and accept his invitation to be a part of his life by the way we live.

Judgment

What is your image of being judged after you die? For some, it is a courtroom scene—God with the gavel,

"When, Lord, did we ever see you hungry?" (Matthew 25:37). Jesus tells us that those who help the poor and needy are actually helping him. He promises that those who respond in love will one day see the face of God in Heaven.

PRAY IT!

Holy God,
You invite me to
spend eternity
with you. You sent
your Son, Jesus, to
restore my relation-
ship with you. Help
me follow the way
of Jesus and be his
disciple. Help me live a
life worthy of the King-
dom of Heaven you have
prepared for me.

Amen

ready to hand down a sentence of eternal damnation in the fires of hell or eternal life in the clouds of Heaven. For others, it is the image of a long line at the pearly gates.

It is important that we not confuse the word *judgment* with the word *condemnation*. The **judgment** that awaits us when we die is not condemnation. Christ, who is the judge of the living and the dead, will judge us at the time of our death by comparing our lives to the Gospel message. This is called the particular judgment. Paul summed it up this way: "For all of us must appear before Christ, to be judged by him. We will each receive what we deserve, according to everything we have done, good or bad, in our bodily life" (2 Corinthians 5:10).

Later in the Gospel of Matthew, Jesus describes the Last Judgment. This is a second judgment that will come at the end of time when God's plan for Creation will be fully realized. The King on his throne —who is Jesus Christ—will separate people into two groups, the righteous people on his right and the

© Arte & Immagini srl/CORBIS

Art can have a big influence on how we picture difficult concepts like Heaven and hell. This portion of a fifteenth-century painting by Fra Angelico shows hell as a place of great agony and suffering.

others on his left. Which group a person is in will depend on the deeds that person did during his or her life. Those on the right will have a place in Heaven because they fed the hungry, gave drink to the thirsty, welcomed the stranger, clothed the naked, cared for the sick, and visited the imprisoned (see Matthew 25:31–40). Those who saw the face of Jesus in the people who were the most poor and vulnerable and reached out to them with love will see

FUN FACT

In Dante Alighieri's *Inferno*, a famous poem written in the 1200s, Dante gives a tour of hell from his perspective. He describes hell using nine concentric circles, like a target, with Satan at the center, or bullseye. Each circle has a different type of sinner, and as the circles get closer to Satan at the center, the sins become more serious.

the face of God in Heaven. Those who turned their backs on those in need will not.

> For all of us must appear before Christ, to be judged by him. We will each receive what we deserve, according to everything we have done, good or bad, in our bodily life.
>
> (2 Corinthians 5:10)

PRAY IT!
Liturgy Connection

Next time you are at Mass, listen for the times when we pray for those who have died. Generally, one of the Prayers of the Faithful is for people who have died recently. Also during the Eucharistic Prayer, we pray in the following or similar words:

Remember our brothers and sisters who have gone to their rest in the hope of rising again; bring them and all the departed into the light of your presence.

This gives us an opportunity to pause and pray for those close to us who have died.

Let's go back to the question the teacher posed to her second-class: "What do you have to be to get to Heaven?" Think about all the times when you have loved well the people you are close to. Think about the times when those who really needed your love received it from you. Think about the times when you and your family helped someone who didn't have a meal or when the toys you donated helped put a smile on a child's face. Think about all the times you helped a person in need or stood up for what is right. These are the times you will tell Christ about on the Day of Judgment, when he will ask you how you have lived your life. You will be able to say, "I was a loving person. I cared for people who needed my help. I respected life, and I stood up for what is right." On that day, each of us will be accountable for our actions.

At the end of time, the world will be the way God wants it. The Kingdom of God will be fully realized. The people who lived faithful, loving lives will be with Christ. Their bodies and souls will be glorified. All of creation will be transformed by God's presence. Imagine that.

Did You Know?

Prayers for the Dead

The Church has always honored the memory of the dead. Prayers for the dying entrust the person to God and call him or her home to be with God, Mary, Joseph, and all the saints and angels. Catholics, in fact the whole "communion of saints" (that is, the living faithful along with all those in Heaven already), pray on behalf of the dead most especially at the celebration of the Eucharist. These prayers reflect the hope that the dead will see God face to face. In our prayers, we hand over the person to God's mercy.

Saints and Mary

Imagine the scene: an invitation is about to be delivered to a girl, about the age you are now. This girl has no idea this invitation is coming. That she is going about her daily chores illustrates she is not expecting anyone to pop in for a surprise visit. In fact, at the moment, she is a bit distracted because she has been thinking about her cousin, who is way too old to be pregnant, but is pregnant anyhow (see Luke 1:5–25). Her mind is also wandering to thoughts of the man she is engaged to, a man named Joseph. (Yes, this girl lives in a time and culture where girls are engaged very young.)

In this chapter you will read about Mary and the saints, close friends of God. Asking saints to pray for you is like asking a friend for prayers.

© Alinari Archives/Corbis

Suddenly, an angel appears from nowhere (because that's what angels do) and says, "Peace be with you! The Lord is with you and has greatly blessed you!" (Luke 1:28). These are powerful words. The angel is telling this girl, whose name is Mary, that she is full of God's grace. She is full of God's life. The Scriptures give us insight into what Mary must have been thinking and feeling after being told that God has greatly blessed her: "Mary was deeply troubled by the angel's message, and she wondered what his words meant" (Luke 1:29).

© Philadelphia Museum of Art/CORBIS

Look carefully at this picture of Mary at the Annunciation. Where is the angel? Consider the look on Mary's face. What is she thinking and feeling as she listens to God's invitation?

The Gospel of Luke describes what happens next. It is the event the Church calls the Annunciation: "The angel said to her, 'Don't be afraid, Mary; God has been gracious to you. You will become pregnant and give birth to a son, and you will name him Jesus. He will be great and will be called the Son of the Most High God. . . . His kingdom will never end'" (Luke 1:30–33).

The angel said to her, "Don't be afraid, Mary; God has been gracious to you." (Luke 1:30)

Mary's Yes

How did Mary react to the announcement that she would give birth to the "Son of the Most High"? Remember that Mary was not yet married, and she had never been with a man. She was a virgin. Because of this, she asked the angel, "How can this be?" He told her she would conceive by the power of the Holy Spirit. God would take care of everything.

At this point, Mary could have chosen not to believe anything the angel was telling her. She could have laughed and said something like, "You've got to be kidding" or "Leave me alone, I'm busy." She could have told him to go find someone else to be the Mother of God. But she didn't. Mary had a deep love for God. She knew nothing was impossible with God. Therefore, we can imagine her taking a deep breath and then proclaiming her response, her yes. The following was her answer to God's invitation: "I am the Lord's servant, . . . may it happen to me as you have said" (Luke 1:38). Mary consented to God's becoming man through her. She

THINK About It!

The Church celebrates the feasts of Mary and the saints throughout the liturgical year. What feast days do you celebrate in special ways in your parish or with your family? How do you celebrate them?

welcomed God into her life completely. With her yes, Mary cooperated in all the work that her Son, Jesus, was to accomplish while on earth.

LITURGICAL CALENDAR

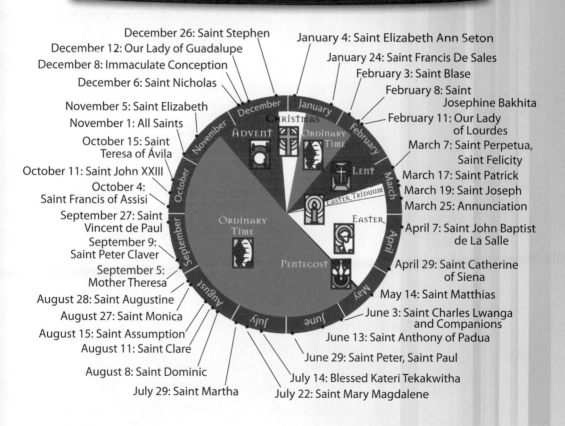

December 26: Saint Stephen
December 12: Our Lady of Guadalupe
December 8: Immaculate Conception
December 6: Saint Nicholas
November 5: Saint Elizabeth
November 1: All Saints
October 15: Saint Teresa of Ávila
October 11: Saint John XXIII
October 4: Saint Francis of Assisi
September 27: Saint Vincent de Paul
September 9: Saint Peter Claver
September 5: Mother Theresa
August 28: Saint Augustine
August 27: Saint Monica
August 15: Saint Assumption
August 11: Saint Clare
August 8: Saint Dominic
July 29: Saint Martha

January 4: Saint Elizabeth Ann Seton
January 24: Saint Francis De Sales
February 3: Saint Blase
February 8: Saint Josephine Bakhita
February 11: Our Lady of Lourdes
March 7: Saint Perpetua, Saint Felicity
March 17: Saint Patrick
March 19: Saint Joseph
March 25: Annunciation
April 7: Saint John Baptist de La Salle
April 29: Saint Catherine of Siena
May 14: Saint Matthias
June 3: Saint Charles Lwanga and Companions
June 13: Saint Anthony of Padua
June 29: Saint Peter, Saint Paul
July 14: Blessed Kateri Tekakwitha
July 22: Saint Mary Magdalene

Christmas
Advent
Ordinary Time
Lent
Easter Triduum
Easter
Pentecost
Ordinary Time

December
January
February
March
April
May
June
July
August
September
October
November

Mother of God

Sometimes, mothers are identified through their children. For example, people might say, "She's the mother of Tom" or "She's Ashley's mom." We read in the Gospels that Mary was the "mother of Jesus." Yet, early in the Gospel of Luke, Mary's cousin, Elizabeth, knew something no one else did about Mary's identity as a mother. Soon after the angel appeared to Mary, Mary went to visit Elizabeth, who was pregnant with John the Baptist. Elizabeth greeted Mary with the following words: "'You are the most blessed of all women, and blessed is the child you will bear! Why should this great thing happen to me, that my Lord's mother comes to visit me!'" (Luke 1:42–43). Elizabeth exclaimed, at the prompting of the Spirit, that Mary

Live It!

At the wedding feast of Cana, the wine has run out. People are scrambling about, trying to decide how to solve this embarrassing dilemma. Imagine Mary, the mother of Jesus, who is at the wedding, nudging Jesus and whispering in his ear, "They are out of wine" (John 2:3). She would like Jesus to do something about it. He tells her, "You must not tell me what to do . . . My time has not yet come" (John 2:4). What happens next is the only time in the Gospels that Mary gives directions. "Jesus' mother then tells the servants, 'Do whatever he tells you'" (John 2:5).

The Blessed Mother Mary points us straight to Jesus. She tells us, "Do whatever he tells you." Spend some quiet time reflecting on Mary's words. What is Jesus telling you to do today?

© Brooklyn Museum/Corbis

"Sorrow, like a sharp sword, will break your own heart" (Luke 2: 35). When Jesus was a baby, Simeon said these words to Mary. As she stood at the Crucifixion and watched her son suffer and die, Simeon's prophecy was all too true. Can you think of other times when Mary was worried or sad about Jesus?

was the mother of the Lord. Mary is truly the Mother of God, because she is the mother of the eternal Son of God made man, Jesus, who is God himself. We call Mary **Theotokos,** which means "God-bearer," or the one who gives birth to God.

PRAY IT!

Holy Mary,
You are my spiritual mother. Be with me today. Protect me and guide me with your love. Show me how to follow your Son, Jesus, in everything I do and say.
Amen

233

When Elizabeth heard Mary's greeting, the baby moved within her. (Luke 1:41)

Mother of the Church

With a mother's love, Mary supports Jesus throughout his life. The Gospels do not tell us much about Jesus' childhood. We can imagine that Mary provides all the guidance and nurturing of the most loving of mothers. Her support and love for Jesus continue throughout his ministry and to his cross, where she stands as he dies. In the final moments of Jesus' earthly life, he gives the Church the gift of his mother. The Gospel of John recounts how Jesus speaks to his mother, and to John, the beloved disciple, as follows: "Jesus saw his mother and the disciple he loved standing there; so he said to his mother, 'He is your son'" (John 19:26). This simple statement shows us that the beloved disciple and all believers are Mary's children. "Then he said to the disciple, 'She is your mother'" (John 19:27). This means Mary is the mother of all Christians; she is our mother. Mary is the Church's model of faithfulness and love. Mary points us straight

PRAY IT!
Liturgy Connection

Because of Mary's holiness and faithfulness, God took her into Heaven, both body and soul, at the end of her life on earth. This event is called the **Assumption.** The significance of this is that Mary shared in Jesus' Resurrection from the dead as soon as her life on earth ended. She is in Heaven waiting for us and for all the faithful to join her. The Church celebrates the Feast of the Assumption on August 15.

to Jesus. For this reason, the Church's devotion to the Blessed Mother is an important part of Christian worship. She is our model of holiness.

Our Heavenly Friends

We've all had the experience of leaning on our friends in time of need. Not only that, but we count on our friends to help us celebrate life's moments. We have a whole other group of friends too, our heavenly friends. Mary is one of these—she is our spiritual mother, and she is joined by the saints, all those who have died and are with God in Heaven.

As Catholics, we have a special connection to those who have died. The Holy Spirit unites all believers, those who have died and are being purified before entering Heaven, and the saints who are in Heaven right now. All of these people are our heavenly friends. Our heavenly friends help connect us to Jesus. Just as we ask our friends here on earth to help us or pray for us, we can ask our heavenly friends to put in a good word for us with God. We can ask them to bring our needs to God. We can also ask them to pray for us when we have difficult decisions to make. We believe that they hear our prayers and are with God in Heaven. It is an especially meaningful prayer to ask our own loved ones who have died to bring our needs before God.

FUN FACT

Have you ever wondered how many official saints there are? It is difficult to arrive at a definitive number. We do know that the names of more than 10,000 saints have been recorded in various historical records during the Church's history.

The Saints

What do you think being a saint means? Saints embody what it is to be holy. To be holy is to seek God and to be filled with God. Mary is the first saint, the queen of all the saints. She was totally filled with God's life. The many saints who have come after her are also examples of what it means to live Christian lives, trying to do what God wants. You'll notice that a number of saints are highlighted in "People of Faith" articles in this handbook. This is because by reading about and studying the lives of the saints, their examples can inspire us.

We witness the Holy Spirit's activity in the Church through her saints. They are our companions in prayer. They, with Mary in Heaven, contemplate God, they

Birthdays of the Saints

Ever wonder how the Church determines on what day a saint's feast will be celebrated? The vast majority of saints are remembered on the anniversary of the day they died. This is a sort of birthday because it is the first day of their new life in Heaven with God. The saints participate in Christ's passage from life on earth, through death, to a new life. Christ's passage is called the Paschal Mystery, and it includes his Ascension into Heaven after his Resurrection. When we celebrate the life of a saint, we affirm our belief in this mystery. Though the births of the saints are significant, by making a special point of remembering them on the anniversaries of their deaths, we commemorate all that Jesus Christ accomplished through them during their lives on earth. This practice also reminds us that they remain alive and offer us their friendship. Death was not the end for them, and it isn't for us either.

praise him, and perhaps best of all, they care for
people like us, who are still living on earth. That's
good news for us. The saints are our holy friends,
looking out for us always. When we celebrate their
feasts and memorials at liturgies throughout the year,
the Church is united with the celebration of God's life
in Heaven. All the official saints of the Church are a
part of our Catholic family. These are the saints whom
the Church has canonized. We can also
use the term *unofficial* with *saint*
to refer to all the people in
the Church who are
living and dead.
This is the whole
communion of
saints.

Did You Know?

The Communion of Saints

When we recite the Nicene Creed at Mass, we
profess our belief in the **communion of saints.**
This refers to the Church. The Church is a communion
of holy people, living and dead (but alive with God).
There is a second, closely related, meaning of communion
of saints. In English *saint* can translate the Latin *sancti*
("holy people") and the Latin *sancta* ("holy things"). The
holy things are primarily the sacraments, especially the
Eucharist. When we profess belief in the communion of
saints, we say something about our relationships with all
faithful people living now and in the past, but that is not
all. We are also saying that "holy things"—especially the
Eucharist—bind us to one another and unite us to
God. When we participate in the sacraments, particularly the Eucharist, we are nourished with the
Body and Blood of Christ, and we become the
Body of Christ for the world.

Remember your former leaders,
who spoke God's message to you.
Think back on how they lived and died,
and imitate their faith. (Hebrews 13: 7)

PEOPLE OF FAITH
Our Lady of Guadalupe

© 2009 Saint Mary's Press/Illustration by Vicki Shuck

On December 9, 1531, a fifty-seven-year-old peasant named Juan Diego, who lived near Mexico City, was on his way to Mass. Suddenly he heard beautiful music and a woman's voice calling to him from Tepeyac Hill. At the top of the hill, he saw a beautiful woman, who revealed that she was the Virgin Mary. She told Juan to go to the bishop and tell him that a church should be built in her honor at the bottom of the hill. Juan went to the bishop and told him about his vision, but the bishop wasn't ready to believe Juan's story. He said he needed a sign to prove Juan's story true. Several days later, Juan's uncle was sick. As Juan rushed to find a doctor, the Virgin appeared again. Juan told her about his uncle. She assured Juan that all would be well. That morning, she appeared to the uncle and cured him. Then she told Juan to go to the top of the hill and in his cloak, gather the roses he would find there and take them to the bishop as the sign the bishop had requested. When Juan opened his cloak, the roses fell out, but the greatest sign of all was the beautiful portrait of the Virgin that suddenly appeared on Juan's cloak. Soon after, a church was built in Mary's honor. The feast of Our Lady of Guadalupe is celebrated on December 12. She is the Patroness of the Americas (adapted from Wintz, "The Story of Our Lady of Guadalupe").

PART 4

LITURGY AND SACRAMENTS

The Seven Sacraments of the Catholic Church

The Sacraments of Christian Initiation
- Baptism
- Confirmation
- The Eucharist

The Sacraments of Healing
- Penance and Reconciliation
- Anointing of the Sick

The Sacraments at the Service of Communion
- Matrimony
- Holy Orders

INTRODUCTION TO LITURGY

Which activities are important for Catholics to do? Your list might include studying the Bible and going to religion classes. You might list feeding the poor. Treating everyone kindly and following the Commandments are probably on your list too. Imagine if a parish did all these things but never got together to pray, especially Mass and the other sacraments. It would be hard to recognize such a parish as Catholic. Getting together for Mass and for the other official prayers of the Church is an essential part of being Catholic.

Mass and the other official prayers of the Church are called liturgies. **Liturgy** is a communal, public,

Participating at Mass involves all five of our senses. Can you name one example of how you use each sense in the Sacrament of the Eucharist?

Bill Wittman

official prayer of the Church. *Communal* means we participate in liturgy together with each other, in communion with the Trinity—God the Father, God the Son, and God the Holy Spirit. *Public* means liturgy is not the private prayer of individuals by themselves. *Official* means liturgy is celebrated under the direction and guidelines of the Church's bishops. In the liturgy, above all we celebrate the Paschal Mystery—the Death, Resurrection, and Ascension of Jesus Christ, through which he destroyed death and restored our life.

There are many different forms of liturgy. Some are sacraments, like Baptism, Matrimony, and the Eucharist, which is the Church's most important liturgy. Other liturgies are special prayers, like morning prayer or blessings. Not all prayer, however, is liturgy. Your nighttime prayers or saying the rosary are good prayers. They are not liturgies, though, because they are not communal, public, and official.

Important though liturgy is, you might struggle to find it interesting. According to a recent survey of American teenagers, 61 percent of Catholic teens find going to Church boring at least some of the time (Smith, *Soul Searching*, page 62). You're not alone if you feel the same way.

The survey also reports that at least 40 percent would

Pray It!

God of time and history,
You walk with me unseen
yet surround me with
your presence.
Fill me with your Spirit
and open my eyes
that I may recognize the
extraordinary love of Christ
in ordinary acts of faith.
May I always praise you with
the saints and angels
every day of my life.
I ask this through Christ,
our Lord.

Amen

Did You Know?

Liturgy Is Work

Liturgy comes from the Greek word *leitourgia*, which is made up of the words for "work" and "people." In ancient Greece, *leitourgia* meant any public work exercised on behalf of the people to serve the common good. This work could be religious, political, or practical. Caring for the poor, serving in the army, or even picking up trash would have been considered a liturgy. These were works of the people for the benefit of the community.

Over the centuries, liturgy became associated only with the religious part of community life. Eventually only the actions of the priests were considered to be the liturgy. Today, however, liturgy is understood as the work of the whole Christ. The whole Christ is the Head, which is Jesus Christ, and the members of the Body, which includes all the baptized and all those who have already died and entered the Kingdom.

choose to go to Mass every week even if it were completely their decision (Smith, *Soul Searching*, page 37). If you fall under this category, you are blessed. You have discovered one of the greatest treasures of the Catholic faith.

As with any treasure worth having, you need to do some work to find it. This section will take you on an adventure in search of the Church's liturgical treasury. It will give you some of the tools to uncover and appreciate its hidden richness. Let's begin.

Reading the Map of the Liturgy

When you start a journey, first you need to know where you are going, right? One of the tools to understanding the Church's liturgy is to realize that the liturgy is not a place we go. Rather, it's an event that involves action. In other words, we don't *go to* Mass so much as we *participate* in Mass. In a sense, *liturgy* is more a verb than it is a noun. In fact, liturgy is work. It is God's work, which we participate in.

In the Church's liturgy, we participate in the work of the Holy Trinity by giving thanks and adoration to God the Father. God the Father is the source of every blessing throughout history. The greatest of these blessings is the gift of his divine Son, Jesus Christ. We become his brothers and sisters through the power of the Holy Spirit.

Bill Wittman

Mass is not a spectator sport. Getting involved in liturgical ministries, like being a lector, can help you appreciate the richness of the Mass. What ministries interest you?

The Key to Unlocking Symbols

If the liturgy had a key, it would be the Holy Spirit. Without the Spirit, we would not see what lies beyond the words, actions, and objects of the liturgy.

Every liturgy is made up of symbols. To understand them, we need to know the symbolic language of faith. In symbolic language, *symbol* doesn't mean "fake." It means exactly the opposite.

Liturgical symbols express a reality that is completely real and deeply meaningful. Yet our attempts to describe these symbols never fully express their meanings. It's like trying to describe your relationship with your best friend or the love you feel for your pet. Try as you might, it's hard to explain it completely. **Symbols** are things visible to us that help put us in touch with something that is real, but invisible, like love. Sounds confusing, right? But our lives are filled with symbols we already understand.

For example, a graduation ceremony uses many symbols: cap and gown, diploma, the march, the graduates themselves. Let's explore one of these symbols.

A diploma is a piece of paper with your name, your school's name and seal, the date, and the principal's signature. All by itself, the paper doesn't mean much. But throw that together with all the years you went to school, your tests, papers, and grades. Add to that all the dreams you have for your future, your school friends and teach-

PRAY IT!

Liturgy Connection

When is your name day? Ask your family how you were named. You may have been named after a saint. Maybe your name is a variation of a saint's name. For example, Beth or Lisa comes from Elizabeth. If you have a saint's name, find out the date of your saint's feast day. If you don't have a saint's name, select a saint to remember and celebrate. For example, you could pick a saint whose life inspires you, a saint who shares your ethnic heritage, or the saint your parish is named after. Find out the saint's feast day and next time it comes around, celebrate it.

iStockphoto

How would you respond to someone who said a diploma was just a piece of paper, worth only a few pennies?

ers, and the ceremony itself. When you combine all this with that simple piece of paper, it becomes a diploma symbolizing everything about that part of your life.

When you look at that diploma, you see your past experience, your present accomplishment, and the possibilities that lie ahead. A meaningful symbol helps us remember the past, appreciate the present, and see future possibilities.

Sacrament and Symbol

Liturgical symbols work in a similar way but are even more powerful. This is because Christ is made real in those symbols and works through the Holy Spirit to transform the present. As we see in the Bible, whenever people encounter Christ, they are changed.

FUN FACT

Did you know that the date of Easter depends on the movements of the sun and the moon? Easter's date does not fall on the same date each year, as Christmas Day does. Rather, it changes each year. Easter is always the first Sunday after the first full moon after the first day of spring.

Jesus heals a blind man. Sacraments help us experience Christ even though we cannot see or touch him.

© Brooklyn Museum/Corbis

When [the blind man] came near, Jesus asked him, "What do you want me to do for you?" "Sir," he answered, "I want to see again." Jesus said to him, "Then see! Your faith has made you well." At once he was able to see. (Luke 18:40–43)

But we can't see Christ today, can we? The risen Christ is unrecognizable to human eyes. This is because his Resurrection has transformed him and because he has ascended to Heaven. Even his closest friends couldn't recognize him at first after the Resurrection. But they did recognize him when he was made known through symbolic actions, gestures, and words.

Today, the Holy Spirit works through our liturgical celebrations to help us see Christ present and active in our midst. We use the adjective *sacramental* to describe these celebrations. Something is sacramental if it makes Christ's presence known. The liturgy is sacramental, because Christ is present and his saving presence is made known to us through the work of the Holy Spirit. The Spirit prepares us to encounter Christ and gives us the eyes of faith to recognize him.

The **assembly,** the people God calls together to celebrate the liturgy—the Church—is also sacramental. It is something with visible characteristics that helps us see the reality of Christ's presence. Because of this the Church is sometimes referred to as a

THINK About It!

How many symbols can you find in your parish church? Pick one or two and discuss what they mean for Catholics. Which is your favorite symbol and why?

sacrament. Through the work of the Holy Spirit, the Church makes Christ, who is invisible, visible to the world.

One of the main effects of liturgy, especially when we celebrate Mass, is that all who participate become one. They are united to each other and to all the saints throughout time. This happens because in the liturgy, they are caught up in the love of the Trinity. Therefore, when we pray the liturgy, we participate in the reality taking place right now in Heaven and on earth, where all the saints and angels are united with us in praising God. When we pray the liturgy, we participate in the work of the Trinity — Father, Son, and Holy Spirit.

[Jesus] sat down to eat with them, took the bread, and said the blessing; then he broke the bread and gave it to them. Then their eyes were opened and they recognized him. (Luke 24:30–31)

Illustration by Elizabeth Wang, 'Through the offering of Jesus our High Priest in the Mass, we are united with all the saints in their praise of God in Heaven', copyright © Radiant Light 2008, www.radiantlight.org.uk

Can you see the saints in this artistic image of a Eucharistic liturgy? The picture illustrates the familiar words we hear at Mass: "Now we join the angels and the saints as they sing their unending hymn of praise: Holy, Holy, Holy . . . "

Unity in Diversity

Many different people from all over the world gather for liturgy. Yet they are one Body united in Christ. The celebrations may differ somewhat due to cultural differences, but the liturgy is legitimate as long as the celebrations follow the Church's official rites.

The Church's official liturgies developed differently in various parts of the world. Many of the symbols, words, and actions were the same ones handed down over the centuries from the Apostles. However, the liturgies looked different depending on which part of the world you were in. A Mass in Greece, for example, was different from one in Rome. *Catholic* means "universal." The variety of official liturgical traditions or rites shows how the Church is indeed universal, because they all express the same mystery of Christ. Therefore, even in diversity, the Church remains one body. This is because we follow the teachings of Christ as we have received them from the Apostles and their successors, the bishops.

Most Catholics in North and South America and Western Europe are Roman Catholics. They are called Roman, because they follow the Roman liturgical tradition, or rite.

Key Words

liturgy
symbols
assembly
sacrament

Time Is a Symbol Too

Time is also a symbol that holds deep meaning. Your birthday, for example, commemorates the day you were born. It's just a date on the calendar. Yet it has

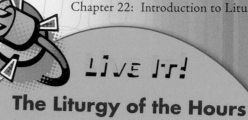

meaning for you and your family. On that day, you remember the past, you celebrate the present, and you hope for the future.

The Church also has special days and seasons during the year when we celebrate particular aspects of the mystery of Christ. On certain days, we also meet the "friends of God"—Mary, the Mother of God, the Apostles, martyrs, and saints. They remind us that we are united in faith even with those who are already in Heaven.

Live It!

The Liturgy of the Hours

One of the liturgies of the Church is called the Liturgy of the Hours. Each day, a liturgy is celebrated at specific times of the day and night. The two most important hours are morning and evening. This is because they represent Christ's Resurrection (seen in the sunrise) and his death (seen in the sunset).

One way you can participate in these liturgies at home is to recite a brief prayer in the morning and at night.

When you wake up, make the Sign of the Cross and say, "O Lord, open my lips, and my mouth shall proclaim your praise." Just before you go to sleep, make the Sign of the Cross and say, "May the Lord Almighty grant us a peaceful night and a perfect end" (Johnson, *Benedictine Daily Prayers*, pages 903 and 932).

Sunday: The First Easter

The most important day in the Christian calendar is Sunday, because it is the day on which Jesus rose from the dead. It is also the first day of Creation and the day of Pentecost. It is called the

Sunrise, sunset. Prayer is the best way to start and end your day with God.

iStockphoto

eighth day, because it is the day beyond time when Christ will come again. Because of all this, we call Sunday the Lord's Day.

Liturgical Seasons

Our liturgies throughout the year unfold the whole mystery of Christ. In Advent and Christmas, we

PEOPLE OF FAITH

Blessed John XXIII (1881–1963; Pope 1958–1963)

© 2009 Saint Mary's Press/Illustration by Vicki Shuck

He was born Angelo Giuseppe Roncalli in Italy. Later he became known as "Good Pope John." During his lifetime, the world experienced two World Wars, communism, and the Holocaust. In the Church, there was fear of the modern world. Yet John XXIII embraced the world and called it "his parish."

When he became Pope at almost seventy-seven years old, many thought he would be "transitional," making little change in the Church. Yet, in his five-year papacy, he revolutionized it.

commemorate how the son of God became one of us, and we wait with joyful hope for Christ's return. In Lent and Easter, we celebrate how Jesus saved us by going to the cross, being crucified, rising from the dead, ascending to Heaven, and sending us the Holy Spirit. Throughout the rest of the year, we experience the joy of living as God's children on earth until we are gathered together into the eternal joy of Heaven.

In 1962, he gathered all the bishops of the world in Rome. He also invited religious leaders, scholars, women, and even the news media. This gathering began four sessions called the Second Vatican Council. He wanted the Church to read the signs of the times and work for unity and peace within herself and with the entire modern world. He died after the first session.

Yet what he began changed the way the Church prayed. It changed how it understood itself and the world. John XXIII paved the way for John Paul II, the ultimate "media Pope," by being the first to welcome TV crews to the Vatican. He let the world see for the first time how the Church worked. Like John Paul II, he also had a sense of humor. When asked how many people worked in the Vatican, he said, "About half."

John XXIII was beatified in 2000. We celebrate his feast day on October 11, the day the Second Vatican Council began.

SACRAMENTS: CELEBRATING CHRIST'S PRESENCE

What have been the most significant events in your life so far? Was it the birth of a baby sister or brother? Did you succeed at something big? Maybe you lost a family member or friend because of a move, divorce, sickness, or death. Did you ever move to a new state?

Did you feel different after the event? Like, you woke up in the morning one person and went to bed at night completely different? The event changed

A new baby brother or sister brings big changes in a family's life. Sacraments celebrate big changes in our life with God.

Shutterstock

you, and you had to live your life in a new way. For example, if a sibling was born, you weren't the youngest or only child anymore. You were now an older sister or brother. You had new responsibilities and a new role in life.

As Catholics, we have moments that also change us, whether we know it or not. But the change is different from anything else in our lives, because it is God who changes us. These unique occasions are called sacraments. Following are the Seven Sacraments: Baptism, Confirmation, the Eucharist, Penance and Reconciliation, Anointing of the Sick, Matrimony, and Holy Orders.

Baptism, Confirmation, and the Eucharist are Sacraments of Initiation. This is because they are the foundation of Christian life. Baptism is always the first sacrament celebrated because it is through this sacrament that we become members of Christ and become part of the Church. Confirmation strengthens us and is necessary to complete baptismal grace. Eucharist completes Christian initiation. It is the high point of Christian life and all the sacraments are oriented toward it. Anointing of the Sick and Penance and Reconciliation are Sacraments of Healing because through them the Church continues Christ's work of healing and forgiving sins. Holy Orders and Matrimony are Sacraments at the Service of Communion. This is because these sacraments contribute to the Church's mission primarily through service to others.

The birth of Jesus shows us that God became man, born as a baby—like each one of us.

Shutterstock

Shutterstock

PRAY IT!

Creator God,
You have made
everything—
time and space, plants
and animals,
even me and
everyone I love.
You called all your
creation good,
and I know you are
with me wherever I go.
Bless this day, which
you have made.
Let me spend it
imitating you
by creating only good
things and blessing the world
with love.

Amen

Humanity, Meet Divinity

In a sacrament, ordinary human beings come face to face with God. No, you don't actually see some guy with a beard and angels. Remember how we said liturgies use symbols to communicate? Sacraments are liturgies that use symbols. This means they use movement, gestures, and things like water and light, in addition to words, to communicate. Sacraments communicate that God is present in the midst of the community. Through sacraments we encounter Jesus Christ and his saving power, called grace.

The amazing thing about sacraments is that they use basic things like water, oil, bread, and wine. Yet these are signs that something extraordinary is present. They are things we can see that help us recognize what we can't see. They help express the divine mystery of God's love. Sacraments are the fullest way we encounter God.

God with Us

The first time we knew fully that God was with us was when God became man. In Jesus' ordinary birth and life, people saw God doing something extraordinary. They saw it in the

iStockphoto

He is risen! This is the most important belief of Christians—that Jesus rose from the dead. During Mass we state this belief in the Nicene Creed: "On the third day he rose again in fulfillment of the Scriptures."

meals Jesus ate with people. They witnessed God's power when Jesus forgave sins. They knew it when Christ's touch healed the blind and the lame. When Jesus Christ rose from the dead and ascended into eternal life, people knew God truly is with us. Therefore, we call Christ the original sacrament, because he is the most basic way we encounter God.

> With a loud cry Jesus died. . . . The army officer who was standing there in front of the cross saw how Jesus had died. "This man was really the Son of God!" he said.
> (Mark 15:37,39).

PRAY IT!
Liturgy Connection

In the middle of every Mass, the priest says, "Let us proclaim the mystery of faith." One of the responses we can make is "Christ has died, Christ is risen, Christ will come again." But all the responses speak of the same thing—Christ's overwhelming love for us, even to death. This truly is a mystery, the mystery of unconditional love. But the mystery goes deeper, because Christ showed us a love stronger even than death. Further, his amazing love transcends time, because Christ promises to come again to gather all of us. This is why the mystery of Christ's love is the mystery of our faith.

Have you ever thought of friendship as a mystery—something you can't quite explain but you know is real?

You're probably thinking, "How can Christ be with us? Isn't he in Heaven?" Yes, you're right. This is where the Holy Spirit comes in. Before Christ ascended to Heaven, he promised the gift of the Holy Spirit. The Spirit is the breath and presence of God. The Spirit changed ordinary disciples into something extraordinary. They became Christ's Body and continued the work Jesus began. Today, through the Holy Spirit, the ordinary works of the Church become the extraordinary presence of God in the world. In this way, the Church is like a sacrament. The Church is a sign of Christ's presence and instrument through which the Holy Spirit still changes the world.

The Church continues to do the things Jesus did: gathering people, eating and drinking, forgiving, and healing. Like Jesus, the Church washes and anoints. She brings people together and inspires

Shutterstock

258

Looking Back

Speechless Before God

Sacrament comes from the Greek word for "mystery." The earliest Christians called the sacraments **mysteries.** But they didn't mean it like a murder mystery or a math problem.

Mystery comes from a Greek word meaning "to stand in silence before." They called sacraments mysteries, because what happens in a sacrament is so profound that, in a way, we're left speechless. No words adequately describe it. Sacraments leave us stunned, because sacraments are mysteries as love is a mystery. It's something you encounter with your heart or your gut. It's not something you solve. It's something you enter into. Only afterward do you use your intellect to reflect on its meaning.

them to continue Jesus' work. Our acts are human acts. But we know that through them, Christ is actually at work because of the Holy Spirit.

Sacred Mysteries

Think of a "best friend" kind of relationship. You share stories and jokes. You laugh and sometimes cry with each other. Even though you can't see it, you know love is there. But the love you share is a mystery. If you tried to tell someone else what you felt, you

The Russian artist Andrei Rublev created this icon as a way to illustrate the mystery of the Trinity. Which figures do you think represent the Father, Son, and Holy Spirit?

Andrej Rublëv, commons.wikimedia.org

couldn't fully describe it. It's as if you have to experience love before you can understand it.

Sacraments work in a similar way. We need to participate in a sacrament before we can comprehend its full meaning. The meaning that is communicated in every sacrament is that God loves us completely. We call this loving relationship with God **grace.** We encounter grace most fully in the sacraments. Through grace, we become part of God's divine life—the life of the Trinity. It is pure love between the Father and the Son poured out to us by the Holy Spirit.

When we celebrate a sacrament, we need to come to it with an attitude of openness to God's love and grace. This isn't as easy as it sounds. Sometimes God's love will challenge us. Sometimes it will make us realize we need to live our lives differently. Every time we encounter God's grace, something changes. Something new is created. Something weak is strengthened. Something dead is brought back to life. If we celebrate a sacrament with the required disposition, or attitude, we will recognize God's grace in us more clearly.

Signs of Grace

In the sacraments, we encounter God's grace in tangible ways. That means that in the sacraments we can see God's love. We can touch it and taste it. We can hear it and smell it. God calls us to participate in the sacraments so we can encounter his loving grace in our lives in unique and powerful ways.

God calls us to encounter new life in Christ through Baptism and Confirmation. Christ's Body and Blood feed us in the Eucharist. God calls us

Live It!

At the Second Vatican Council, held in the 1960s, the bishops said, "It is necessary that the faithful come to it [the liturgy] with proper dispositions, that their minds should be attuned to their voices" (*Constitution on the Sacred Liturgy* [*Sacrosanctum Concilium*], number 11). To be attuned means to be "in sync or in harmony." It's like a band. If the members want to make good music, their instruments need to be in tune with each other. The bishops ask that our minds be in tune with our voices when we celebrate the liturgy. This means we should pay attention to what we say and sing at Church. Next time you participate in a liturgy, listen to what you say and sing. Find ways to sync your actions and thoughts during the week with what you pray on Sunday.

Bill Wittman

Do you think most people realize that sacraments like the Eucharist are encounters with God? If not, what might help them see this?

FUN FACT

Following are some things the Church blesses: homes, engaged couples, pets, church bells, farm fields, boats, cars, rosaries, rings, throats, altars, organs, church doors, children, parents, pregnant couples, birthday celebrants, seeds, water, oil, statues, travelers, parks, cemeteries, schools, palm branches, and ashes.

back to him in the Sacrament of Penance and Reconciliation and heals us spiritually in the Anointing of the Sick. God calls us to lives of service and commitment in the Sacraments of Matrimony and Holy Orders.

Some of these sacraments are celebrated many times over a lifetime. Others are celebrated only once. Christ instituted all the sacraments. Look in the Gospels, and you can find how Christ established each sacrament's meaning. Christ commissioned his disciples to continue his work, trusting them to celebrate the sacraments.

For God loved the world so much that he gave his only Son, so that everyone who believes in him may not die but have eternal life. (John 3:16)

What You See Is What You Get

The sacraments show how God is changing us. It's like the computer term WYSIWYG—"what you see is what you get." In the Gospels when Jesus said a person's sins were forgiven, they were really forgiven. When he touched sick people and said they were healed, they really were. Jesus' actions and words weren't just for show. They did what he said they would do.

It's the same in a sacrament, because Christ is at work in the Church. When the Church pours water over someone and says the person is a new creation, the person really becomes something new. When the Church asks the Holy Spirit to change bread and wine into the Body and Blood of Christ, they really do change.

Now, you're thinking that the Body and Blood still look like bread and wine. Exactly! Remember how you were different after your sibling was born? Outside, you looked the same. Inside, you were different. It's not a change in appearance. To see the change in the bread and the wine in Eucharist, you need the eyes of faith. This is why sacraments are different from tricks

Did You Know?

You Can Write a Blessing

Almost all blessings have the same structure. Once you learn this easy four-part structure, you can write your own blessings. Just remember: "you–who–do–through."

You: Begin by naming God. Think of a description of God, like "God, our Father" or "Creator God."

Who: Now remember something good God has done. For example, "You made all the creatures of the earth" or "You give me many friends and companions."

Do: This is where you ask God to do something good again, like, "Please bless my dog and all animals."

Through: Finally, end the prayer by asking it through Jesus. "We ask this in the name of Jesus, the Lord. Amen."

Now what and whom will you bless?

Did You Know?

Blessings

Among the many kinds of sacramentals, blessings hold an important place. God blesses creation with his grace, calling it good. In turn, people bless God by praising him and remembering all the good things he has done. They also bless other people, asking God to help them live the changed lives they have received or will receive in a sacrament. We can also bless places and objects, asking God to help us use them wisely for the good of all people.

Anyone can do a blessing, even you or your parents. A deacon, priest, or bishop specifically leads particular blessings. These blessings are liturgies of the Church (that means they are public prayers) and often include some Scripture readings and spoken prayers.

you see in magic shows. The changes God makes aren't illusions. They are real. The difference is that God doesn't try to deceive our vision. Instead God calls us to faith so we can see God's real actions in the sacraments.

A parent can bless a child. You can bless your parents. Blessings are simple ways to communicate God's love.

Shutterstock

"Go, then, to all peoples everywhere and make them my disciples: baptize them in the name of the Father, the Son, and the Holy Spirit, and teach them to obey everything I have commanded you." (Matthew 28:19–20)

Living a Changed Life Every Day

You don't have to wait for the celebration of a sacrament to encounter God's grace. Over the centuries, the Church instituted and began using sacred signs called **sacramentals.** These signs prepare us to receive grace. Sacramentals prepare us to celebrate the sacraments with the attitudes we need to let the sacrament do what it's meant to do. They make us ready to cooperate with the grace we receive. Sacramentals also ask God to bless the different events and stages of our lives

Sacramentals include things like making the Sign of the Cross on another person, signing yourself with holy water, marking your forehead with ashes, or blessing your home, car, or pet. You might use a sacramental each day. For example, your parents could make the Sign of the Cross on your forehead and say a prayer before you leave for school. At meals, you can pray a blessing. Often, a sacramental includes a symbol related to one of the sacraments, for example, holy water (Baptism) or food (the Eucharist).

THiNK AbouT IT!

Some people mistakenly think of blessings and sacraments as magic. How are our rituals different from magic? What's the difference between our sacramental symbols and objects some consider to be lucky charms, like a rabbit's foot? Do you treat blessings superstitiously?

24

The Eucharist: The Heart of All Liturgy

Can you say "thank you" in a different language? If you can say "Eucharist," then you can. In Greek, "to give thanks" is *eucharisto*. This is what we do in the sacrament called the Eucharist or Mass.

The **Eucharist** is the most important sacrament we can celebrate. Could we say anything better to God, who created everything and gives us life? The

At a Seder supper, the youngest child asks a series of questions that prompt the adults to tell the story of Passover.

© Leland Bobbé/Corbis

What can I offer the Lord for all his goodness to me? I will bring a wine offering to the Lord, to thank him for saving me. (Psalm 116:12–13)

best response is to give thanks. Sometimes we say "thanks from the bottom of my heart." This means we want to show gratitude by giving our truest, fullest, best selves.

We do the same in the Eucharist. The Eucharist is the heart and high point of the Church's life. We gather in response to God's love. We try to bring our best selves and give heartfelt thanks to God. But our thanksgiving falls short of the extraordinary goodness of God. Because we are members of the Body of Christ, however, our thanks are joined to Christ's sacrifice of praise to the Father. Christ gave his fullest, best self in thanksgiving to the Father when he offered himself on the cross, once for all. Through Christ's perfect offering, we receive the grace of that perfect love between the Father and Son in the Holy Spirit.

Making the Past Present

Jews and Catholics do a special kind of remembering called **anamnesis.** Every year at **Passover,** Jewish people tell the story of how their ancestors escaped slavery in Egypt on the night the angel of death passed over the land (see Exodus, chapter 12). But the Jews don't tell the story as if it were only a past event. They believe that the same thing that

PRAY IT!

Lord Jesus,
Sometimes it's hard
to pray at Mass.
I get so distracted,
and sometimes I don't
understand what
is happening.
Help me just to
respond as best I can,
to believe what I pray,
and to live what I believe,
so I can be your
Body for all those who
need you most.
Amen

PRAY IT!
Liturgy Connection

Before Communion we sing, "Lamb of God, you take away the sins of the world. Have mercy on us." The image of Jesus as the Lamb of God comes from the ancient Jewish Passover ritual. In the spring, the Jews killed an unblemished lamb and smeared its blood on the doorposts of a family's house. In the Exodus story (chapter 12), the sign of the blood saved the family from death and freed them from slavery.

For Catholics the sacrifice of Jesus frees us from the slavery of sin. That is why the Eucharist is a sacrifice that forgives our venial , or less serious, sins and helps us avoid committing mortal sins in the future. It also brings us heavenly and earthly blessings. This is why we send Mass cards when someone dies and why Masses are often celebrated in remembrance of someone who has died.

happened in the past is happening again right now in the present. Just as he did their ancestors, God frees them.

"On that night I will go through the land of Egypt, killing every first-born male. . . . The blood on the doorposts will be a sign to mark the houses in which you live. When I see the blood, I will pass over you and will not harm you." (Exodus 12:12–13)

In the Eucharist, we recall the past in a similar way. We remember Christ's Passover, when he passed over from death to eternal life. His blood, which he poured out on the cross, is the blood that saves us, like the blood of the Passover lamb in Exodus. In the Eucharist we recall what he did in the past through his life, death, and Resurrection, but we also celebrate that his saving action is present today. We call this kind of remembering anamnesis because it reminds us who we are: children of God. It reminds us to whom we belong: Christ. The meaning of *anamnesis* is easy to remember if we recognize that its opposite is *amnesia*. People with amnesia can't remember who they are or to whom they belong.

You Are What You Eat

What the Church says God does in a sacrament really happens. What you see is what you get. In the Eucharist, when we eat and drink the consecrated bread and wine, we eat and drink the Body and Blood of Christ. This is called **Communion.** Communion transforms us, unites us more closely with Christ, and enables us to become more fully a part of the Body of Christ. This is because we are being intimately united in love with Christ. We actually become more like Christ when we do this. One reason this happens is because sharing Communion forgives our venial, or less serious, sins. Our union with Christ also strengthens us to avoid more serious sins.

The bread we break: when we eat it, we are sharing in the body of Christ. (1 Corinthians 10:17)

Bill Wittman

What you see is what you get: the Body of Christ. Better yet, you become the Body of Christ. What can you do to make Holy Communion all it is meant to be?

Key Words

Eucharist

anamnesis

Passover

Communion

preside

But this union goes even further. We're united in love not only with Christ but also with all his members—everyone who shares in his Body and Blood. In Communion we are also united to everyone in all time who has shared Christ's Body and Blood. We are in union with our ancestors who believed in Christ. We are united with our descendants who will come after us.

The word *communion* means "union with." When we celebrate Eucharist, we are in union with all the faithful who have gone before us, all who will come after us, and, of course, all who are with us now.

Illustration by Elizabeth Wang, "With the Angels we celebrate Christ's glorious Resurrection', copyright © Radiant Light 2008, www.radiantlight.org.uk

Call and Response

Communion is only one part of the Sacrament of the Eucharist. First, Christ gathers us into an assembly. We hear God's call to worship, and we respond by coming together on Sunday. Then we listen to the Word of God proclaimed in the Scriptures. We listen especially to Christ, who speaks to us in the Gospels.

Next we respond by giving thanks to God the Father for everything he has done. Most of all, we thank God for sending us his Son, Jesus Christ. In our thanksgiving we remember how Jesus took bread and wine and blessed them. We remember how he broke the bread and poured the wine and how he shared

Did You Know?

Remembering the Future

In Mass we remember the past. But when we participate in Communion, we also "remember" the future. This means that even though the future hasn't happened yet, we have a sense of what to expect. This is because God has revealed some things about it to us. In Communion we are united with those in Heaven who are fully one with Christ, because they have died like him. They now share his eternal life. These are the martyrs, saints, and the dead who "have gone before us marked with the sign of faith" (Eucharistic Prayer I). With Christ and the angels, they give perfect thanks to the Father. They are doing now what we hope to experience fully in Heaven. When we remember Christ's sacrifice and share in it through the Eucharist, we become part of this Mystical Body of Christ in Heaven. We participate in the unity of the Church and witness a glimpse of our future already taking place in Heaven.

Bill Wittman

The Word of God, proclaimed by a priest or deacon, is an essential part of the Mass, not to be missed.

Did You Know?

Source and Summit

Everything we do as the Church is geared toward giving thanks to God through the Eucharist. Everything we do flows from it. This is why Catholics call the Eucharist "the source and summit." It is the source, because it is where the Church gets the power and inspiration to carry out her mission. It is the source, because we receive life from it. The Eucharist is the summit, because it is the high point of the Church's life. It is our reason for living.

When we celebrate the Eucharist, we fulfill Jesus' command to "do this in memory of me" (Luke 22:19).

them with his disciples. We follow his command and do the same.

The priest on our behalf asks the Holy Spirit to change the bread and wine into the Body and Blood of Christ. Over the bread and wine, he says the words that Jesus said at the Last Supper: "This is my body which will be given up for you. . . . This is the cup of my blood." Through the action of the Holy Spirit, the bread and wine become what the priest says they are—the Body and Blood of Christ. The high point of the Eucharist is when we share in the banquet prepared by Christ, who gives us his Body and Blood to share. After this, Christ calls us to go and love God by being the Body of Christ for the world.

Even though there are a number of important parts to the liturgy, the celebration of the Eucharist is one single act of worship and praise of the Father through the Son, in the love of the Holy Spirit.

Who Celebrates the Eucharist?

When you participate in Mass, who is doing the celebrating? You might think that the Mass is primarily the action of the priest, because he says most of the words and stands at the altar. The priests and bishops **preside** over the celebration of Mass. The role of the presider at Mass is unique and essential because he represents Christ, acting in the person of Christ. The priest is so essential that without a priest we cannot celebrate the Eucharist. Only validly ordained priests can preside at the Eucharist. They are the only ones who can consecrate the bread and wine so they become the Body and Blood of Christ.

Mass is not the action of the priest alone, though. Who else is involved in the action of the Mass? Perhaps you are thinking of the choir or music director. Musicians contribute a lot to Mass. They sing and lead many of the responses, but Mass involves the action of others too. Perhaps now you are thinking of the readers, altar servers, Communion ministers, other liturgical ministers, or even the assembly. The fact is, all these people assembled celebrate Mass and each person is called to actively participate.

Liturgy is sometimes described as the work of the people, and you can see why. No one is meant to be a spectator. But above all, Mass is

THiNK About It!

How does participating in the Eucharist make you thankful? What are you thankful for? How does the Eucharist help you feel more united to Christ and the Church? What is your favorite part of Mass and why? How does this part of Mass help you live as Christ for others?

Altar serving is a liturgical ministry that many young people enjoy. Being involved in this way can make the Eucharist even more special.

Bill Wittman

God's work, which we participate in. When we celebrate Mass we participate in the work of the Trinity. It's really Christ who is doing the work in communion with the Father and the Holy Spirit. Christ is the most perfect priest. He is the eternal high priest who offers the perfect sacrifice—his own self—to the Father. In the Mass, Christ acts through the priest to offer his Body and Blood in thanksgiving to the Father. All the members of his Body participate in the work of the Eucharist by joining with Christ through the priest.

The Role of the Assembly

If Christ is doing the work of the Eucharist, we can sit back and relax, right? Guess again. Saint Teresa of Ávila is believed to have written, "God has no body now on earth but yours; no hands but yours; no feet but yours." Christ leads, enables, and directs us. But we, the members of his body, must do work too. This is why the bishops at the Second Vatican Council said: "[The] Church earnestly desires that all the faithful should be led to that fully conscious, and active participation in liturgical celebrations which is called for by the very nature of the liturgy. Such participation by the Christian people . . . is their right and duty by reason of their baptism" (*Constitution on the Sacred Liturgy [Sacrosanctum Concilium]*, number 14).

The first way we participate is by coming to the Eucharist with an open and humble attitude. We need to be open to listening for God's voice. (This is the meaning of *obedience*, because *obey* is related to the Latin word *audire*, meaning "to hear"). This helps us be ready to receive the grace of God in the sacrament.

If anything in our life seriously prevents us from listening to and obeying God, we must address it before we share in Communion. This is because receiving Communion is a public statement. It is like Jesus' words. They do what they say they do. By sharing Communion we say we are completely united with Christ and with each other. If we have sinned so seriously that we have built a barrier between us and God or others,

Live It!

Sunday is the most important day of the week, because it's the day Jesus was raised from the dead. Sunday is actually the most important day of the year. (Easter is just a very big Sunday.) For this reason Sunday is the most significant time to celebrate the Eucharist. For the Christian family, it's a day of joy and rest from work.

Following are some ways you can make Sunday a more significant part of your week: be sure to participate in Mass. Rest from something you normally do during the week, such as watching TV, playing video games, or using your cell phone. Instead, spend that time doing something nice for someone else. During the day, look more closely for God's presence in everyone around you.

You have every right to sing. Have you ever considered that participation at Mass is both your right and your duty by reason of your baptism?

Bill Wittman

FUN FACT

The essential signs of the Eucharist are bread and wine. The bread must be made with only wheat flour and water. Nothing else can be added. The wine must be made from grapes only and contain at least 5 percent alcohol. If it becomes vinegar or if too much water is added so it is no longer wine, it cannot be used for Mass.

then we are not speaking the truth if we participate in Communion.

This is why people who know they have sinned mortally must not share in Communion until they have received absolution in the Sacrament of Penance and Reconciliation (see chapter 30).

We also participate in the Eucharist by joining in the responses, songs, silences, and gestures. This kind of participation is really not optional. It puts us in touch with the Christian spirit. Our participation in the liturgy helps us learn how to be Christian.

Finally, we participate by leaving the Eucharist, promising to do in the world what we have done at Mass—live as Christ for others.

Mother Teresa spoke to the graduating class at Harvard University, in Cambridge, Massachusetts, in the 1980s. She urged them to care for the poor, using what they had learned in their studies. In the liturgy, we learn how to live as Christ.

Mother Teresa's words are also for us, as follows:

> You and I have been taught to love, to love one
> another, to be kind to each other, not with words
> but in real life. To prove that love in action as
> Christ has proved it. That's why we read in the
> gospel that Jesus made himself the Bread of Life, to
> satisfy our hunger for love. For he says, "whatever
> you do to the least of my brethren, you do to me."
> (Monroe, *Finding God at Harvard*, page 318)

Looking Back

The Easter Duty

In the early Church, people shared in Communion every time
they participated in the Eucharist. However, over the centuries,
for various reasons, more and more people stopped receiving
Communion, even though they might attend the Eucharist each
week or even each day. By the sixteenth century, most people were
receiving Communion only outside Mass or as they were dying.

In more recent times, the Church has been encouraging
everyone who has celebrated First Communion and is free of
mortal sin to share in Communion whenever they participate in
a celebration of the Eucharist. At least once per year, during the
Easter season, all Catholics who are able to receive Communion
are obligated to do so. This is called the Easter duty. It is best to
think of this as the bare minimum and best to strive to participate in
Communion every Sunday.

25

The Eucharist: The Liturgy of the Word

Do your family members have favorite stories to tell about one another—stories that everyone has heard over and over but are still worth telling?

© Rob Lewine/CORBIS

When you get together with your family or friends, do you tell or hear stories often? Like the one about when your grandparents met for the first time or your best stories about your favorite pet?

These stories help communicate who your family is. They are your shared history and identity. That's why they are retold at family gatherings. When newcomers join your family, they hear these stories too. Telling, listening, and retelling these stories helps tie families together.

The Church has its own family stories. Every time the Church gets together to pray, one or more of these stories is told. In the sacraments, these stories are organized into a section called the **Liturgy of the Word.** Every sacrament includes a Liturgy of the Word. In fact, in the Eucharist, the Liturgy of the Word is such an important part of the celebration that you cannot have the Eucharist without it. The Liturgy of the Word consists of readings from the Bible, a homily by a bishop, priest, or deacon, the Creed, and prayers for the Church, the world, and people in need.

> In the beginning, when God created the universe, the earth was formless and desolate. . . . Then God commanded, "Let there be light"—and light appeared. (Genesis 1:1–3)

Jesus, the Word of God

The Book of Genesis tells the story of God's creating the world by speaking. "God commanded, 'Let there be light'—and light appeared" (Genesis 1:3). The Word of God creates something new. God's Word brings order where there was only chaos. God's Word is life.

Pray It!

Jesus,
Word Made Flesh,
Even though you
are God, you chose
to become like me.
Dwell again in human
skin and use my voice
to speak your Word. Let
me proclaim your Good
Newswhere there is hunger, and let me hear your
voice where there is suffering. Help me be a part of
your Word, spoken to bring
new life.

Amen

In the beginning the Word already existed; the Word was with God, and the Word was God. . . . The Word became a human being and . . . lived among us. (John 1:1,14)

Illustration by Elizabeth Wang, 'A Worthy Mother Of A Divine Son', copyright © Radiant Light 2008, www.radiantlight.org.uk

Jesus Christ is God's Word made flesh. God created something new when he raised Jesus from the dead. Jesus reordered the way we live. This is so we would live for God and not ourselves. God's Word, made flesh in Jesus Christ, gives us new life.

Jesus is called the **Logos,** a Greek word that translates as "word." Its meaning, however, is more like "thought," "logic," or "meaning." Jesus is the *Logos,* because when we see Jesus and listen to him, we can begin to see the mind of God and understand God's logic.

Think back to your family's stories. Some of them serve as reminders about your past that give meaning to your present. For example, the members of a family without enough money for necessities might remind one another of the stories of their family's past struggles. In difficult times, they would tell these stories again to remind themselves that they don't give up during hard times. These stories give everyone strength and hope.

The stories of Jesus and our ancestors in faith do the same thing. When we hear them, we are able to look at our present situation and see it in light of the story or "logic" of Christ. The stories of the Church are like lenses or filters that we can place on a camera that allow us to see the world the way God sees it. For example, whenever we share a meal, we see that meal through the lens of the Last Supper and all the meals Jesus shared. Because of the meal stories we find in the Bible, we see how eating with others shows our love for others.

The Bible

All the stories or readings we hear in the Liturgy of the Word come from the Bible. The Bible is made up of many books and letters. These writings are inspired by God and reveal God and God's plan of salvation to us.

PRAY IT!
Liturgy Connection

Sometimes at Mass after the homily, special people are called forward. They are blessed, and then they leave the Mass following a person carrying the Lectionary or the *Book of the Gospels*. These people are the catechumens. They are preparing to be baptized. They are dismissed from the Mass with a catechist to reflect on the Liturgy of the Word. One way to think about this is that they continue feeding on Jesus, the Word of God. Once they are baptized, they will stay for the whole Mass and feed on Jesus, the Bread of Life. They prepare for Baptism by praying and "digesting" the words they have heard in the Scriptures that day.

This Bible looks old and well used. How used is your Bible?

iStockphoto

THiNK About It!

Do you have a favorite Bible story? Who are the main characters in the story and what happens to them? Are you like any of the characters, or has a similar event happened to you in your own life? What if you were actually in the story—what would you do?

The Bible includes many different kinds of writings. There are letters, religious histories, songs, and poems. There are books filled with laws and other books filled with wise sayings. The Bible's writings often use symbols to tell stories. The heart of the Bible is the four **Gospels** of Matthew, Mark, Luke, and John. These are the stories Jesus' followers wrote after he was raised from the dead.

A Jewish youth reads from the Torah, which consists of the first five books of the Old Testament.

© Claudia Kunin/CORBS

The Bible is divided into two main sections—the Old and the New Testaments. The Old Testament was written before the birth of Christ and includes the Jewish law, or Torah, as well as the other books of the Hebrew Bible. The New Testament includes the Gospels, the Acts of the Apostles, and the letters of early Church leaders written after Jesus' Resurrection. Both parts of the Bible are necessary for Christians to understand the full meaning of Christ's life.

The Gospel Reading

Whenever the Scripture readings are proclaimed at Mass, we believe it is God speaking to us, especially in the Gospels. Whenever the Gospel is proclaimed, we show this in a special way by adding more festive elements to the proclamation.

Just before the proclamation of the Gospel, we stand and sing an acclamation to Christ, the Word. Usually, it's "Alleluia!" During the acclamation, a deacon, priest, or bishop takes a book called the *Book of the Gospels*. This book contains only the readings from the four Gospels. He processes with it to the ambo.

Did You Know?

Lectionary ABCs

The Sunday readings are arranged in a three-year cycle. In Year A, the Gospel reading is from Matthew. Year B is Mark, and Year C is Luke. John's Gospel is read throughout the year on certain Sundays. Each year begins on the First Sunday of Advent, which falls in late November or early December.

The first reading usually comes from the Old Testament. It is related in theme to the Gospel. Next, the psalm summarizes the theme. The second reading comes from one of the New Testament letters. It doesn't always relate to the theme because it is read continuously. That means we start at the beginning of the letter and read a portion each Sunday until we come to the end. The last reading is always from one of the Gospels.

The **ambo** is a reading stand where the Scriptures are proclaimed. In some parishes, altar servers carrying candles and sometimes incense accompany him.

Did You Know?

The Lectionary:
A Calendar for the Bible

Although all the readings we hear in the Liturgy of the Word come from the Bible, we don't read directly from the Bible itself. We read from the **Lectionary** (and the *Book of the Gospels*, which contains only the Gospel readings from the Lectionary). The Lectionary is a little bit like a calendar with readings. It shows the parts of the Bible we are to read on specific days of the year. Every day of the liturgical year and every sacrament and special liturgy have assigned readings. These readings are the same for all Catholics throughout the entire world. Only on rare occasions, and usually only with the permission of the bishop or pastor, can the assigned readings be changed. The assigned readings can never be replaced with nonbiblical texts, even if they have a religious theme.

You must not depend on bread alone to sustain you, but on everything that the LORD says.
(Deuteronomy 8:3)

The devil tempts Jesus to turn stones into bread, but Jesus replies that we need the Word of God as much as bread. Why?

© Brooklyn Museum/Corbis

A deacon incenses the
Book of the Gospels.
Using incense helps
express the importance
of the Word of God.

Bill Wittman

Feeding on the Word

The Word of God is more than just stories handed down to us. It is the bread that sustains us from day to day. Both the Word of God and the Eucharist feed us in Mass. This is why the Liturgy of the Word and the Liturgy of the Eucharist are closely connected to each other. In the Liturgy of the Word, Christ, the *Logos* of God, feeds us. This prepares us to be fed by Christ, the Lamb of God. Therefore we show reverence to both the Word and the Eucharist, because both give us life.

In addition to hearing the Word proclaimed in the Scriptures, the Word feeds us through the homily. A bishop,

FUN FACT

Before 1969 when the Second Vatican Council revised the way we do the Mass, people heard only one New Testament (NT) and Gospel reading at Sunday Mass. The Old Testament (OT) was proclaimed only on weekdays. Back then, if you went to Mass every Sunday for a year, you would hear only 1 percent of the OT and 17 percent of the NT. Today, if you go to Mass every Sunday for three years, you will hear 14 percent of the OT and 71 percent of the NT (USCCB Committee on the Liturgy, *Newsletter*, page 27).

Key Words

Liturgy of the Word
Logos
Gospels
ambo
Lectionary

priest, or deacon takes the readings we have just heard and helps us look at our lives through the lens of those readings. In a way, he takes the lens of the Scriptures and places it over the pictures of our lives. Then he shows us how the readings tell us about our lives today. Therefore, the preacher's task is not primarily to teach us about the Scriptures but rather to interpret our lives, using the Scriptures as the key.

"This passage of scripture has come true today, as you heard it being read." (Luke 4:21)

Having been fed by the Word, we respond by publicly stating our core beliefs. We do this by saying the Creed or by renewing our baptismal promises. We conclude the Liturgy of the Word by praying intercessions (or Prayers of the Faithful) for the Church. Our intercessions include prayers for the world, for people in need, and for our community's particular

During the homily the priest shows us how the Scriptures, even though they were written thousands of years ago, apply to our lives today.

Bill Wittman

needs. We name those things in our world that are in need of God's life-giving Word. We ask God to help us be like Christ, the Living Word, so we can be a life-giving word to all those in need. When we pray the intercessions, we imitate Christ, who prayed to the Father for those he loved and for those who were suffering. Praying for others is one way we exercise the responsibilities of our Baptism when we were recreated to be like Christ.

Live It!

To make the readings come alive on Sunday, try an adapted form of an ancient type of prayer called *lectio divina* (from the Latin for "holy reading").

First, choose one of the readings for the upcoming Sunday. Find it in a Bible and sit in a comfortable, quiet place to read it. Close your eyes and breathe deeply. Open your eyes. Slowly read your reading several times. Try reading it once out loud. Listen with your heart.

Second, ask yourself, "What does this mean for me? What is God trying to say to me?" Journal your thoughts if you like.

Third, respond with your heart. God has spoken to you with his heart. What would you like to say to God at this moment with yours?

Fourth, rest in silence with God. Breathe deeply and give thanks for your conversation with God.

This is what is written: the Messiah must suffer and must rise from death three days later, and in his name the message about repentance and the forgiveness of sins must be preached to all nations. (Luke 24:46–47)

People of Faith

Saint Anthony of Padua

© 2009 Saint Mary's Press/Illustration by Vicki Shuck

"Saint Anthony, Saint Anthony, please come around. Something is lost and needs to be found." You might hear this rhyme when someone has lost something, like car keys. That's because Saint Anthony of Padua is the patron saint of searchers of lost articles.

Saint Anthony is revered as one of the Church's greatest preachers, who brought many lost people back into the faith. He had a beautiful voice and a captivating way of speaking. His homilies were well written and made people think. He was known as the "hammer of the heretics," because his sermons helped people bring their thoughts and actions into line with Church teachings.

His original reason for becoming a priest was to become a martyr. Martyrs were people who were killed because they believed in Christ. Anthony was moved by the recent martyrdom of five Franciscans. Inspired by their order's public way of living like Christ, he left his comfortable life in Portugal to join the Franciscans in Africa in hopes of dying for the faith. His poor health, however, changed his plans. Instead, he spent his short life with the Franciscans in Italy to become one of the greatest spiritual writers of the Church, venerated for his great teachings.

Less than a year after Saint Anthony's death, Pope Gregory IX canonized him. His feast day is June 13.

26 THE EUCHARIST: THE LITURGY OF THE EUCHARIST

There's a Jewish saying: The person who eats without first thanking God is a thief. Ouch! But you know it's true. You've probably been taught to say thank you whenever you receive a gift. Well, everything we have, even our food, is a gift from God. Therefore, it's only right to thank God before we share a meal. We do just that in the part of the Mass that follows the Liturgy of the Word. It is the **Liturgy of the Eucharist.** Let's take a closer look at each part of the Liturgy of the Eucharist.

Have you ever been asked to bring up the gifts at Mass? It is an honor to represent the faith community in this way.

Bill Wittman

Giving Back to God What God Has Given Us

The Liturgy of the Eucharist begins with the Preparation of the Gifts. Here, representatives from the assembly bring bread and wine to the altar, and money is collected from the people. This money will go toward helping people who are poor and toward supporting the work of the Church.

When we bring bread and wine to the altar and collect money, we show that it is God who has given us these gifts. It is God who cares for our every need.

What shall I bring to the Lord, the God of heaven, when I come to worship him? . . . What he requires of us is this: to do what is just, to show constant love, and to live in humble fellowship with our God. (Micah 6:6,8)

Did You Know?

The Dinner Table and the Altar Table

The basic parts of the Liturgy of the Eucharist might look a lot like a special meal at your home. First, you need to set the table. At Mass, we place bread and wine on the altar. At home, you say grace before eating. At Mass, we pray a long prayer of thanksgiving to the Father for all his blessings. In this special prayer, we ask the Father to send the Holy Spirit to change the bread and wine into the Body and Blood of his Son. At home, you might end your prayer with the Lord's Prayer. At Mass, we also pray this prayer that Jesus taught his disciples. Then comes the best part—the meal. At Mass, we eat and drink the consecrated bread and wine. Finally, after this meal, we end with a short prayer of thanksgiving to God. At home, you might say thank you again to the person who provided the meal.

Looking Back

The Work of Human Hands

In the early Church, instead of money, people brought the actual fruit of their labor—livestock, produce, handicrafts, whatever they had. Special ministers called deacons collected these offerings. They set aside for Mass some of the bread and wine the people offered. Also set aside were some of the gifts the Church could use throughout the week. Then the deacons gave the rest of the people's gifts to the poor of the town.

Today, instead of bringing things like sheep, chickens, tomatoes, or clothing, we bring money to represent our concern for the poor and to advance the work of the Church.

The Eucharistic Prayer

The next part of the Liturgy of the Eucharist is the core of the Mass. Here, the priest leads the assembly in the **Eucharistic Prayer,** which is the Church's great prayer of thanksgiving to the Father. Since the Eucharistic Prayer is so important, let's look more closely at its main parts.

Giving to people in need goes beyond the collection during Mass. Anytime we give to those in need, we are being Gospel people, loving one another as Christ has loved us.

Preface and Holy, Holy, Holy

"On your mark! Get set! Go!" When you hear these words at the start of a race, your ears perk up. Your eyes focus, and your entire body is alert. Something big is about to happen.

At the beginning of the Eucharistic Prayer is a special dialogue between the priest and the people, as follows.

> **Priest:** The Lord be with you.
> **People:** And also with you.
> **Priest:** Lift up your hearts.
> **People:** We lift them up to the Lord.
> **Priest:** Let us give thanks to the Lord, our God.
> **People:** It is right to give him thanks and praise.

This dialogue is a little like a signal to us that something important is about to happen. So listen up. With these words, the priest invites us to pray with him.

KEY WORDS

Liturgy of the Eucharist

Eucharistic Prayer

epiclesis

transubstantiation

293

The artist illustrates the connection between the community gathered for the Eucharist on earth and those in purgatory and in Heaven. Can you see the image of the Trinity? Mary and the saints? the souls in Purgatory?

Illustration by Elizabeth Wang, 'the one Sacrifice of Christ, represented at every Mass, we are united with the Heavenly Court and the souls of Purgatory', copyright © Radiant Light 2008, www.radiantlight.org.uk

Holy, holy, holy! The Lord Almighty is holy! His glory fills the world. (Isaiah 6:3)

Even though he will do most of the speaking, the Eucharistic Prayer is the prayer of everyone gathered. He speaks on behalf of the comunity, and we pray with him. All of us, together with the priest, focus on God and join our prayers with those of the angels and saints in heaven.

The next part of the Eucharistic Prayer is called the Preface. This is a summary of the good things the Father has done for us throughout history. It is called the Preface because it will lead us to the main reason we are so thankful—the gift of God's Son, Jesus.

FUN FACT

"The Lord be with you." "And also with you." This dialogue happens four times in the Eucharist: at the start of Mass, before the Gospel reading, at the Preface, and before the end of Mass. This dialogue reminds the priest and the people that the Holy Spirit is present in our midst as we celebrate the Eucharist.

You'll hear many different prefaces throughout the year, but you'll always know it's the Preface because it begins right after the dialogue above. Every Preface says why we are grateful to God. Listen to the Preface of the Eucharistic Prayer for Masses with Children (I), as follows. What are we thanking God for here?

> We thank you for all that is beautiful in the world and for the happiness you have given us. We praise you for daylight and for your word which lights up our minds. We praise you for the earth, and all the people who live on it, and for our life which comes from you.

At the end of the Preface, we are so thankful that we can't help but burst into the song of the angels, "Holy, holy, holy Lord . . ." This acclamation is sometimes called the Sanctus and may be spoken if no one is available to lead the singing.

Send Down the Spirit

The next section of the Eucharistic Prayer is often brief, and if you tune out, you might miss it. It's

PRAY IT!
Liturgy Connection

Some see the collection as a payment to their parish for the things they get from the parish, like Mass, the sacraments, and religious formation. But giving money at Mass is different from buying stuff at the mall. That's because giving money at Mass is not about getting stuff. It's about giving thanks to God for everything he has given us. All we have comes from God. God gives all our gifts to bless us and those in need. When we give money at Mass, we show we want to participate in God's care for those in need.

You don't need to give much. Just give something. If you receive an allowance, give a percentage of it each week. When you are planning the activities of your week, include your parish. Give your talents and time.

called the **epiclesis**, a Greek word meaning "calling upon" or "invocation." Watch and listen to the priest here. He asks the Father to send down the Holy Spirit over the gifts of bread and wine. As he does this, he places his hands over the gifts, with his palms facing down.

The priest is asking the Father to send the Holy Spirit to change the bread and wine into the Body and Blood of Christ. Later in the prayer, there will be another epiclesis. At that time, the prayer will be for the Father to send his Spirit upon us. You see, in the Eucharistic Prayer, we get changed too. The Holy Spirit changes us from individual people into one body. The Holy Spirit changes those who eat the consecrated bread and wine into the Body of Christ.

Did You Know?

Using Our Gifts

If Jesus had taken up a collection at the Last Supper, what do you think he would have asked for? It probably wouldn't have been money. Instead, he gives us a clue about what he wants from his disciples when he says, "Do this in memory of me." That is, if we want to remember Jesus, we do what he did on the night before he died. He took bread and wine, blessed them, broke the bread and poured the wine, and then shared them in a new way, calling them his Body and Blood.

He also wanted us to remember him by doing what he did throughout his life. He cared for the poor, took care of the sick, and shared his life with strangers and friends. In other words, he used his gifts to help those in need. So we do the same. We take the gifts God has given us—the ability to work and the talents we have—and give them back to God to help those in need.

Bill Wittman

The priest is at a moment of *epiclesis* during Mass. Find this key word and read why *epiclesis* is so important.

"On the Night Before He Died . . . "

The institution narrative is probably the most familiar part of the Eucharistic Prayer. It recalls Jesus' words at the Last Supper on the night before he died. Through the power of the Holy Spirit the bread and wine are changed into the Body and Blood of Christ in the institution narrative.

This change in the bread and wine is called **transubstantiation.** This means that the essence or substance of the bread and wine changes into the Body and Blood of Christ. However, the appearance, smell, and taste of the elements do not change.

When the words of Jesus are spoken over the bread and wine by a validly ordained priest, they become Christ himself. He becomes present in a true, real, and

THiNK ABouT IT!

In an old Mass book from the ninth century, called the *Stowe Missal*, part of the Eucharistic Prayer is titled "The Most Dangerous Prayer." Why do you think the Mass, and in particular, the Eucharistic Prayer, would be dangerous? Who or what would be threatened today by the prayer we make?

Although there were no photographers at the Last Supper, many artists have depicted the occasion when Jesus instituted the Eucharist. What do you think it would have been like to be at the table with Jesus at the Last Supper?

© Historical Picture Archive/CORBIS

Live It!

If we mean what we say, then the Eucharistic Prayer and our Amen will require us to sacrifice like Jesus. We will need to sacrifice our selfishness, give up our comforts and prejudices, and take up Christ's cross. This prayer can really change the world, because God changes us too.

The best way to live this prayer is by giving our fullest attention to it during Mass. This is hard to do for such a long prayer, so at first try focusing as best you can at the beginning and end of the prayer. When the priest begins the Preface dialogue with "The Lord be with you," that's your signal to listen up. When you begin this dialogue, stand tall with your head held high. Then at the end of the prayer, sing your Great Amen as though you mean it.

concrete way. He is fully present in Body, Blood, soul, and divinity.

Here we don't pretend to be at the Last Supper. We remember Jesus' words because he is the Father's best gift to us. We remember so Christ will be present again today and his Spirit can continue to bless the world.

The Eucharistic Prayer isn't over yet. We still need to be as attentive to the entire prayer as we are during the institution narrative. The institution narrative is followed by the proclamation of the mystery of faith. This is called the Memorial Acclamation. Here, in song or spoken word, we remember Christ's love for us on the cross. We remember that the Father raised him from the dead. We remember that Christ will come again to unite us all forever.

Giving, Receiving, and Interceding

We're not done yet. We remembered Christ's sacrifice on the cross so we might live. In this next part, called the offering, we ask God to receive our own sacrifice.

The sacrifice we offer to the Father in the Eucharist is the sacrifice of our praise. This sacrifice is represented by our thanksgiving to the Father, our remembrance of his Son, and the gifts we have placed on the altar, which the Holy Spirit changes. What we actually offer to God is our lives lived as his children.

Next we ask the Father to remember his Church. We pray that the Church on earth will be united with Mary and Joseph and all the Apostles and saints. We ask God to bless our Church's leaders.

PRAY IT!

Blessed are you,
God of everything.
You gave me all I have,
even my life.
I want to say thank you
by offering you my life
lived well.
Use me and my talents
and give me only
what I need,
so I can always be grateful
to you
and attentive to those
who have so little.
Amen

We also pray that God remember us. Finally, we pray for all the dead and ask God to unite us again in his Kingdom.

Tapestry of "The Communion of Saints" by painter: John Nava. From the Los Angeles Cathedral.

The tapestry called "The Communion of Saints" hangs in the Cathedral of Our Lady of the Angels, in Los Angeles. Notice the ordinary-looking people walking beside canonized saints. What do you think the artist is saying?

Saying Yes

When we come to the end of the Eucharistic Prayer we can't lose focus, because it's perhaps the most critical part of the prayer. Here we summarize our thanksgiving into a doxology. A doxology is a statement of praise to the Trinity. We gather all we have said, sung, and hoped for in the Eucharistic Prayer and give all glory and honor to the Father. We do this through Christ, with Christ, and in Christ. And we do this all in the unity of the Holy Spirit.

The last part of the doxology is the Great Amen. Here we sing or say "Amen." This Great Amen is like our stamp of approval on the prayer. When we say "Amen," we mean, "Yes, make it happen." We really want what we have prayed for—to be one with Christ and each other. Imagine that. When we are completely united with Christ and each other, we would love everyone as Christ loves us. The world would look like God's Kingdom on earth.

Think about that for a moment. When Jesus talked about the Kingdom, some people weren't happy about it. That's because the Kingdom favors people who are poor and weak. It demands that people with power sacrifice their lives for others who are poor. The Kingdom turns the world upside down for both the poor and the powerful.

© Brooklyn Museum/Corbis

Jesus offered his love and healing to those who were poor and the sick, caring for them and healing them. He asks us to do the same.

THE EUCHARIST: COMMUNION AND SENDING FORTH

If you were hosting Thanksgiving dinner, what would you need? Food, of course. Special, fancy food, probably, and dessert. What else? A dinner table with nice plates, utensils, and glasses. Anything else? Oh yes, people to eat the food. So now you have a complete Thanksgiving dinner, right? Hmm. Something seems to be missing. What could it be? What would the people do? Just eat? Of course not. They would laugh, tell stories, give thanks, and have a good time with one another. After dinner, they would probably hang around and talk even more with one another or watch a movie together or a football game on TV.

The word *Eucharist* means "giving thanks to God." When we celebrate Mass, it is something like sharing a great Thanksgiving feast.

© Larry Williams/CORBIS

There might even be times when an old grudge or hurt gets forgiven or new friendships are made. Whatever the people do, it's safe to say that to have a Thanksgiving dinner, you need more than just food.

It's a little bit the same when we talk about the Eucharist and Communion. Both words mean more than the Body and Blood of Christ we eat and drink in the sacrament. Thanksgiving is more than the meal. It's the same with the Eucharist and Communion.

Eucharist also means "giving thanks to God." The Eucharist is not only the consecrated bread and wine—the Body and Blood of Christ—we eat and drink. It's the whole event. It's gathering and greeting each other at the doors of the church. It's hearing our Church family's stories and all the good things God has done for us throughout history. It's blessing God and all the gifts God has given us, especially the bread and wine that become the Body and Blood of Christ. It's sharing our life together the way a family shares its life—by eating together.

In a similar way, *Communion* means more than the sacrament we receive. It also means our union with Christ and each other, especially when we eat and drink his Body and Blood. Like Thanksgiving dinner, Communion is more than the meal.

PRAY IT!

Jesus, Son of God,
  Teach me to pray with
    open hands and an
  open heart.
Jesus, Lamb of God,
    Nourish my body
    that I may do
    your will.
Jesus, Love of God,
    Send me where you
    need me to go
    and help me give others
    the love and joy you
    give me.
This I pray in your
    holy name. Amen.

In this chapter, we'll look at the high point of the Sacrament of the Eucharist—the Communion Rite.

FUN FACT

What do children do when they want to be picked up? They reach their arms up above their heads and open their hands. We do something similar, called the **orans** posture, when we pray to our Father during the Lord's Prayer. Early Christians used this posture too. We raise our eyes and hands, imitating the image of Christ on the cross. The posture also looks like a cry to our Father to hold us.

Our Family Prayer

The Eucharistic Prayer asks God to change not only the bread and wine (see chapter 26). It also asks God to change us so we might become one body in Christ. This is like becoming one family.

After the Eucharistic Prayer is finished, our next action is to pray out loud as one family to our one God, our Father. We use the words Jesus taught his own disciples—the **Lord's Prayer.**

Our Father in heaven: May your holy name be honored; may your Kingdom come; may your will be done on earth as it is in heaven. (Matthew 6:9–10)

A woman prays the Lord's Prayer in the orans position. Read the "Fun Fact" article on this page to find out more about this gesture.

Bill Wittman

One of the lines we pray is, "Forgive us our trespasses as we forgive those who trespass against us." Have you tried sharing a meal with someone who hurt you or someone you hurt? It's not easy, is it? But once we forgive the other person or receive forgiveness, eating together is much easier. Therefore, we ask the Father to forgive any wrongs we have committed. At the same time, we promise to forgive others.

A Sign of Peace

We put our promise into action with a sign of peace. In the **Rite of Peace,** the deacon or priest invites us to share a sign of Christ's peace with one another. This can be a handshake, kiss, hug, or some other gesture. Usually, we say "peace be with you" as we share the sign.

Bill Wittman

The Rite of Peace reminds us that the Eucharist is not just about God and me. Loving our neighbor is essential to loving God.

Jesus, the Paschal Lamb

Next is the Fraction Rite, when the priest, with the help of a deacon or other priests, breaks the consecrated bread into smaller pieces so it can be shared with everyone. A fraction is a portion of a whole, a term that is also used in Math.

During the Fraction Rite, we sing a litany to Jesus, the Lamb of God. A **litany** is a form of prayer,

Did you know that when the priest breaks the consecrated bread into smaller pieces, it is called the Fraction Rite?

© Pascal Deloche/Godong/Corbis

spoken or sung, in which a leader begins a dialogue, often using different phrases, such as various names for Christ. The people respond to each phrase by repeating the same words. In the Lamb of God, we recall how Jesus is our Paschal Lamb, whose blood frees us from the slavery of sin. (*Paschal* comes from a Greek term that means "Passover.") The cantor or choir

LiVE It!

It's fun to greet friends during the sign of peace. But this ritual isn't about catching up. It's actually a serious gesture.

Remember that in the liturgy, Christ is acting and speaking. When we say "Peace be with you" and shake a person's hand or hug the person, it is really Christ's peace we are sharing. That's a powerful thing, because Christ's peace changes the world! It turns enemies into friends. It heals wounds and hurts. It ends war and injustice. Sharing Christ's peace is serious business.

It may be more important to share a sign of peace with people you aren't friends with or people with whom you need to reconcile. But this isn't always possible. Next time you share the sign of peace, also think about the person you need to reconcile with, and pray for him or her. Do something during the week to move closer toward reconciliation with the person.

addresses Jesus, the Lamb of God, who takes away our sins. Sometimes the cantor includes other names for Jesus, like Bread of Life or Saving Cup. Each time, we respond "Have mercy on us." As the priest finishes breaking the consecrated bread, the Body of Christ, our response changes to "Grant us peace." This reminds us of our hope for unity and peace with each other.

Communion: Becoming One Body

Now we come to Communion, the high point of our entire Eucharist. It's the main reason we come to Mass and the thing that gives us strength throughout the week. This is when we become what we have been praying for by the power of the Holy Spirit. It is when we become one with Christ.

Becoming one with a person means knowing that person will never leave you. The person will never reject you or make fun of you. The person will

Did You Know?

Sealed with a Kiss

The sign of peace was originally called the kiss of peace. The priest kissed the altar and then passed that kiss to the ministers around him. They in turn passed the kiss of peace to the assembly. Doing the sign of peace this way signified the sealing of Christ's promise to unify all God's people with his peace. It's like sealing an envelope with a letter inside—we're sure Christ's peace is here with us and never leaving us. Or its like a seal on a certificate. It's a stamp of approval proving that indeed Christ's peace is here. In a way, we seal with a kiss our commitment to strive for close relationships with Christ and one another.

When we say "Amen" at Communion, we are saying "Yes, this is the Body of Christ" and "Yes, we promise to be the Body of Christ."

© P Deliss/Godong/Corbis

love you no matter what. In Communion, we become one with Christ, who will do all this and more for us. Communion is eating and drinking with the one who knows everything about us and loves us no matter what. When we receive the Body and Blood of Christ, we receive Christ, real and present, and he will never leave us. When we receive Christ, our connection with the Church also grows stronger. This is why Saint Augustine called the Eucharist the "mystery of unity" (Sermon 272).

> Because there is the one loaf of bread,
> all of us, though many, are one body,
> for we all share the same loaf.
> (1 Corinthians 10:17)

This is also why we sing as we share Communion. When we sing together, our individual voices become one voice. Singing together shows our union with one another through the Holy Spirit. Singing also expresses joy in a fuller way than speaking does.

The *Body of Christ* refers to both the consecrated bread and wine and to all the people who are part of the Church—the Body of Christ. In Com-

KEY WORDS

orans
Lord's Prayer
Rite of Peace
litany

munion when we come forward and look into the eyes of the ministers, who say, "Body of Christ," "Blood of Christ," the ministers are talking about the Eucharistic elements and us. We respond "Amen." That is, "Yes, let it be so." In our response, we promise to be the Body of Christ in the world.

In the gifts of his Body and Blood, we see clearly Christ's love for us. When we say "Amen" and eat his Body and drink his Blood, we become united completely with Christ and his mission. His mission is to show everyone the immense love of his Father. He did that by loving others, even if it meant suffering and dying for them. Jesus himself had a cup to drink, which is a way of saying he had a sacrifice to make. He knew much would be required from him (see Matthew 26:39). Yet he drank from that cup. He accepted the mission his Father gave him. Jesus showed the world the Father's love, which is stronger than death.

Once everyone has shared in Communion, we pray together in silence or sing together a song of praise. In the silent prayer or song, we give thanks to God for giving us the gift of the Eucharist. Finally, we end the Communion Rite with a prayer asking that the Communion we have shared will indeed change our lives.

PRAY IT!

Liturgy Connection

After the Fraction Rite, the priest says, "This is the Lamb of God who takes away the sins of the world. Happy are those who are called to his supper."

Who are "those"? Of course, he means us and everyone else gathered for Mass. The priest is inviting all who are present who are Catholic to participate in Communion.

He also means those all over the world gathered for Mass. He also means those who are in Heaven. These words remind us that the Church is bigger than just our own parishes. The Church is worldwide and heavenwide. The Church is all who respond to Christ's invitation to the banquet.

Sent to Love and Serve

"As the Father sent me, so I send you." (John 20:21)

How does the Eucharist change our lives? The Eucharist unites us with Christ and nourishes our souls. But will people recognize that we are members of the Body of Christ? Will we be different after we share in all these graces of the Eucharist?

In one of his writings on the Eucharist, Pope John Paul II described the Eucharist in many ways. He said it was a call for Catholics to tell others about Jesus. He said it was the way all people will begin to care for one another. He said it was the way Christians promise to make the world a better place. But all these things are actions we do outside the Eucharist. In a way, the Eucharist never ends. It continues even after Mass.

Pope John Paul II also said that the Eucharist doesn't isolate Catholics from the world. It doesn't turn them into a clique, separate from everyone else. Instead, the Communion we share and the unity we encounter with Christ and one another help us bring people together. The loving unity we share is like a magnet that draws others into the same loving relationship we have with Christ. That's why almost immediately after we share in Communion, the final part of the Eucharist sends us out "to love and serve the Lord." This reminds us to love and serve God not only at Church but also in the world. We will find God in the world most clearly in people who are poor.

In fact, the "Eucharist commits us to the poor" (CCC, number 1397). This means that when we say yes to Christ in the Eucharist, we say yes to people who are poor. We promise to think about others who are in need and to do what we can to help them. That's why we leave Mass to share with others the gifts we have received there.

The Mass sends us out to give the gifts of the Eucharist to others. These are love and friendship, attention and care for

Did You Know?

A People on the Go

Have you ever noticed that the Church walks a lot when it prays? At Mass, there are five processions—at the gathering, before the Gospel, when the gifts are brought to the altar, at Communion, and at the dismissal. Whew! That's a workout.

Sometimes the Church is called the Pilgrim People of God. You may have an image in your mind of the Pilgrims who settled part of the English colonies in North America hundreds of years ago. The key is to realize we call them Pilgrims because they were travelers rather than because they were settlers. We are pilgrims because we are on a journey, not because we've arrived. Does that mean we're always going on a trip? Not really. It means that while we live on earth, we are making our way to Heaven.

The pilgrim image also refers to the Israelites wandering in the desert for forty years as they journeyed to the Promised Land (see Deuteronomy 2:7). It refers too to the disciples on the road to Emmaus. On the way, they met a stranger who turned out to be the risen Christ (see Luke 24:13–35). All of us are disciples on the way to Heaven. Along the way, we meet Christ.

others, forgiveness, hope, and joy. When you see a person who is lonely, you can give him or her the gifts of love and friendship you received in the Eucharist. You can treat the person as part of your family, because you are part of God's family. You can be kind to her or him, even if the person is mean or cold to you, because you have received forgiveness yourself in the Eucharist. You can do something to help that

People of Faith

Saint Augustine

"Be what you see, and receive what you are."

CITY OF GOD
The Confessions
The Blessed Trinity

© 2009 Saint Mary's Press/Illustration by Vicki Shuck

Saint Augustine might be the world's most reluctant saint. From the age of seventeen, Augustine lived a wild life. He also searched for the truth and meaning of life. His mother, Saint Monica, was a devout Christian who prayed each day for her son's conversion to Christianity.

After studying the writings of Saint Paul and Saint Ambrose, Augustine realized that Christianity was the answer. He was still reluctant to be baptized, because then he would have to give up his

person feel happy, because you have received so much joy from Christ. This is how the world will be changed. It will change because of God's love we encounter in the Eucharist.

"Whenever you did this for one of the least important of these brothers of mine, you did it for me!" (Matthew 25:40)

undisciplined lifestyle. Eventually, he was baptized at the age of thirty-four by Saint Ambrose himself. At thirty-eight, Augustine became a priest, and by forty-three, he was the Bishop of Hippo in North Africa.

Saint Augustine is known for his sermons to those preparing for Baptism (the catechumens) and those recently baptized (the neophytes). He gave one of his most famous instructions to the neophytes as they were standing near the altar to receive Communion for the first time. He pointed to the consecrated bread and wine on the altar and said, "Be what you see, and receive what you are" (Sermon 272). From this phrase of Saint Augustine, we get the saying, "You are what you eat." Saint Augustine's point is that we receive the Body of Christ, and we become the Body of Christ.

Saint Augustine is venerated as a Doctor of the Church and as one of the great Fathers of the Western Church. His feast day is August 28.

28 The Sacrament of Baptism

It can be as light as air, yet as hard as rock. Two-thirds of your entire body and three-fourths of your brain are made up of it. A trillion tons of it disappear into the air each day. Yet 75 percent of the earth is covered by it. You can't go a week without it. But too much of it can kill you.

What is it? It's water. Water makes life possible. When scientists search for life on other planets, they look for signs of water. Water makes all things grow. We live and breathe in water before we're born. After that we enjoy it when we swim, surf, soak, or sail.

Water also kills. Hurricanes and floods have destroyed entire cities. Overwatering kills plants. Drinking too much water can be fatal. People die each day from drowning. Water gives life. It also destroys life.

The waters in the Sacrament of Baptism are like that. They give us new lives. And they end our old ones. Let's look at how Baptism does this.

Key Words

Original Sin
Baptism
catechumenate

The Birth of a Catholic

In the Sacrament of Baptism, new Christians are born. In Baptism, we leave our old lives behind in those waters. We are born into new lives in Christ. We become like Christ, who died on the cross. Like Christ, we are resurrected to a completely new and eternal life.

Bill Wittman

What do these symbols say about what it means to be Christian?

By our baptism, then, we were buried with him and shared his death, in order that, just as Christ was raised from death by the glorious power of the Father, so also we might live a new life. (Romans 6:4)

People don't literally die when they are baptized. So what does it mean to die and rise again in Baptism? Think about it as follows.

Have you ever thought you were really going to die? Maybe you had an awful plane ride that left you wondering if you would land safely. Many people who have near-death experiences come away from them wanting to live their lives differently. They feel as though they get a second chance at life, and they don't want to miss a second of it.

Life without Baptism may be thought of as a life lived sort of half awake. We're

PRAY IT!

God of Heaven and earth,
You made the waters
and filled the seas
with life.
Shower your mercy
upon me
and wash me clean
of my faults.
Refresh my spirit and
fill my thirst
that I might live each day as
your child, dead to sin
and alive for you alone.
Amen

not equipped to see all the ways God is present in our lives. But in Baptism, we are awakened. We start new lives, and we clothe ourselves with Christ. We see the world the way Christ saw it, as filled with the Father's goodness. We are able to live as Christ did by loving others. In Baptism we become sons and daughters of the Father and brothers and sisters of Christ. Like Christ, we begin to see ourselves as filled with the Holy Spirit. Through Baptism, we become part of the Body of Christ, the Church, and we share in Christ's priesthood. That means we are people who, through Christ, know the Father and help others know him too.

Baptism enables us fully to become the people God created us to be. It frees us from sin and makes union with God, or salvation, possible for us. We need the Church for salvation, because it is the Church, through Christ, that baptizes.

Did You Know?

Emergency Baptism

The Church can baptize someone immediately if the person is in danger of death. Any person can baptize someone in danger of dying if no priest or deacon is available as long as that person has the intention of doing so and pours water on the person's head, while saying "I baptize you in the name of the Father, and of the Son, and of the Holy Spirit."

Watermark

Water also cleans. We bathe and shower in it. We wash dishes with it. Rain cleans the air and makes everything fresh.

Baptism also washes us clean. The waters of Baptism wash away sin. It is the first sacrament we receive and the first way our sins are forgiven. Most important, it washes away **Original Sin,** the sin every human being inherits from Adam and Eve. Humans are imperfect, because to be human is to not be God. Our first parents, Adam and Eve, proved that, even when everything else is perfect, we can still make mistakes and bad choices. But Baptism removes the stain of Adam and Eve's sin from our human natures and gives us a second chance. The waters of Baptism change our natures so completely that it leaves a new kind of mark on our souls. It leaves a permanent spiritual sign on our human natures. This sign consecrates us. That means it makes us holy. It changes us forever into adopted children of God. It sets us apart to worship him. The mark that Baptism makes on us is permanent and can never be removed. This is why Baptism cannot be repeated.

"No one can enter the Kingdom of God without being born of water and the Spirit." (John 3:5)

Did You Know?
Infants and Baptism

From the earliest times, the Church has baptized infants in the faith of the Church with the hope that one day they will make the faith of the Church their own. God's love is a pure gift to us, which means we don't need to do anything to earn it. This is why we don't wait to baptize until people are older. Nothing we could do at any age makes us any more deserving of God's love than we already are at birth. By baptizing babies we show our trust in God's goodness even when we don't deserve it or ask for it. As members of God's family, they will learn to love and respond to God. God will love them as his own forever.

Styles of baptismal fonts vary. What type do you have at your parish?

Bill Wittman

PRAY IT!
Liturgy Connection

Jesus was baptized in a river. Today, we use baptismal fonts. Some of the early fonts were round to imitate the shape of a womb. This showed that Baptism is like rebirth. Others were rectangular like a tomb or shaped as a cross to show our death to sin. Still others were octagonal. The number 8 has important symbolic meaning for Christians. Our seven-day week reflects the Bible's account of seven days of Creation. Referring to an eighth day is a way of saying something is really new in creation. That new, wonderful thing is Christ's Resurrection. Fonts with eight sides symbolize this. How does your parish font look?

Rite of Baptism

Ever since her beginning, the Church has been celebrating Baptism. The way the sacrament has been celebrated has changed throughout the centuries. But the primary action in the rite of Baptism has stayed the same. We immerse a person in water or pour water over his or her head, while we call upon the name of the Trinity: the Father, the Son, and the Holy Spirit.

The process for initiating a person in the Catholic Church varies according to age. Infants and young children celebrate the Rite of Baptism for Children. They are baptized and anointed with Chrism. When they get older, they will celebrate the Sacraments of Eucharist and Confirmation, typically in that order. Adults and older children go through a similar process, but the rite that is followed is called the Rite of Christian Initiation of Adults (RCIA). The candidates are baptized, confirmed, and given the Eucharist all at the same liturgy.

In both ways of initiation, **Baptism** is the first step to becoming united with Christ through the Church. It is the beginning of a Christian's life. Confirmation strengthens people for their new lives. The Eucharist unites them in Christ and nourishes them for their new lives in him with his Body and Blood. Christian initiation is accomplished through these three sacraments, whether celebrated in one liturgy or several liturgies spread out over many years.

For adults, many rituals are celebrated over a long period of time leading up to their Baptisms. Their preparation is called the **catechumenate.** It is how an adult learns the Christian way of life.

Did You Know?
Baptism Without Water

Although water and the Trinitarian formula ("I baptize you in the name of the Father, and of the Son, and of the Holy Spirit") are essential for Baptism, God doesn't need them. If you lived an extraordinary life of faith but didn't get to be baptized, God's love could still save you. This is because the way you lived proved that God was already a huge part of your life. It showed that God had anointed you in a special way. Unbaptized people who die for the faith, adults who have begun the process for becoming baptized, and those who seek God and strive to live out values consistent with the principles that Jesus taught can be saved if they sincerely desire to know God in their lives and try to live as God would have them live.

God wants all to be saved. His love can find a way to save us even without Baptism. Therefore, when a baby dies before being baptized, or an older person dies without knowing Christ or the Gospel, we pray for their salvation and trust in God's mercy. We also trust that God's plan of salvation includes people from other religions.

THiNK ABOUT IT!

How many different ways can you name to show how water gives life? How do you think these life-giving uses for water are related to the Church's understanding of Baptism? Are there any ways that water kills or destroys? How do you think these deadly images for water are also related to Baptism?

After Baptism, a baby learns how to be a Christian from his or her parents, godparents, and other Christians. Infants don't go through a catechumenate like adults. But their parents and godparents do spend time preparing themselves so they can be good teachers for their children as they grow.

You were probably baptized as a baby. So let's look at some of the symbols from the Rite of Baptism for Children.

Meeting at the Threshold

Stand in a doorway. It's a bit uncomfortable because it's an in-between space. You're in neither one room nor the other. The time of your life that you're in right now might feel a little like a doorway. You're not really a child. You're not an adult either. Sometimes it might be hard to know where you fit in. Doorways are also powerful places, because they are how you move to a new space. They let you out when you feel confined. They bring you in when you feel left out.

An unbaptized person is spiritually outside the Church. But Jesus called himself the Door. Through him, we enter his family and find where we belong (see John 10:7–9). This is why the Baptism ritual begins with the celebrant going to where the parents, godparents, and child are and greeting them. This may be at the Church entrance or in specially designated seats.

Bill Wittman

The priest or deacon comes to greet a family seeking Baptism for their child. Baptism is like a door that opens to all other sacraments of the Church.

Giving Your Name

It is no longer I who live,
but it is Christ who lives in me. (Galatians 2:20)

After being welcomed by the celebrant, the baby's parents announce to the assembly their baby's name. They also ask the Church to baptize their baby. The priest or deacon asks the parents whether they understand the responsibility that comes with their request. Baptizing their baby means they promise to bring up their baby to love Christ. They will need to teach their child what it means to follow Christ.

The parents aren't the only ones with a big responsibility. All those gathered for the Baptism are asked whether they will help the parents bring up the child in the Christian faith. If you're at a Baptism, you also share in this responsibility.

Marked with the Cross

When we enter the Church, we make the Sign of the Cross on ourselves. We do the same for those

Many people do not realize that each time they make the Sign of the Cross, the action expresses their Christian identity.

Bill Wittman

who are about to be baptized. The priest or deacon and the baby's parents and godparents make the Sign of the Cross on the baby's forehead. This shows that the baby now belongs to Christ.

FUN FACT

When people rejected Satan in the early Church, they meant it. Before Baptism, they faced the west, where the sun sets. When asked if they rejected Satan, they spat in that direction, as if they were spitting into the devil's face! Then they turned toward the east, where the sun rises, and professed their faith in God.

Rejecting Satan and Accepting Christ

Part of belonging to Christ means rejecting anything that isn't Christ. Just before the baby is baptized, he or she has to publicly reject Satan and accept Christ.

"Now wait a minute," you're thinking. "Babies can't talk." That's why the priest or deacon asks the parents and godparents to renew their own baptismal promises or vows, when they first rejected Satan and accepted Christ. These are the promises they will teach their child. He asks them: "Do you reject Satan, all his works, and all his empty promises?" Then he asks: "Do you believe in God the Father? in Jesus Christ? in the Holy Spirit and the holy catholic Church?"

Baptized in the Name of the Trinity

The baby is baptized in the baptismal font. The infant may be immersed in the baptismal water three times, or the minister may pour water over the baby's head three times. As he does this, he says, "I baptize you in the name of the Father, and of the Son, and of the Holy Spirit." The words of this Trinitarian formula cannot be changed.

Live It!

Easter is so special that we even have to wait for the heavens to be just right. It happens once a year on the first Sunday after the first full moon after the first day of spring. The Easter Vigil is a special Mass that is the start of Easter. It begins after sunset when it's dark on the night before Easter Sunday. This is the night when the Church baptizes adults.

This is one liturgy you don't want to miss. Find the date for the next Easter Vigil and plan now to participate.

Anointed with Chrism

The title *Christ* means "anointed." Therefore, in the next part of the rite, the baby's head is anointed with Chrism (See chapter 29 for more about Chrism.) This anointing shows that the baby is now part of Christ and has a new name, "Christian."

Shutterstock

You were baptized into union with Christ, and now you are clothed . . . with the life of Christ himself. (Galatians 3:27)

If you were baptized when you were too young to remember, ask your family to share their memories of the celebration with you.

323

Clothed in Christ

With all this water, the baby can get pretty wet. The baby, therefore, is given a white garment to wear. The practical act of changing the baby's clothes also takes on special meaning. This garment's color—white—symbolizes the purity of a new Christian life. Even when a baby is not baptized by immersion and doesn't get wet enough for a change of clothes, the baby is clothed in white to symbolize new life in Christ.

PEOPLE OF FAITH

Saint Elizabeth

© 2009 Saint Mary's Press/Illustration by Vicki Shuck

Most everything we know about Saint Elizabeth comes from the beginning of Luke's Gospel. In it, Elizabeth is married to Zechariah, a priest of the Temple in Jerusalem. She is also the cousin of Mary, the Mother of Jesus.

One day as Zechariah is in the Temple, the angel Gabriel appears to him and says Elizabeth will have a son. Their child will grow up to become John the Baptist.

Christ, Our Light

The newly baptized baby is now a child of the light. He or she receives a candle lit from the Paschal candle. The baby can't hold the candle, of course. Instead, the candle is given to the baby's parents or godparents. The priest or deacon asks them to keep the flame of faith alive for the baby until the baby meets Christ in Heaven.

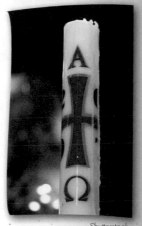

Flame from the Paschal candle is passed to the families of the newly baptized along with a challenge: keep the flame of faith alive.

Shutterstock

Elizabeth is old, so Zechariah doesn't believe Gabriel. As punishment, Gabriel takes away his voice. Sure enough, Elizabeth becomes pregnant, and poor Zechariah is mute the whole time. After John's birth, Zechariah gets his voice back.

Elizabeth is best known for being the first to recognize Jesus as the Messiah even before his birth. While they were both pregnant, Mary visited Elizabeth, and John leapt in Elizabeth's womb when Mary arrived. Elizabeth announced that Mary and her unborn child were blessed. She also called Mary blessed for having believed God's promise. Elizabeth's proclamation has become part of the Hail Mary.

Elizabeth's name means "God is faithful." Her feast day is November 5.

29 The Sacrament of Confirmation

Pray It!

Spirit of God,
You anoint me
with your gifts
and empower me
to use them.
Set your seal
upon me
and bless my words
and deeds
that all may know
I am your child
and your witness
to the world.

Amen

You might not realize it, but you use oil almost every day. How many ways can you think of? Many foods you eat are probably cooked with it. If you love French fries, they are likely cooked in oil. Soap has oil for cleaning. Oil in your conditioner keeps your hair soft. Lip balms heal your lips. Cars break down without oil. Bike chains need oil to keep moving. Did you ever put ointment on a cut? That's made with oil. Have you used perfume or cologne? That has oil too.

Oil is everywhere. We wouldn't live well without oil. It's essential for life. It's essential for the Church too.

Water and Oil

Do you ever use lotion or moisturizer after a shower? You know how it keeps your skin from becoming dry and stiff. Lotion seals in the moisture from the water. In a way, the Sacrament of Confirmation does the same thing. In this sacrament, a baptized person is anointed with a consecrated oil called Chrism and strengthened with the Holy Spirit.

iStockphoto

Did you know that you must be baptized before you are confirmed? The water of Baptism is the gateway to Confirmation and all other sacraments.

Confirmation is so closely tied to Baptism that it is almost impossible to speak about it without also talking about Baptism. This is because Confirmation adds to the gift of new life we received in Baptism. When we were baptized, we received the Holy Spirit. Confirmation is like getting an extra gift. It deepens and seals in the Gift of the Holy Spirit that we receive in Baptism. The oil used in Confirmation symbolizes the power of the Holy Spirit. The Spirit keeps us close to the Father and his Son, Jesus Christ. It also gives us a stronger tie to the Church. It sends us out strengthened to carry on the Church's mission. Confirmation helps us put our faith into words and actions.

Set me as a seal on your heart, as a seal on your arm. (Song of Songs 8:6, NRSV)

327

Stained for Life

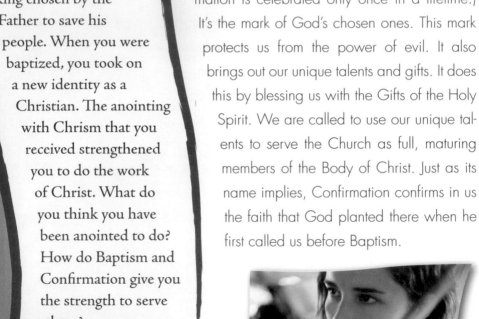

THiNK About It!

The title *Christ* means "anointed one." Jesus Christ is the anointed king chosen by the Father to save his people. When you were baptized, you took on a new identity as a Christian. The anointing with Chrism that you received strengthened you to do the work of Christ. What do you think you have been anointed to do? How do Baptism and Confirmation give you the strength to serve others?

Have you heard of people staining wood with oil? Perhaps you have furniture or flooring made of stained wood where you live. The oil protects the wood and brings out its unique grain. It also gives the wood an aged look.

Confirmation marks us in a way that is similar. Like Baptism, the Sacrament of Confirmation places a permanent mark on our souls that can never be taken away. (For this reason, Confirmation is celebrated only once in a lifetime.) It's the mark of God's chosen ones. This mark protects us from the power of evil. It also brings out our unique talents and gifts. It does this by blessing us with the Gifts of the Holy Spirit. We are called to use our unique talents to serve the Church as full, maturing members of the Body of Christ. Just as its name implies, Confirmation confirms in us the faith that God planted there when he first called us before Baptism.

How do you use your God-given talents to serve the Church and other people?

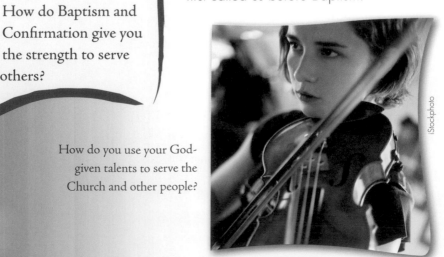

328

"The Spirit of the Lord is upon me,
because he has chosen me to bring good
news to the poor." (Luke 4:18)

East and West

In the earliest centuries of the Church, the anointing with oil of the newly baptized was done by the bishop immediately following Baptism. But as the Church grew larger and as more people were being initiated, bishops couldn't be everywhere to baptize and anoint all the new Christians. Two different practices emerged as a result.

The Church in the West (that's the former western part of the Roman Empire) still wanted the bishop to confirm the newly baptized. This was because the West focused on the connection the bishops had to the Apostles of Jesus. Jesus commissioned the Apostles. They, themselves, commissioned new bishops. Those bishops ordained new bishops. Therefore, every bishop is directly connected in a long line to Jesus. Because of this connection, Western Churches delayed the Confirmation until a point in time when the bishop could do the anointing. This practice eventually led to the separation of Confirmation from Baptism by many years.

The Churches in the East (that's the former eastern part of the Roman Empire) also valued the connection to the Apostles. But for them, the connection was less in the presence of the bishop and more in the oil he blessed. Therefore, whether or not the bishop was present, Eastern Churches continued to confirm immediately after Baptism as long as they had oil blessed by the bishop. Confirmation was then followed by the Eucharist, when the newly baptized person received Communion for the first time. This practice clearly shows the close connection and unity among the three initiation sacraments of Baptism, Confirmation, and the Eucharist.

Age and Confirmation

In the Eastern Churches today, anyone who is baptized is immediately confirmed and given the Eucharist. It doesn't matter if the person is a baby or an adult.

Live It!

A teen was chosen by his pastor to carry the Chrism for their parish in the diocese's **Chrism Mass.** In this annual celebration, the bishop blesses all the oil to be used in the diocese for the following year. The teen's pastor told him that the Chrism had perfume in it. Immediately the teen wrinkled his nose and imagined his mother's perfume—a little too sweet and strong.

As he carried the Chrism for his parish, the teen took a big whiff, and his eyes lit up. After Mass he ran to his pastor and exclaimed, "You mean I'll smell like that when I'm confirmed? That's the best thing I've ever smelled in my life!"

How can your life be like the awesome perfume of Chrism? Find out when your diocese celebrates the Chrism Mass and plan to participate.

Bill Wittman

The ages of Confirmation candidates vary. How old are most candidates in your parish?

Today, most dioceses in the West (this includes the United States) continue to separate the celebrations of Baptism and Confirmation by many years. If you were baptized as a baby, this is probably your experience too. In fact, most Catholics in the United States today do not celebrate Confirmation until their teens. U.S. bishops determine the age for their own dioceses.

If you were baptized after you reached what we refer to as the age of reason, however, your experience probably reflects the typical practice in the Eastern Churches. That is, when you were initiated, you likely celebrated Baptism, Confirmation, and the Eucharist in that order in the same liturgy. The **age of reason,** usually considered age seven, is when a person is old enough to understand what she or he is doing. The person is capable of knowing the difference between right and wrong. Adults who are baptized are also confirmed and given the Eucharist at the same liturgy, typically the Easter Vigil.

Rite of Confirmation

Because most people in the United States today are confirmed many years after their Baptism, let's look at that way of practicing Confirmation.

Before you can be confirmed, you need to have reached the age of reason. This is because in the rite, you must also profess your faith. If you have committed any serious, or mortal, sins, you would need first to celebrate the Sacrament of Penance and Reconciliation. (See chapter 30.) Next, you have to ask for the sacrament freely. That means no one can force you to celebrate it. Last, you need to be ready to live your life as a disciple of Christ. Confirmation calls you to speak about your faith both in the Church and in your daily life.

Did You Know?

Who's Who in Confirmation

The ordinary minister of the Sacrament of Confirmation is the bishop. However, he can give priests permission to confirm. Priests do not need permission to confirm someone if they are also baptizing that person. This usually takes place at the Easter Vigil with catechumens.

Each Confirmation candidate has a sponsor. This person is usually the person's godparent from Baptism. During the rite, the sponsor stands with the candidate as a sign of support and a reminder of their baptismal relationship. Who is your godparent?

The essential parts of the Sacrament of Confirmation are the anointing of the forehead with **Chrism** (in the East, other parts of the body are also anointed) along with the laying on of hands and the following words: "Be sealed with the Gift of the Holy Spirit."

Did You Know?

Three Oils of the Church

The Church uses three different types of holy oils in her liturgies, as follows:

+ **Sacred Chrism,** consecrated olive oil with perfume, represents the sweet fragrance of Christ and the good works of his Body, the Church. **Chrism** is used in the Sacraments of Baptism, Confirmation, and Ordination and to consecrate objects for sacred work.

+ **The Oil of Catechumens** is blessed olive oil used to anoint those preparing for Baptism. The anointing helps the person battle evil. It's like ancient athletes who oiled their bodies before competitions. This made it harder for their competitors to grab and hold them.

+ **The Oil of the Sick** is blessed olive oil used in the Sacrament of Anointing to anoint the forehead and hands of people who are seriously ill or near death. The anointing strengthens the sick and prepares those who are dying for death.

Read about these three sacred oils in the "Did You Know?" article above. How many of these oils have you been anointed with in your lifetime?

PRAY IT!
Liturgy Connection

Confirmation isn't the only time we use Chrism. When babies are baptized, they are anointed with Chrism on the top of the head. This anticipates their Confirmation later in life. The hands of newly ordained priests and the foreheads of newly ordained bishops are also anointed with Chrism. When a new altar is dedicated, the bishop rubs Chrism all over the top of it. The bishop also uses Chrism to make twelve crosses on the walls of new churches. Sometimes these spots where he anoints the walls are later marked with an actual cross. (Does your church have these?)

The Chrism, along with the Oil of the Sick and the Oil of Catechumens, is kept in a box called an ambry. A church's ambry is often found near the baptismal font or in a wall niche within the worship space.

Renewal of Baptismal Promises

Because Baptism is closely connected to Confirmation, the Confirmation rite includes some reminders for us. Let's imagine now that you're about to be confirmed. One of the things in the Confirmation rite that would remind you of your Baptism is the renewal of baptismal promises. Here, the bishop asks you the same questions your parents were asked back when you were a baby about to be baptized: "Do you reject Satan? Do you believe in God the Father? Do you believe in Jesus, his Son? Do you believe in the Holy Spirit? Do you believe in the catholic Church?" Because you couldn't even talk yet at your Baptism, your parents responded to these questions for you. At your Confirmation, you speak for yourself and publicly renew your baptismal promises.

> For this reason I remind you to keep alive the gift that God gave you when I laid my hands on you. For the Spirit that God has given us does not make us timid; instead his Spirit fills us with power, love and self-control.
> (2 Timothy 1:6–7)

Laying On of Hands

Next the bishop extends his hands over you and all the candidates. This is a powerful gesture. It is a sign that the bishop is asking the Holy Spirit to come upon you and be with you. You see this gesture often when someone or something is being blessed with the Holy Spirit. As the bishop does this, he leads a prayer that puts into words the request that the Father send the Holy Spirit upon you. He also asks the Spirit to help and guide you with the spiritual gifts you will need to live your faith fully.

What are some things these spiritual gifts help you do? They help you feel more confident and courageous about your faith. This lets you talk about your faith more easily with your friends and with those who ask you

Did You Know?

The Awesome Gifts of the Spirit

Seven gifts of the Holy Spirit are given to the newly confirmed: wisdom, understanding, right judgment (counsel), courage (fortitude), knowledge, reverence (piety), wonder, and awe (fear of the Lord). (See chapter 16 for descriptions of all the gifts.)

This last gift, awe, is closely tied to fear, as in "fear of the Lord." But this doesn't mean that we should be afraid of God. It means we realize how awesome God is. God is much greater than anything we can think of. In fact, a definition of God by Saint Anselm was "that than which greater cannot be thought" (*St. Anselm's Proslogion*, page 117). Think of the greatest thing ever. Then try to imagine what is beyond that—that's God. Magnificent and powerful though God is, he still cares for each one of us. Now that's an awesome God.

FUN FACT

What do Jesus and an olive tree have in common? Ask Saint Cyril, who lived in the fourth century AD, and he'd say "lots." The oil used in Confirmation comes from olives, which come from olive trees. The Holy Spirit we receive comes from Jesus. Therefore, if oil is like the Spirit, the olive tree is like Jesus. For Saint Cyril, we become a part of Jesus, like branches on his tree, when we are anointed with his Spirit.

about your Catholic beliefs. The gifts help you know how to use your talents to serve the Church and others in need. They help you be able to make better decisions between right and wrong.

Anointing with Chrism

Finally, the bishop anoints you, making the Sign of the Cross on your forehead with Chrism. As he does this, he calls you by your name, saying, "Be sealed with the Gift of the Holy Spirit." You respond "Amen." Then you and the bishop share a sign of peace. All the Gifts of the Spirit are yours. Are you ready to use them?

Read the "Fun Fact" above to find out what kind of tree this is and how it is like Jesus.

Shutterstock

336

"When the Holy Spirit comes upon you,
you will be filled with power, and you will be
witnesses for me." (Acts 1:8)

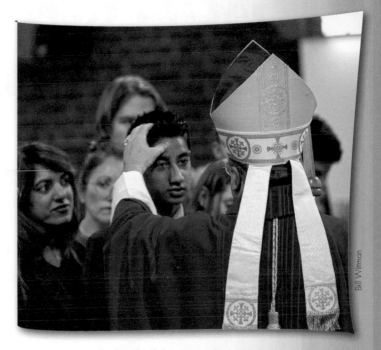

Which gift of the Spirit do
you most need?

The Sacraments of Healing

Have you ever been so sick you had to stay in bed all day? You couldn't go to school or see your friends. Forget about going outside or watching TV. Even talking on the phone hurt. You felt so awful you just wanted to curl up into a ball.

Have you ever felt guilty? You know, the kind of guilt where you couldn't even show your face to anyone? It seemed like everyone knew what you had done, and you felt terrible about it. You just wanted to hide forever.

Everyone has days like these. This is not, though, what God wants for us. God wants us to live every day as fully and joyfully as possible. Yet sometimes, because of sickness, we can't fully enjoy the gift of life God gives us. Any joy we do feel is limited. This is because we're suffering, and we're away from friends and the things that make us happy.

Sometimes because of sins we have committed, we separate ourselves from others out of guilt or shame. This separation is not the kind of life God wants for us either.

Serious sickness and sin separate us from others. We aren't the person we know we are. At these times, the Church offers us two Sacraments of Healing. These sacraments reconnect us to the community and to the life we know God wants us to live. These are the Sacrament of Penance and Reconciliation and the Sacrament of Anointing of the Sick.

Have Mercy on Me, a Sinner

When we have sinned, the Church provides several sacraments for God's forgiveness. The first is Baptism. It washes away Original Sin and our personal sins. It unites us to Christ and gives us the Holy Spirit. In the Eucharist we can ask for and receive forgiveness for venial sins. These sins are not serious. But serious sins committed deliberately after Baptism are called grave sins, or **mortal sins.** For these sins, God provides the Sacrament of Penance and Reconciliation. This sacrament is also called conversion, confession, **Penance,** or Reconciliation.

It was the will of Jesus that the Church be able to forgive sins through the ministry of priests and

PRAY IT!

Jesus, Healer and Savior,
Only you know what
is in my heart
and what I need to
be whole again.
Open my eyes to see
myself as you see me—
forgivable and blessed.
Touch my heart
and bless all who suffer
in mind, body, or spirit,
that together we might
praise you
with all your people for your
great and immense love.
Amen

339

bishops. When we celebrate this sacrament, God forgives sins and wipes away the hurt that sin causes in our relationships with God, ourselves, and others. Through the sacrament God strengthens us to live as he wants us to live.

This sacrament is about conversion or change. But conversion doesn't just happen, like turning on a light switch. It is a process, a change of heart that turns us away from sin and toward God. It's like a journey. You walk down one path. Then you slowly realize you're going the wrong way. You notice that things don't look right. You can choose to keep going. Or you can decide to stop, turn around, and go a different way.

iStockphoto

Conversion is not as easy as turning on a light switch, but it does involve seeing our relationship with God in a new light.

Through the process of conversion, we change our points of view and return to God. With the help of the Holy Spirit, we can begin to undo the harm our sins cause. Hopefully, we start to feel sorrow for what we have done. Once we decide to avoid sinning again and make up for what we have done, we are ready to turn around. We are ready to celebrate the Sacrament of Penance and Reconciliation.

"Turn away from your sins and believe the Good News!" (Mark 1:15)

A change of heart leads to repentance, or **contrition.** This means we feel sorrow or remorse. Sometimes, we feel sorrow because we're afraid of being punished. It's like when you apologize to your sibling for something you did only because your parents will ground you if you don't. It is called imperfect contrition. Then there are other times we feel so bad about something we did that we run to our parents. We want them to comfort us. We know they will understand and make things right again. This is the kind of remorse that comes from faith in our parents' love. This kind of contrition comes from our love of God and our trust in his mercy. When our repentance arises from our love of God, it is called perfect contrition.

There is no imperfection in us that God cannot heal. Nothing is so wrong in us that God cannot love us. We can do nothing so terrible that God cannot forgive it. We aren't perfect, but God is. Thank God!

© Francis G. Mayer/CORBIS

The Spanish painter Goya painted "Saint Peter Repentant." Even great saints like Peter were sinners. We all need God's mercy.

Reconciliation in Four Movements

Reconciliation is a process with several steps or actions. In the Sacrament of Penance and Reconciliation, there are four basic actions. Three are actions of the penitent (the person who wants to confess). The fourth is the action of the priest (or confessor). All these movements, with a reading from the Scriptures and possibly a song, make up the Sacrament of Penance and Reconciliation.

ThiNk AbouT IT!

Some people think of God's grace as they think of the electric company. If they don't pay their bills, their electricity gets turned off. In other words, if they don't do the right things, God stops loving them. What would you say to someone who thinks about God's love in this way?

Step One: Being Sorry

You have to be sorry before you can be forgiven. The penitent, with the help and encouragement of the priest, expresses sorrow. This is called an act of contrition. You can do an act of contrition by saying a prayer, like the *Confiteor* ("I confess to Almighty God . . .") (See appendix A, Catholic Prayers). Or you might just say in your own words how sorry you are. Then the priest helps you remember that in Penance, as in Baptism, you get to wipe the slate clean and start over again. That is, you die to sin and rise to new life. The priest might also help you do an examination of conscience. This is not a test, like final exams. It's more like a review of your life. The priest helps you look at your life and the areas where you haven't lived the way God wants you to live. Doing this helps you remember how loving God is and always will be, no matter what.

Step Two: Confessing Sin

You can't just be sorry. You have to say what you're sorry for. In the Sacrament of Penance and Reconciliation, we say out loud what we are sorry for because we believe in God's mercy. In this second step, we confess to the priest all the grave sins we can remember. It isn't necessary to confess venial sins, but the Church strongly encourages this.

PRAY IT!
Liturgy Connection

Have you seen people being dismissed from Mass after Communion? They carry small cases in which the priest places the Body of Christ—the consecrated hosts from the Mass.

These are extraordinary ministers of Holy Communion who visit parishioners who can't attend Mass due to sickness. The Communion ministers share with them some of the readings and songs from the Mass. They also pray together. Then the Communion ministers give them the Body of Christ.

These special ministers go to hospitals, nursing homes, and anywhere people need our care. They take with them not only our greatest gift—the Eucharist—but also the Word of God and our prayers for them.

Bill Wittman

Confessing our sins to a priest is something like having a conversation with Jesus.

Step Three:
Repairing the Damage

Reconciling with others when we have hurt or been hurt is essential to healthy relationships.

© Leah Warkentin/Design Pics/Corbis

"Above everything, love one another earnestly, because love covers over many sins." (1 Peter 4:8)

If we call someone a name, confessing that to a priest is good. But we also need to do something to heal the pain we cause. In this third step, the priest helps us think of things we can do to make up for, or repair, the damage that was done because of our sin. This is called reparation, satisfaction, or Penance. For example, we might go to the person we hurt and say we're sorry. We could do something nice for him or her. We could also pray more, be nicer to others, or give up something we like for a while. The more serious the sin, the more we need to do to fix the damage. Although it might be hard or even impossible to fix things completely, making up for what we did helps us live the lives God wants for us.

Did You Know?

The Effects of the Healing Sacraments

The Sacrament of Penance and Reconciliation has a number of wonderful effects on us, such as the following:

+ It turns us away from sin and toward God, reuniting us and strengthening our relationship.
+ It restores our relationship with the Church.
+ It saves us from eternal separation from God (hell) if we are in state of mortal sin.
+ It frees us from some of the consequences of our sin, such as weakening our resistance to temptation and having unhealthy attachments to things and other people.
+ It gives us peace of mind and spiritual comfort.
+ It give us strength to resist sin in the future.

When we are sick, the special grace of Anointing of the Sick helps us in the following ways:

+ It helps us see that Christ knows what we are going through, because he also suffered.
+ It joins our suffering to his.
+ It strengthens us and gives us peace and courage to bear suffering with faith in Christ.
+ It forgives our sins.
+ It brings us back to health if that is God's will.
+ It prepares us for the day when we will die and pass to eternal life with God.

Bill Wittman

Receiving absolution is a sign of God's love and forgiveness.

Jesus heals people with leprosy. Every time Jesus miraculously cured people, he healed them spiritually as well as physically.

© Brooklyn Museum/Corbis

Did You Know?

Reconciliation in Three Forms

Penance and Reconciliation happens in three ways. The first way is individually with a priest. Usually, the priest and the person sit face to face. Many parishes have a special room designated for this called a reconciliation room. Sometimes, the priest and the person sit or kneel in a confessional. They can't see each other, but they speak through a small opening in the wall.

Did you celebrate your first Reconciliation in a liturgy with other people? In this second form, a group prays, sings, and listens to Scripture readings. Then, each goes to a priest for individual confession. Even though it's a group liturgy, the confessions remain private.

The third way is one you have probably never seen because it is used only in extreme circumstances, which are indentified in the Church's law. It involves general absolution. This means that the priest absolves the penitents together. The people then celebrate individual confession at a later time.

Step Four: Being Forgiven

The one thing I do . . . is to forget what is behind me and do my best to reach what is ahead. (Philippians 3:13)

When we've done something wrong, there's nothing like hearing "I forgive you." This final part is the gift of the sacrament. Here our sins are pardoned or forgiven. This is called **absolution.** *Absolution* means "freeing from guilt." Because God loves us so much, he forgives us through the words of the priest. These ritual words are called the prayer of absolution. As he says this, the priest places his hands over our heads in a gesture of forgiveness.

We are reconciled with God and the Church when we honestly confess all our grave sins to a priest and receive absolution. Only priests who have been given permission by Church authority to forgive sins in the name of Christ can do so. However, they can forgive sins even without permission if someone is in danger of death.

Brought Back to Life in the Community

Sin is a spiritual sickness, and it separates us from the community. Physical sickness in our bodies also keeps us away from the community—literally. In

FUN FACT

The priest who hears your confession is bound by Church law never to say anything to anyone else about what you confessed in the Sacrament of Penance and Reconciliation. No exceptions. This is often called the sacramental seal, because all knowledge about what you said is sealed up. The priest's lips are sealed.

Looking Back

Misery Loves Company

Early Christians believed Christ would return soon and the world would end. They believed the baptized had to live upright lives for only a short time. After a while it was clear that Christ was not returning right away. Rituals and regulations emerged to guide the celebration of the Sacrament of Penance and Reconciliation as more and more Christians who had sinned sought to restore their relationships with God and the Church.

By the fourth century, Penance was public and often severe. Sinners had to endure long and harsh penances before they could be forgiven. These penitents often wore ashes (we still do this on Ash Wednesday), rough sackcloth, and even chains. They did not have wine or meat. Sometimes as a sign of their sorrow, they didn't even bathe or cut their hair. Because Penance was so hard, many waited until they were near death to confess their sins.

Jesus' society, those who were sick were in some way separated from the community too. These included people with leprosy, people who were blind or deaf, those possessed, and those whose bodies were paralyzed. They were reunited to the community's daily life of prayer and work by the healing love of Christ. Jesus' healing cured them. But it did more than that. It brought them back to life in the community. Jesus healed them to restore their relationships with God and the community.

When the Church prays for people who are sick and when she celebrates the Sacrament of Anointing of the Sick with them, we aren't just hoping for a miracle—although miracles sometimes happen. When we pray with those who are sick, we are, more important, asking God to heal the person who is sick to be reunited with the community. In Anointing of the Sick, those who are sick and those who are healthy are reunited to worship God.

Anointing of the Sick

The Sacrament of Anointing of the Sick is for Catholics who are seriously ill or in danger of death because of either sickness or old age. The sacrament can be repeated if the person's condition gets worse.

> "When one of [the lepers] saw that he was healed, he came back, praising God in a loud voice."
> (Luke 17:15)

The sacrament can take place in a church, a hospital, or even a home. It is important that members of the person's family and other members of the Church are present to pray with and for them. But only bishops and priests can give the sacrament.

Parishes sometimes celebrate a communal Anointing of the Sick in conjunction with Mass. Those who are sick are invited to come forward for anointing.

The liturgy has several parts. The essential parts are the anointing and the prayer of the bishop or priest over the person who is sick. This prayer asks God for the special grace of the sacrament.

Prayer of Faith

Trusting in God's mercy, the people who are gathered pray a short litany for the person who is sick. The entire Church is present in this community, and the people who are sick, even in their illness, are united in prayer with them.

Laying On of Hands

Then the minister lays his hands on the head of the person who is sick. This gesture, called the **laying on of hands,** shows that the sick person is the focus of the prayer. It is a sign of the healing power of God and a silent calling of the Holy Spirit upon the person. It is the way Jesus healed many of those in his own community.

[The disciples] drove out many demons, and rubbed olive oil on many sick people and healed them. (Mark 6:13)

Bill Wittman

A priest performs the laying on of hands during the Sacrament of Anointing of the Sick. Jesus often touched the people he healed.

Anointing

Next, the minister anoints the forehead and hands of the person who is sick. (In the Eastern rite, other parts of the body are also anointed, especially those parts that are in pain or need healing.) The oil used for the anointing is olive oil usually blessed by the bishop at the Chrism Mass (see chapter 29). If the bishop has not blessed the oil, the minister of the sacrament may bless the oil himself. The prayer said during the anointing asks God to help the person with his love and mercy and to save and raise up those who are sick.

The Sacrament of Anointing of the Sick is not just for people who are dying. A person may receive the sacrament before surgery, when seriously ill, or because of old age.

Bill Wittman

Live It!

Catholics are called not only to celebrate the Sacrament of Penance and Reconciliation but also to live a penitential lifestyle. To live a penitential lifestyle means to remember every day that we are not perfect. It also means remembering that the goal of our lives is not to be perfect but rather to praise God for his love. In other words, God does not expect us to be perfect. He wants us to be faithful. Does this mean we have to be gloomy every day and think we are awful? No. Actually, these disciplines are good habits that help us live more faithfully and joyfully. Following are some ways you can live a penitential lifestyle:

- make up with friends and family
- cry when you feel sorrow
- care for others
- pray to the saints
- accept suffering

- defend the poor
- admit when you're wrong
- gently correct others and accept correction yourself
- give and ask for forgiveness
- live your Christian faith

Prayer After Anointing

Finally, the bishop or priest prays a special prayer over the person who is sick. The prayer expresses the Church's hope for the person and its trust that God will strengthen the person in his or her sickness.

Did You Know?

The Role of People Who Are Sick

As the Body of Christ, we believe that every person, no matter how weak or small, is important. Infants, those who are sick, the elderly—anyone the world might consider weak or useless—are valuable to the Church, because each person in his or her own unique way builds up the Body of Christ.

Therefore, even in their weaknesses, people who are sick have important roles to play in the Church. When we see them suffering, we are reminded of how precious and fragile life is. They also show us how strong God's love in Christ can be even in the middle of so much pain. They help us think of what is really important in life—not material things, but the love we can share with one another. Their sickness also reminds us that we depend on God for life and that we are given that life through Christ's death and Resurrection. The Church needs the powerful witness of those who are sick. Therefore, in the Sacrament of Anointing of the Sick, God gives them sacramental grace to help them through their sickness or old age.

THE SACRAMENTS OF MATRIMONY AND HOLY ORDERS

Have you ever made a really big promise, one that would cause you or others pain if you broke it? Has someone ever made an important promise to you? Promises help us know how to live, and they help us in our relationships.

The first promises we make as Catholics are in Baptism, when we promise to believe in the Father, Son, and Holy Spirit. All the other promises we make as Catholics are based on these baptismal vows (see chapter 28).

A couple spends a lifetime living out the vows they made in marriage.

Let's look at two sacraments adult Catholics can celebrate that help them live out their baptismal promises—the Sacrament of Matrimony and the Sacrament of Holy Orders.

Shutterstock

I Promise to Be True to You

Do you have a best friend or someone you like more than a friend? All of us need special people in our lives. This is because God wants us to find relationships. They help us know his love. Of course, our relationships aren't always perfect, because we're not perfect. Married people know this well. They love each other completely. But there are days when that love is tested or even absent. When a baptized man and woman celebrate the Sacrament of Matrimony, however, Christ takes their imperfect love and joins it to his perfect love. It's like taking two pieces of thread. Try to twist the two pieces together, and they just keep unraveling. But add a third piece of thread and braid them. The threads won't come apart. Christ's love is that third thread. His divine promise to love us strengthens our human promises to love each other. Christ's promise to the Church—his Bride—is stronger than any promise we can make.

PRAY IT!

Father God,
You promise me
light and life,
and each day
you fulfill your
word.
Help me keep my
own promises
and let my word
always be true.
Strengthen all who
have promises to
keep and bless them
with your Spirit
so they may serve
you faithfully.
Amen

For this reason a man will leave his father and mother and unite with his wife, and the two will become one.
(Ephesians 5:31)

When you see a man and woman celebrate the Sacrament of Matrimony, you are actually seeing a sign of Christ's love for the Church. The sacrament strengthens them to love each other with the love Jesus Christ has given to the Church. Through their promises, Christ blesses them to love deeply and live faithfully until they live eternally with Christ.

In Good Times and in Bad, in Sickness and in Health

Do you think this means keeping the promise is easy? Hardly. But Christ's promise to his Church—and the spouses' promise in marriage—is a **covenant.** A covenant is stronger than a contract. In a covenant each party keeps the promise, no matter what the other party does. In the Bible, God made a covenant with his people always to love them as his own. But they often ignored God. Sometimes they even fell in love with other things they thought were better than God. Yet God kept his promise and loved them, no matter what.

God never forces anyone to love him. It's the same in a marriage. To be a real covenant, each person must enter marriage willingly. They need to give their lives freely and totally to each other.

In their covenant, the husband and wife give everything they have to each other in a personal way. They share everything, not just what they own but also who they are—the good and the bad. They promise to love each other, no matter what.

KEY WORDS

covenant

vocation

ministerial priesthood

common priesthood of the faithful

God created marriage for us. Christ took our need to be close to another person and made it into a symbol of his love for us. In the marriage covenant between a husband and wife, we see the true love of God. God's love blesses and brings new life. The marriage enables the husband and wife to share life and love with any children they are blessed with. In fact, a child is the supreme gift of married life. Being open to children is essential to marriage, but those who are not blessed with children have the opportunity to share their love in other ways.

LIVE IT!

The homes of Christian families are also churches. We call them domestic churches. This is because Christians first hear about Christ and learn their faith at home. The home is meant to be a community of grace and prayer and a school of Christian love. Make your home life more like Church. As a family, designate one place in your home as the family prayer center. Place on it a candle, a Bible, and a cloth matching the color of the liturgical season. Include pictures of people you want to pray for and a bowl of holy water. Use the water to bless yourself and one another. Gather there with your family on special days, like birthdays, to pray a blessing.

"Happy are those who have been invited to the wedding feast of the Lamb." (Revelation 19:9)

I Will Love You and Honor You All the Days of My Life

Marriage is a vocation. A **vocation** is a way of life people choose in response to God's call to live out their faith. Pope Benedict XVI called vocation "God's task for each one of us" (papal greeting, March 25, 2007). Some join a religious group of brothers or nuns and serve the Church with them. Some become deacons, priests, or bishops, while others get married. Some remain single, living their faith through deep friendships. All these, except being single, are vocations for life.

Because marriage is a lifelong vocation, it is meant to be permanent. Divorce involves a separation of what God joins together through marriage. Those who get divorced and marry other spouses go against God's

Did You Know?

Who Ministers at a Marriage?

In Matrimony, the ministers are the two people in the couple because they—not the priest or deacon—give their vows to each other. Of course, it is Christ who is doing the promise-making. But the two being married, through Christ, make their promises to each other.

In the sacrament, the priest or deacon is the Church's witness and leads the blessing over the couple. The couple selects its own witnesses (usually the best man and maid of honor) who fulfill the required legal roles. The witnesses support the couple throughout its married life. Finally, the assembly is a community of faith ready to help the couple keep its promise.

logic or plan. Their actions contradict our faith. It is painful, but this is why the Church asks them not to receive Communion. Yet the Church still loves them. They are called to live out their faith by continuing to educate their children in the Catholic faith.

Couples exchange rings at their wedding as a sign of their love and faithfulness to each other.

Shutterstock

Those who are divorced can marry and remain in communion with the Church if they receive an annulment. This involves having the previous marriage declared null by the Church. Such a declaration means that when the wedding took place, the standards for a sacramental marriage did not exist. This doesn't mean that a civil marriage didn't exist. And it doesn't mean the husband and wife didn't love each other or that their children are illegitimate.

The Rite of Marriage

Marriage is a public vocation. So the marriage vows are made publicly in a liturgy called the Rite of Marriage.

FUN FACT

Have you seen a bride walk down the aisle with her father to meet her groom? This practice comes from a time when daughters were considered family "property." The father was giving away his property to the groom's family. The Catholic marriage rite emphasizes the couple's freedom and equality. It suggests that both the bride and groom walk down the aisle. They can be escorted by both sets of parents.

Have you ever been to a Catholic wedding? What symbols and actions do you remember most? Let's look at some of them.

A nuptial blessing asks God to send his Spirit upon the couple. What a sacred way to begin married life!

Bill Wittman

Intentions and Consent

The most important action is the consent (or vows). These are the promises the man and woman who are getting married make to each other. First, the priest or deacon has to be sure they are not being forced into the marriage. So he asks them the following:

1. Do you really want to give your lives to each other?
2. Will you be faithful to each other until death?
3. Will you accept children and raise them in the Church?

If they say yes, they make their vows. They declare that they are making a covenant with the other person to love and be faithful to him or her.

Blessing and Exchange of Rings

You can't see a promise. We use the symbol of rings to represent it. Rings show who you are and whom you belong to. The Church blesses the rings, and the bride and bridegroom place them on each other's fingers.

Nuptial Blessing

The last part of the rite is the nuptial blessing. In this prayer, the priest or deacon asks God to send his Spirit upon the married couple. He prays that they may be faithful to each other.

Look for these symbols next time you're at a Catholic wedding.

Holy Orders

Married persons enter into a covenant to serve the Church by serving their families. Those ordained to be bishops, priests, or deacons also enter into a covenant to serve. They promise to serve the People of God in a more public role.

You are the chosen race, the King's priests, the holy nation,
God's own people, chosen to proclaim the wonderful
acts of God, who called you out of darkness into his own
marvelous light. (1 Peter 2:9)

THiNK About It!

Imagine you were getting married. Which symbol from the wedding would be most important for you and why? How could you make the vows the high point of the liturgy?

Imagine you were being ordained. How would it feel to lie facedown on the floor as you heard the Litany of the Saints? What does this unusual posture mean? Do you see this done at other times during the year?

361

Some baptized men are called to share in Christ's mission of service as priests. They are ordained into **ministerial priesthood.** They serve in the name of Christ and represent him in the community.

The work of the ordained priest is different from what other Catholics do. A priest receives a sacramental grace. This gift is a sacred power that enables him to serve in a unique way. Priests lead the Church's prayer, especially the sacraments. Priests also teach the faith received from the Apostles and work to nourish the spiritual lives of everyone who is part of the Church.

Since the beginning of the Church, there have been three types of ordained ministers: bishops, priests, and deacons. We can't be the Church without all three. While there are three degrees of ordained ministry—bishop, priest, and deacon—it is only the bishop and the priest that are part of the ministerial priesthood. It is the deacon's role to help and serve them.

Did You Know?

We Are Priests Too

Did you know that if you're baptized, you're a priest in a way? All of us, by Baptism, share in the priesthood of Christ. We call this the **common priesthood of the faithful.** Christ is called priest, prophet, and king. To share in his priesthood means we participate in his mission. In his name, we are sent into the world to worship, witness, and serve. The common priesthood and the ministry of ordained priesthood can't exist without each other.

Bill Wittman

In this picture, who belongs to the common priesthood of the faithful and who belongs to the ministerial priesthood?

Rite of Ordination

There is an ordination rite for each of the three types of ministerial service—deacon, priest, and bishop. Let's look at some of their symbols and actions.

Examination and Promise

At every ordination, the ordaining minister is a bishop. He asks the candidate to promise to serve the Church. After making the promise, the candidate admits he can keep it only with God's help.

Litany of Saints

In the Litany of the Saints, we ask all the saints to pray for the man being ordained and for the Church. As we do this, he lies facedown on the floor. This shows his obedience to the Church. It symbolizes his weakness and need for God. It shows his humility.

Laying On of Hands and Prayer of Consecration

Next, the bishop lays his hands on the candidate's head. It brings the power and blessing of the Holy

PRAY IT!
Liturgy Connection

At Baptism, you received a white garment called an alb. Ordained men also receive special garments to signify their roles in the Church.

Deacons wear a stole (a long, thin cloth) over one shoulder and a dalmatic, a tunic with large sleeves.

Priests also wear a stole, but it drapes over both shoulders like a yoke. They also wear a chasuble, which is a round, sleeveless garment.

Bishops wear the dalmatic and the priest's stole and chasuble. They also wear a ring symbolizing their promise and a miter (a liturgical headdress) showing their governing office, and they carry a staff, or crozier, because they are shepherds of the Church.

Why are these men facedown on the floor? Find out by reading about the Rite of Ordination.

© Alessandra Benedetti/Corbis

Spirit. The Holy Spirit gives the candidate the grace he will need to do his ministry.

Do you remember where we've seen this gesture before? If you said Confirmation, you're right (see chapter 29). As in Confirmation, the Holy Spirit leaves a permanent, invisible mark on the candidate. This mark identifies him as a minister dedicated to serve God's people. By the laying on of hands and the special prayer that follows it, he is ordained. Because the mark is permanent, he can never be ordained again for that order.

Servant of the Gospel

Imagine walking around with a book over your head. In a symbolic way, bishops do. When a bishop is ordained, two deacons hold open the *Book of the Gospels* over his head during the consecration prayer. This shows that the bishop is always supposed to live out the Gospel in the way he leads the Church. He must proclaim the Gospel in everything he does.

The bishop receives the fullness of Holy Orders. This means he gets his mission directly from Christ through the line of bishops. If you trace the bishops backward, looking at who ordained whom, you'll end up at the Apostles—whom Jesus personally sent to continue his work. This makes a bishop a successor to the Apostles. Each bishop is a member of the community of bishops. They are the visible leaders of the Church. Each bishop is obedient to the Pope, who is the successor to the first Pope, Peter.

At their ordination, deacons are given the *Book of the Gospels*. They take on tasks of service to the Church and the world that demonstrate their commitment to the Gospel. Deacons do not receive the ministerial priesthood, however, through their ordination they share in Christ's mission in a special way. They serve the Church as ministers of the Word by proclaiming the Gospel and preaching. They assist with liturgies by distributing Communion, presiding over funerals, and assisting at and blessing marriages. They dedicate themselves to numerous other ministries of service. All of the deacon's tasks are carried out under the authority of his bishop.

Did You Know?
Everybody Is a Symbol

The Church takes our bodies seriously. For example, your body needs to be at Church if you want to participate in the liturgy. (You can't participate via satellite!)

In marriage, the bride and groom give each other promises, rings, and their bodies. They represent Christ to each other, who gave up his own body on the cross because of his love for us.

Because a priest represents Christ in bodily form, and Jesus was male in body, the Church ordains only baptized men. Although everyone is called to a vocation, only bishops have the responsibility and right to call someone to ordination.

Anointed to Be Servants

At their ordination, the priests' hands are anointed with Chrism. This gives them the authority to lead Mass. Into their hands, the bishop places the bread and wine that will be consecrated for Communion.

Priests are the bishop's coworkers. With him they form a community that takes responsibility for caring for a diocese. The bishop puts each priest in charge of a parish or gives him another function in the diocese. The priests rely on the bishop for their authority as they carry out their ministry.

PEOPLE OF FAITH

Saint John Baptist de La Salle (1651–1719)

© 2009 Saint Mary's Press/Illustration by Vicki Shuck

"Let us remember that we are in the holy presence of God." Saint John Baptist de La Salle spoke this prayerful reminder often in his work as a priest and advocate for schoolteachers and the children they serve.

John Baptist was born in France to a wealthy family. After ordination, he gave up his comfortable life and devoted his energy to schools for those who were poor.

Fraternal Kiss

The rite ends with the fraternal kiss. Fraternal means "brotherly." The newly ordained share this sign of peace with the brothers in their order. This embrace shows their permanent bond to the Church and each other.

When deacons are ordained, they are given a *Book of the Gospels*.

He gave his wealth away and devoted his life to training teachers. He developed new ways of teaching that we still use today. For example, he created the grade system, grouping students of similar abilities together. He also directed his teachers to teach only in the language of the people instead of in Latin.

He began the Institute of the Brothers of the Christian Schools (Christian Brothers). They are dedicated to teaching people who are poor. He knew what kind of commitment was required to be a teacher. John Baptist worked hard to support them in their commitment to educating children.

His feast day is April 7. He is the patron saint of teachers.

PART 5

CHRISTIAN MORALITY AND JUSTICE

1. I am the LORD your God: you shall not have strange Gods before me.
2. You shall not take the name of the LORD your God in vain.
3. Remember to keep holy the LORD's Day.
4. Honor your father and your mother.
5. You shall not kill.
6. You shall not commit adultery.
7. You shall not steal.
8. You shall not bear false witness against your neighbor.
9. You shall not covet your neighbor's wife.
10. You shall not covet your neighbor's goods.

32 LIVING THE MORAL LIFE

"Where are you going?" You'll be asked this a lot as you grow up. Often the answer is easy: "Out with my friends, Mom." At times, the question becomes harder, like if you're deciding whether to go to college or to get a job. Sometimes you just feel lost in life, and it seems like not even a global positioning system (GPS) could give you a clue.

God gives guidance that can lead us closer to him. God wants us to draw nearer to him in this life and to live with him in happiness forever in Heaven.

Maps can help us get where we want to go. Morality can get us where God wants us to go.

Shutterstock

Gifts and virtues, along with God's laws found in the Scriptures, help get us there.

In this section, we'll explore what it means to live the life of morality and justice that God intends for us.

> "I chose you before I gave you life, and before you were born I selected you to be a prophet to the nations."
>
> (Jeremiah 1:4)

Off to a Great Start

God has a plan for us even before we are born. God forms us in our mother's womb with a spiritual soul, an active mind, and a free will. These gifts draw us toward God. They allow us to respond with love to God's love and seek true, never-ending joy in his presence in Heaven.

Free will, the gift from God that allows us to choose what we do, is the basis for our moral responsibility. This doesn't mean we can do whatever we want. God's law obligates us to do good and avoid evil. This moral law is the inner voice, or conscience, that we hear when we have to choose between right and wrong.

This choice is made harder by Original Sin, the wound

Pray It!

Loving God,
Let me never forget
that you made me
wonderfully, loved
me from the start,
and gave me great and
countless gifts.
When temptations and
hard times come, as I know
they will, help me remember
your gift of fortitude. Give
me the strength to make
good choices that lead to a
holy life, today and always.
Amen

that all humans have that makes us open to choosing wrong and evil options.

> "Happy are those who know they are spiritually poor; the Kingdom of heaven belongs to them!" (Matthew 5:3)

Despite this hurdle God has always promised us salvation. Think back to Abraham, who pleased God and was promised countless descendants. Ever since that time, God has made and kept promises. Ultimately, God's promises lead to the Beatitudes, promises Jesus makes in the Gospels of Matthew and Luke. He promises true happiness, or beatitude, in the Kingdom of Heaven—a desire God has put in our hearts. Jesus shares the Beatitudes to help us connect the desires in our hearts with where we're going. Our final destination is the Kingdom of Heaven, where we will see God and live forever as his children. The Holy Spirit will give us the grace to help us make better moral choices and lead us to the glory of Heaven.

Walking the Talk

It's easier to talk about what's good and right than actually to do it. Jesus realized how hard it was to follow the Old Law, the first rules God gave for living a moral life, which is summed up in the Ten Commandments. Jesus also surely prayed the Psalms, one of which tells us that God's word "is a lamp to guide me and a light for my path" (Psalm 119:105). He challenges us to look deeper at God's laws. We need to understand

People gather around Jesus, listening to him teach. One of the most important teachings Jesus shared with his followers was the Beatitudes, rules for living that will bring true happiness.

© Brooklyn Museum/Corbis

not only what they say but also how they bring us closer to God and others. Then we put them into practice. This is how we build a strong and accurate conscience.

Ultimately, Jesus makes the law simple to understand: "Do for others what you want them to do for you" (Matthew 7:12). We have the freedom to choose whether to follow Jesus. This freedom makes us responsible for what we choose to do.

That's a powerful responsibility, and Paul encourages us to take it seriously. The Scriptures tell us God guides us,

Live It!

We talk a lot in this chapter about good habits. You know there are plenty of bad habits too. Some even become addictions, and addicts often join support groups to try to break bad habits.

Doesn't it make sense to form a support group with friends who will help you avoid bad habits or even practice good ones? Maybe you and your best friend can help each other give up caffeine—even if it's just during Lent—by taking turns buying juice at lunch. Maybe you and a friend can help each other avoid name-calling if that's a habit you struggle with. Even prayer habits, like learning the rosary, are easier when someone prays with you.

as the Father he is, with laws that call us to follow the path to eternal happiness and avoid evil ways.

> Keep on working with fear and trembling to
> complete your salvation, because
> God is always at work in you
> to make you willing and able
> to obey his own purpose.
> (Philippians 2:12–13)

FUN FACT

Certain orders of religious women, or nuns, wear clothing called a habit. If you haven't met a nun in a habit, perhaps you've seen the movie *Sister Act*.

Just as virtues are behavioral habits we practice until they become a way of life, a nun's habit symbolizes her choice of a holy lifestyle. She chooses each day to wear a habit, just as she chooses virtuous habits such as prayer and simple living.

You're Born with It

Though the Bible often is called God's instruction manual for life, everyone already is equipped at birth with an understanding of what is good. We call this the **natural law,** because it's part of our human nature. God made us in his image, and natural law lets us take part in God's wisdom and goodness. It's the basis of our human dignity and rights, as well as the duties that come with our rights. We can know natural law by using God's gift of reason.

Because natural law expresses God's moral vision, it never changes. The rules that support natural law are always correct throughout all time. Do you treat people the way you want to be treated? That's a common example of natural law that doesn't change, no matter your circumstances. Natural law brings people together and should form the basis for society's laws.

Of course, with all the troubles in the world, it's clear that some people are ignoring natural law. In fact, God's Chosen People, the Israelites, wandering the desert with Moses, chose to ignore moral rules that should have come naturally. Amid the chaos, God gave Moses the Ten Commandments. God wanted to give his Chosen People all the help possible in knowing the rules that already are part of our human nature but that sin often obscures.

The Ten Commandments were written on stone, and they're about pretty heavy stuff, such as murder. But we can disobey the Fifth Commandment, for example, without someone dying. Things we say or do can hurt or kill someone's spirit. We must be careful about our words and actions and their intentions. Following the Ten Commandments in ways great and small brings light and peace into our lives.

Shutterstock

The Ten Commandments are laws for everyone, for all time. No wonder they are "written in stone."

Higher Love

God uses the teachings and prophecies of the Old Law to prepare us for the Good News of Jesus in the Gospels. About 1,300 years after Moses went up Mount Sinai and received the Ten Commandments, people were continuing to search for God's guidance. They found it in Jesus Christ.

They too sought freedom from oppressive rulers, and the similarities don't end there. Despite natural law and the Ten Commandments, people still needed more help. The Roman Empire wasn't their biggest problem—sin was. They had the Commandments but needed the grace of the Holy Spirit, which comes from faith in Jesus, to live lives of selfless love. This is the New Law, God's moral law made perfect.

The Sermon on the Mount is the ultimate expression of the New Law. In it Jesus teaches us to love our enemies, avoid greed and revenge, and live humbly. This is what must be done, and we get the power we need to do it each time we receive the sacraments.

> Fill your minds with those things that are good and that deserve praise: things that are true, noble, right, pure, lovely, and honorable. (Philippians 4:8)

Good Habits

Most people don't like to be told what to do, but laws do just that—they are outside influences that help us live out our inner goodness.

Can't we just take control of our own goodness?

Virtues are habits we develop to help us consistently do the right thing. They allow us to use our minds and our free wills in a more perfect way. Because these virtues come with being human, they can be acquired by human efforts.

Virtues may not seem easy at first, but over time, with practice, they come more naturally. It's like how your teachers stretched you from three plus three to three times three. You practiced multiplication over

THINK & ABOUT IT!

Temptation is all around us. Some of our favorite activities can become bad habits that lead us to sin if we don't control our use of them.

Discuss with your friends or family how bad practices can hurt your relationships with them and with God.

Then talk about best practices that you and others use to avoid temptation. If you can't beat a problem on your own, maybe somebody you love will have a solution. You may not know until you discuss it.

and over. If you've mastered it, it makes more complex math easier.

Human virtues are like that. They grow as we learn more about life, do good acts, and keep trying when things get tough. With God's grace, they become holy habits that make it easier to be good.

Chief among the many human virtues are four Cardinal Virtues, on which the other virtues depend. *Cardinal* comes from the Latin word for "hinge," because Cardinal Virtues are pivotal to our moral lives. Like hinges, these habits are stable and guide our behavior to swing in the paths of faith and reason. To learn more about Cardinal Virtues, see the article "Cardinal Virtues."

We have to work to get virtues and work to keep them. Remember, though, that God is with us in our quest to live a holy life.

Shutterstock

Cardinal virtues are like hinges: they help open the door to a good life. Read about them in the "Did You Know?" sidebar on the next page.

Always Closer

"Come near to God, and he will come near to you" (James 4:8). This call captures the magnetic energy of God's love. Faith, hope, and love—called the Theological Virtues—help us come near to God to live in relationship with the Holy Trinity. The wonderful thing is that God himself is the source of these virtues. We know God by faith, we hope in God's promises, and we can't help but love God, for God is love.

Faith, hope, and love guide and energize the human virtues. They make our relationships with God and our neighbors more perfect. To learn more about the Theological Virtues, see the article "Theological Virtues."

Living a moral life is one way we worship God. We become a living sacrifice, along with other members of the Body of Christ. Our celebration of Mass and the nourishment of the Eucharist fuel our efforts to live Christian lives.

Did You Know?

Cardinal Virtues

The four Cardinal Virtues are prudence, justice, temperance, and fortitude.

Prudence is good judgment, exercised with caution. It sets the pace for the other virtues. Instead of just rushing into a choice, prudent people think before they act.

Justice is all about giving both God and our neighbors what is due to them. It goes beyond just giving our fair share and stretches us to put the needs of others before our own.

Temperance means balance and self-control. We like to eat and play, but we can hurt our bodies with too much of either. People may find work to be rewarding or they may enjoy alcohol, but temperance helps us avoid addictions to them.

Fortitude gives us the strength to overcome temptations to do wrong, no matter how intense they are. It helps us overcome fears and make sacrifices.

MORAL DECISION MAKING

Have you ever felt tangled in temptation or tied up in a knot of lies? You may at times find yourself cornered by conformity or choosing something convenient instead of what you know is right in God's eyes. The good news is that God offers us all kinds of help to be good—to be what he knows we can be.

Wouldn't it be nice to have a tool to cut through the tension and challenge of making good, moral decisions? Well, you do. It's your conscience. That's the God-given voice inside you that helps you use reason to judge whether an act is right or wrong.

How is your conscience like a knife? Find out by reading this page.

iStockphoto

As with any good tool, you must not let your conscience get dull or rusty. Your conscience must be kept sharp to cut through life's challenges. A well-formed conscience is truthful and solid. It doesn't conform to peer pressure or popular trends but rather to the true good for which God made us. Conscience makes its judgments based on reason in a world that's not always reasonable. It's important to do all you can to sharpen or form your conscience.

The peace that Christ gives is to guide you in the decisions you make. (Colossians 3:15)

The Sources of Moral Actions

We consider three things when we judge the morality of an act: the object, the intention, and the circumstances. Let's use an actual tool—a hammer—as an example to explore the morality of human acts. A doctor can whap your knee with a rubber hammer to test your reflexes. Your little brother can whap the same knee, causing you serious pain while giving him a twisted sense of joy.

The object, or what's happening in both examples, is the use of a hammer to whap your knee. The intention differs. Your doctor cares about your health, unlike

Pray It!

Lord,
Sometimes it's hard to do the right thing. Help me be stronger, so when I have a tough decision to make, my choice will please you. When I mess up and sin, give me the strength to say I'm sorry. Your love will restore me, Lord. Bring me back to you.

Amen

your brother! Circumstances also are important. They can change the degree of goodness or evil in an act. For example, if your brother is only three years old, your pain may still be great, but he's not as guilty.

All three sources must be considered to make a judgment about the moral goodness of an act. Let's consider the following examples:

Object. Some choices are always wrong, no matter what good might come of them. Moral evil isn't justified even if some good results. Scientists, for example, might cure diseases by research done on stem cells taken from human embryos (unborn babies), but human life is lost in the process. A good intention doesn't make an evil object good. People sometimes make this point by saying "the end doesn't justify the means."

Did You Know?

Sins Both Great and Small

Venial sins are less serious sins. They are offenses against God's will that weaken our relationships with God and others, as well as hurting our personal characters. Sin is rooted in our free will, which is found in our hearts. Charity, or love, also lives in our hearts. Venial sin wounds charity but does not destroy it. In fact, with God's grace, charity can repair damage that venial sin does.

Ultimately, a person might commit a **mortal sin,** choosing on purpose to do something that goes seriously against God's Law. A mortal sin requires that you know you are committing a serious sin and that you freely choose to do it. You cannot commit a mortal sin by accident or if someone is forcing you to do it. This type of sin is called mortal because it can cause eternal death. If we don't seek forgiveness, mortal sin can mean eternal separation from God. It also destroys charity, which helps us love God. Without charity, we can't experience eternal happiness with God.

Intention. It's wrong to pull a fire alarm at school to avoid taking a test, because your intention is bad. But it's a good act if there really is a fire and your intention is to warn people—the object, intention, and circumstances are all good.

Circumstances. There are times when responsibility for our actions is lessened or wiped out due to circumstances like ignorance, fear, or threats. For example, what if a school bully threatened to hurt your best friend if you refused to share test answers? If you help the bully cheat, the threatening circumstance lessens your responsibility for your actions.

We always have the right to exercise freedom, especially in moral and religious matters. But freedom doesn't give us the right to do or say anything we want. We may have freedom, but this does not lessen the importance of making good decisions.

It all comes down to having a conscience that is well formed. Our consciences can help us make the right choices by following God's law and human reason, or they can stray from reason and law and do wrong. Our consciences are like moral muscles. The stronger the muscle is, the more we can trust it. When our consciences are strong, we must obey their certain judgment. We exercise our consciences by thinking about the good and bad of every situation we encounter. But we're not on our own

FUN FACT

In 2005 the U.S. Supreme Court ruled that the Ten Commandments could not be displayed in public buildings if the main purpose were to promote religion. Things were different in 1956. To publicize his classic movie *The Ten Commandments*, director Cecil B. DeMille had public displays of the Ten Commandments erected around the country. Most were placed in or near government buildings.

Pray It!
Liturgy Connection

If you mess up in a team sport, you might say "My bad" to your teammates. It's a quick way to admit something's your fault.

At the start of Mass, we pray for forgiveness, admitting that we are sinners in need of God's love and mercy. One prayer we sometimes say is the *Confiteor*, Latin for "I confess" (see appendix A, "Catholic Prayers"). It's a way to admit to poor moral choices we've made or good things we've failed to do. It's important to think about these words, because they help us remember that our poor choices hurt our relationships not only with God but also with the whole community.

Though this penitential rite seems routine, the act of publicly admitting our wrongs is a good spiritual exercise. It gears us up for the examination of conscience that we do before the Sacrament of Penance and Reconciliation.

to figure things out. The Scriptures, Church teachings, prayer, and the guidance of holy people and the Holy Spirit all help us form our consciences and live the "good life." That's what God wants for us.

If we ignore our consciences and fail to develop them, we don't escape responsibility for our actions. We are still responsible for our choices and any wrong we do. It is said that ignorance of the law is not an excuse for breaking it. A poorly formed conscience is no excuse for sinning either.

Aiming for God

If your life were an arrow, what would your target be? The Greek word we translate as *sin* was originally an archery term. It meant how far you missed the mark, or bull's-eye. If eternal happiness with God is our target, sin is a sign we've gone astray.

Sin is anything we say or do that goes against God's law. As followers of Christ, sin is a step off our path of following Jesus,

iStockphoto

If your target is to be the kind of person God created you to be, how close are you to being "on target" in your everyday decisions?

who always obeyed God. Sin is a failure to love not only God but also our neighbors. This hurts our human nature and our relationships with others.

Jesus shows us that our relationships with God, others, and ourselves should be the focus of our lives. He teaches us that we must love God with all our beings and love our neighbors as we love ourselves. Christian morality aims for this target, that is, choosing to be the people God made us to be.

Sin often starts in small ways. Focusing too much on money and the things we want, for example, can come between us and God, as well as between us and our neighbors. Things, or the money needed to get them, become too important. We want more or better things than our friends have. Our things start to make us feel superior to some people and envious of others.

If you want to, you can keep the Lord's commands. You can decide whether you will be faithful to him or not. (Sirach 15:15)

THiNK About It!

Paul shared advice in his letter to the Colossians that's still important to us today. Read Colossians 3:1–17, then think about the things Paul says we need to get rid of and the traits we need to clothe ourselves with.

Paul tells us to "teach and instruct one another with all wisdom" (Colossians 3:16). What wisdom can you share with others that will help them live in a way that's pleasing to God? What is one thing that's worked for you as you seek Christ's peace?

Is it wrong to feel this way? For an answer, look to the Tenth Commandment, which tells us not to covet our neighbor's goods. Repeating sins may seem harmless, but doing so leads us to form bad habits called vices. Unlike virtues, vices make it easier to commit sin. They can become deadly sins called capital sins that distance us from God and others. (See the article "The Seven Deadly Sins" in this chapter.)

Whenever our sin separates us from God and from others, God wants to bring us back together. Through a process called **justification,** God restores our broken relationships after we have sinned. *Justification* is a word that refers to God's act of making us worthy of being united with him. God forgives our sins, makes us holy, and renews our spiritual lives. God gives us love, which helps us turn toward him and away from sin.

God's love makes all the difference. We are freed from sin, and we enter new lives made possible through Jesus' Passion, when he suffered and died for our sins. Our lives, now on earth and forever with God, are gifts given to us out of immense love. It is this love that supports and sustains us as we strive to make good moral decisions—decisions that keep us turned toward God, as well as those that get us turned back around after we do something wrong.

A good example of justification is Peter. He betrayed his friend—Jesus himself. On the night before Jesus died, Peter three times denied that he even knew Jesus. What could be worse? Yet after the Resurrection, Jesus welcomed Peter back and restored their relationship.

Rock-solid Guidance

Making good decisions is not always easy, but God and the Church offer us support. Natural law, the Ten Commandments, and, of course, God's grace help us. Something else the Church offers is a set of guidelines that help us grow in our love of God and neighbor. These are called the precepts of the Church (see appendix B, "Catholic Beliefs and Practices"). The precepts encourage us to do things that help us live the right way, such as worship with the community and seek forgiveness when we sin. When we participate in the life of the Church and make friends with people who are also trying to live the good life God wants for us, our decision making can be much easier than if we try to go it alone.

The teachings of the Pope and the bishops are a huge help to us too. In fact, their teachings are essential if we are to live as God wants us to live. They help us understand Christ's teachings and how they apply to the situations we encounter today. This is an important responsibility, and their

Key Words

venial sin
mortal sin
justification
Magisterium
doctrine

teachings have an important-sounding name to match: the Magisterium. The **Magisterium** is the official teaching authority of the Church. We can rely on the Magisterium's explanation of **doctrine**—teachings based on God's Revelation by and through Jesus Christ—because the Magisterium is infallible. This means the Magisterium is without error when it speaks about doctrine, including the teachings related to moral living. The Pope and the bishops uphold and explain the Church's moral teachings, helping us all to understand and live out these teachings.

Live It!

Moral decision making affects every part of our lives. Our consciences, and therefore our decisions too, can get clouded by advertising messages. We can't escape it, but we can control it.

Consider some of the following common things and the messages we get about them. How could you respond?

Clothing. Do fashion designers care about what clothing says about you, or do they just want their logos on your shirt? You can find great, inexpensive clothes at thrift shops.

Food. Companies may package and market their food to look cool or sexy, but is it good for you? Read labels and choose healthy options.

Technology. Does it make you cooler or actually distance you from "real time" with your friends? Set down the cell phone or MP3 and just enjoying being with people.

Brian Singer-Towns, Saint Mary's Pess

"Peter: you are a rock, and on this rock foundation I will build my church" (Matthew 16:18). With these words Jesus made Peter and all the popes that have followed him the spiritual and moral leaders of the Church.

Did You Know?

The Seven Deadly Sins

The Church warns us about seven very harmful sins. We call them capital, or deadly, sins because they lead us toward other sins and away from God. For example, the drive to have more and better stuff might lead us to steal, disrespect our parents, or value things over God. Following is a quick look at these sins:

- **pride:** the belief that you're better than others
- **greed:** an unhealthy desire for money and things
- **envy:** resentment against people who have more things, privileges, or success than you
- **wrath:** intense anger that leads us to get even instead of making things right
- **lust:** the out-of-control desire to enjoy yourself, especially in sexual ways
- **gluttony:** the practice of eating or drinking too much
- **sloth:** laziness, or slacking when action is needed

Honoring God

Praising and respecting God are important. Maybe your family made an extra effort on vacation to find a Mass on Sunday. Perhaps you've set aside your ego and taken the risk of singing in church, despite what your friends might think. Things like this may not seem like a big deal, but they're pleasing to God. Keep up the good work.

The First Commandment: For Starters, Honor God

In these next few chapters, we'll explore ways to live out the Ten Commandments, starting here with the commandments that focus on our love of God.

The First Commandment, "I am the LORD your God. You shall not have strange gods before me," calls us to love, believe, and hope in God.

When we pray to God, worship him as he deserves, and keep the promises we make to him, we're obeying the First Commandment.

Whenever we pray, whether at church or in a private place, it's important to give our full attention and try to block out distractions that might get in the way of our focus on God. Those distractions could include our cell phones or thoughts about that cute star in the movie you saw last week.

The First Commandment is first for a reason. Our happiness in life is based on it. Our relationship with God brings us great joy.

God makes it clear that he will "tolerate no rivals" (Exodus 20:5). That was the case when the Israelites broke the First Commandment by worshiping a golden calf. The story presents God as being so angry with his people that he threatens to destroy them.

"'Love the Lord your God with all your heart,
with all your soul, with all your strength,
and with all your mind'; and 'Love your
neighbor as you love yourself.'"
(Luke 10:27)

With stories like these, the Bible warns us against the dangers of false gods. Things like money, possessions, and popularity can become our golden calves—our idols.

PRAY IT!

O, God,
You are my God.
There are no others
in my life.
Give me the strength to
keep it that way.
Help me avoid things
that distract my focus
from you.
Keep my language clean
and my schedule clear.
Let my words and worship
praise only you.
Let nothing come between us.
Amen

Making these things more important than God is **idolatry** and violates the First Commandment. Another form of idolatry is superstition, which is the belief that a person or object has powers that actually belong only to God. A lucky rabbit's foot isn't lucky for the rabbit that lost it, and it won't do you any good, either. Likewise, a baseball slugger who taps his crucifix necklace three times before batting may be sad to know that God likes players on the other team too. Some people go much further, trying to foretell the future or placing their trust in some type of magic. All these practices deny the power of God and his plan for each of us.

It's wrong to disrespect or abuse religious practices. You may hear comedians ridicule the Catholic faith or

Did You Know?

Do the Math: The Eighth Day

Both Christians and Jews see Sunday as the first day of the week. It is the day of the Sun, the light that broke through the darkness on the first day of Creation.

Jews observe their Sabbath on Saturday, because God made it holy by resting on the seventh day from all the work he'd done. The Gospels tell us that Jesus rose the day after the Sabbath.

Saint Justin, who wrote the earliest description we have of the Lord's Day, noted that Christians gather on Sunday instead of the Sabbath not simply because it recalls the light of God's first Creation but also because we celebrate the Resurrection of Jesus, the Light of the World.

Though Sunday is the first day of the week in the calendar, the Church considers the Lord's Day to be the eighth day. Because the Bible speaks of seven days of Creation, the "eighth day" is a way of referring to the first day of a new creation.

Bill Wittman

We might think it strange that the Israelites worshiped a golden calf. But how can money, power, possessions, and popularity be the "golden calves" of today?

see artists do disgusting or violent things with crucifixes or holy statues. This is sacrilege, and it violates the First Commandment. Buying and selling spiritual favors also is a sin against the First Commandment. For example, a preacher should not promise to cure your illness for a $50 donation, nor should you believe you can buy your way into Heaven. Salvation and miracles come only from God, and it's wrong for humans to believe they can buy or control God's will.

Atheism, which is the denial of God's existence, is the most extreme way to break this commandment. Any person or political system that rejects God takes a tragic turn from God's love and other gifts.

Catholics make an important distinction between idolatry and veneration. Some Christians do not keep holy art or statues in their churches because they consider them close to idolatry. But look around most Catholic churches and you'll see a crucifix, statues of Mary and other saints, and other sacred images. Do we worship these things, as the Israelites bowed

FUN FACT

Catholics do a great job of keeping Ash Wednesday holy, even though it isn't a Sunday or a holy day of obligation. Catholic churches are usually packed that day. It's a great way to begin Lent. We are encouraged to attend Mass that day and receive the mark of the cross in ashes on our foreheads.

to the golden cow? No, we **venerate,** or meditate on these images as we pray. We believe that doing this is a way of honoring the presence of God in the world. Christians have rejoiced for nearly two thousand years that the Word of God became flesh when Jesus was born. Our belief in God's loving presence is strengthened by the ability to see God among us. We adore only God, but we respect God's presence in the life of Mary and the saints by praying with sacred images—this is not idolatry.

The Second Commandment: Don't Defame the Name

What's in a name? We like it when our friends call us by our names or by favorite nicknames. It can hurt when someone abuses our names, maybe by putting a mean adjective in front of them. We want people to respect our names and use them with love.

The Second Commandment, "You shall not take the name of the LORD, your God, in vain," is a clear call to respect God's name. It is so sacred that even today, some Jews will not speak or write God's name.

It is holy for us too, as Jesus teaches in the Lord's Prayer: "hallowed [holy] be thy name."

Listen to some everyday conversations, and you can hear that certain people struggle with the Second Commandment. Jesus invites us to call God by name but only in ways that respect and please God. Keeping this in mind helps us avoid abusing God's holy name.

And so, in honor of the name of Jesus all beings in heaven, on earth and in the world below will fall on their knees, and all will openly proclaim that Jesus Christ is Lord, to the glory of God the Father. (Philippians 2:10–11)

There are random and trivial uses of God's name, sometimes to get a laugh or sound cool. It's not cool to use God's name improperly, or in vain, which means for no real value. It's even worse to use the name of God, Jesus, Mary, or the saints in ways that are intentionally offensive. That's called blasphemy,

LIVE IT!

It's hard to change habits, especially when our language gets bad. Following are some ideas to try:

Find new ways to express frustration. Some people substitute similar words, like "gosh," "darn," and "snap," but these make it too easy to slip back to actual bad words. Try "Heavens!" instead. It sounds corny and may inspire you to say nothing at all.

Hold yourself accountable. Ask friends to join you in cleaning up your language. Make a "swear jar" and put a quarter in it whenever your friends catch you swearing. Give the money to a charity.

Remember God loves you. When Jesus faced his worst stress (see Mark 14:32–36), he called out to his Father, "Abba." You are a child of God. Call God's name with love when you need his help.

and you'll hear it on concert stages, from coaches in stadiums, and sometimes popping up in conversations among folks you hang out with. It's important to avoid the casual abuse of God's name before it gets out of control. (See the "Live It!" article.)

Sometimes a person will blurt out "I swear on the Bible" to try to convince you something is true. What's true is that there are only two times to take such oaths: either when you are testifying in court or when you are promising to uphold a law. Oaths like these are sacred promises, because they call on God to make sure that the witness tells the truth or the leader lives up to a commitment. If they don't, it's a false oath, calling God to be a witness to a lie. Lying under oath, which is called perjury, is a serious sin. It disrespects God, who is always faithful to his promises.

Think About It!

The Church requires that we observe the Lord's Day by attending Mass every Sunday or Saturday night. Unfortunately, not all Catholics attend Mass regularly. What are some reasons you could give someone for attending church every Sunday?

The Third Commandment: Keep Sunday Sacred

Sunday is supposed to be a day of rest, right? It may not seem that way when your parents wake you up for church on Sunday morning. But rest is more than just sleeping. Sunday is a day to celebrate our love of

© Andy Aitchison/Corbis

No 24/7 for my people! When God gave us the Sabbath, he gave us a break. A Jewish family lights the Sabbath candle at sundown on Friday.

God and re-create ourselves by refreshing our minds, bodies, and spirits, all for God's glory.

God rested on the seventh day, after the hard work of the first Creation. He established the **Sabbath** as "a day of rest dedicated to me" (Exodus 20:10). In the Jewish tradition, the Sabbath is from sundown Friday to sundown Saturday. Jews still observe the Sabbath through prayer, fasting, and worshiping together on Saturday. How did we Christians wind up with our holy day on Sunday?

The Third Commandment, "Remember to keep holy the LORD's Day," has a fresh ring to it, because what we're observing reflects the Christian practice of the Jewish Sabbath tradition. We celebrate the day on which Jesus rose from the dead to new life. It's a day on which we recall the new creation that started with his Resurrection.

The main way we keep the Lord's Day holy is by celebrating the Eucharist. Sunday is the Church's most important holy day, and going to Mass on Sundays and other holy days of obligation is a serious

People greet each other just before Mass begins. You wouldn't be late for a movie or a concert. Being on time for Mass on Sunday is important too.

© SW Productions/Brand X/Corbis

obligation for Catholics. Attending Mass on Sunday is one of the Precepts of the Church and to miss Mass without a serious reason is a sin (see appendix B, "Catholic Beliefs and Practices"). There's a reason behind this rule. You can stay in your room and pray for an hour every Sunday, but your Catholic faith is bigger than just you and God. There's something special and pleasing to God when his people come together with one heart, join their voices in song and prayer, hear God's Word proclaimed, and share the Body and Blood of Christ. It's important for the family of God to come together regularly, just as many families try to gather for meals as often as they can. God insists we make a date—Sunday or Saturday evening—to get together with each other and with him.

Along with avoiding activities on Sundays that keep us from going to Mass, we also should make time to relax our minds and bodies. Our lives are busier than ever, and God didn't make us to be slaves to our calendars and activities. For example, you could mow your neighbor's lawn on Saturday or on Monday after school instead of on Sunday. Your coach might keep scheduling practices on Sundays until you and your teammates explain why Sunday is important to you. It's a day to rest and catch up with your family, friends, and faith. We should strive to avoid making demands of other people that hinder them from observing the Lord's Day. Keeping Sunday holy in these ways brings us closer to becoming the people God made us to be.

KEY WORDS

idolatry
atheism
venerate
Sabbath

LOOKING BACK

Be Glad You Live Now

We can learn something by recalling how intensely God's laws are written and enforced in the Bible. For example, when it comes to working on the Sabbath, Moses quotes God as saying "You have six days to do your work, but the seventh day is to be sacred, a solemn day of rest dedicated to me, the LORD. Anyone who does any work on that day is to be put to death" (Exodus 35:2).

Blasphemy also was not taken lightly. In John's Gospel, a crowd asks Jesus whether he is the Messiah. When he replies, "The Father and I are one" (John 10:30), they pick up stones to kill him because they think he is blaspheming.

People aren't killed for such sins these days, but the zeal of the past might inspire us to take the first three commandments more seriously today.

PEOPLE OF FAITH

Saint Peter Claver

© 2009 Saint Mary's Press/Illustration by Vicki Shuck

Imagine being captured and thrown into a dark, dirty ship for a horrible two-month voyage. That was reality for some slaves brought to the New World in the 1600s.

When these slaves finally saw the sun again, they'd also see a smiling priest, Fr. Peter Claver. He was the "saint of slaves" in Cartagena, a major city in Colombia, in South America. He gave the newly arrived slaves food, medicine, and hope.

Peter was born in Spain. He was just 14 years old when he began

Saint Peter Claver is known as the "saint of slaves." Read about how Peter Claver was a small ray of hope for slaves after the torturous journey from freedom in Africa to slavery in the Americas.

© Bojan Brecelj/CORBIS

studying in Barcelona, in Spain, to be a priest. He felt a call to become a missionary. When it came time to set sail, Peter was so excited that he didn't say good-bye to his family.

Neither could the slaves he'd serve. They'd be chained with hundreds of others and packed into ships. They got little food or water, and many got sick or died. Father Peter and his helpers rushed to the ships to bury the dead, feed the living, and heal their wounds.

"This was how we spoke to them," Father Peter wrote, "not with words but with our hands and our actions" (Knights of Peter Claver, "St. Peter Claver, 1581–1654"). He sucked poison and tiny bugs from people's wounds. His Christian example was so powerful that he baptized more than 300,000 slaves, converting them to Christianity—the faith of their captors.

Father Peter knew slaves would never have freedom, but he worked tirelessly to give them hope. He led them to Jesus, who suffered like them and for them, and he prepared them for joy in Heaven.

HONORING FAMILY

Not that they'd admit this publicly, but in surveys, most teens say that one of their parents is their hero. They also rate family unity as their biggest value. The need for a strong, loving family is so great because God created us that way.

Of course, family life doesn't always seem so wonderful. For example, when a parent tells you "I'm doing this for your own good," it usually doesn't feel good. Some families have serious problems.

Eating together is healthy for both parents and children: physically, emotionally, and spiritually.

© Charles Gullung/zefa/Corbis

Most parents try hard to give their children all they need, especially love. Sometimes their love means the children won't get what they want. It's obvious that if a six-year-old wants to play with matches, a loving parent would never let that happen. But it might be less obvious to you that a loving parent would not let a thirteen-year-old stay out without a curfew. We often take for granted the good things parents do and focus too much on the times they don't let us do what we want to do. At such times, it helps to remember a few of the following things:

- **Only God is perfect, and God is love.** But sometimes even God says no.

- **Parents are older and wiser in many ways.** They got some of their wisdom by learning from their mistakes, which they do not want you to repeat.

- **Parents have authorities over them too.** The government is supposed to do what's best for everyone, and surely your parents doubt this at times. Ultimately, your parents must answer to God, who put them in charge of you.

PRAY IT!

Heavenly Father,
You use parents to create us.
You call parents to guide us.
Please strengthen our parents to be strong for us,
especially when we need them most.
Help us appreciate their patience and sacrifices.
Help us be patient and learn from their strengths and their mistakes
so we might someday be good parents too.
Amen

The Fourth Commandment: Honor Your Parents

Understanding this may help you respect your parents more. Through the Fourth Commandment, God calls us to honor our parents.

Honor means "to show great respect or courtesy." It's what we try to do on Mother's Day and Father's Day, but it should happen every day. You can honor your parents by doing chores the first time you are asked. Better yet, do things without being asked, or do more than they expect. If they ask about your day at school, share something interesting. They really do care. God put them in your life to care for you.

Our Church draws some clear connections between itself and the families that come together to worship and serve.

The Church is the family of God. The core of the Church, from its earliest days, has been families. In the Acts of the Apostles, we see entire families who become Christian at the same time. (See Acts 18:8.)

Our Church also looks at families as the domestic church. It looks at the way Jesus chose to grow up as a member of the Holy Family. Our families too are called to learn together by word and example.

Parents are called to teach their children about our faith and encourage them to consider how they might serve the Church. Parents also should introduce children to daily prayer and daily reading of the Scriptures.

Catholic parishes and schools can help parents fulfill the promise made at their child's Baptism: to raise their child in the faith.

Bill Wittman

Teach children how they should live, and they will remember it all their life.

(Proverbs 22:6)

When two people marry and have children, they take on a sacred responsibility. Every new life they bring into the world is a miraculous gift from God. Your parents have the duty to provide for your physical needs, like food, clothing, and shelter. They also are supposed to meet your spiritual needs. This includes teaching you about faith, prayer, and the virtues.

In fact, the Church wants each family to be a school of virtues. Your parents teach virtues through their words and actions. Simple words such as "I love you" or "I forgive you" teach powerful lessons. So does discipline.

THiNK ABoUT It!

Mary and Joseph surely were shocked when they discovered she was pregnant with Jesus. However, an angel told each of them, "Do not be afraid" (Matthew 1:20, Luke 1:30). While their child and their challenges were unique, they knew God would support them.

When people become parents, life is never the same. What are some ways your life might change if you someday became a parent? How could God guide and strengthen you for this task?

KEY WORDS

honor
discipline
society

You may see discipline as punishment, but think of it as a way of learning. In fact, the word *discipline* comes from the same root as *disciple*, which means "learner." **Discipline** simply means learning self-control by accepting the authority of your family. You and your parents are learning in a faith community called a family in the same way that disciples like Peter, John, and Mary Magdalene learned from Jesus.

They loved Jesus too, and their love inspired others to follow him. As a sign of your love, you give your parents respect, gratitude, obedience, and help. Your respect for them makes family life go more smoothly.

"Respect your father and mother" is the first commandment that has a promise added: "so that all may go well with you, and you may live a long time in the land." (Ephesians 6:2–3)

Celebrating milestones, like graduation, are opportunities for a parent to say, "You are my beloved child, with whom I am well pleased."

© Rob Lewine/CORBIS

Being Family Is Hard Work

Of course, respect between children and parents is a two-way street, as Paul writes to the Colossians: "Children, it is your Christian duty to obey your parents always, for that is what pleases God. Parents, do not irritate your children, or they will become discouraged" (3:20–21).

Your parents try to meet your basic needs, and that includes respect and encouragement. They should support you in your studies, your activities, and your plans for a vocation. They should teach and remind you that your first calling is to follow Jesus.

FUN FACT

It may seem odd that the Fourth Commandment relates to both our parents and our country. But people often use family terms such as *fatherland* when talking about their countries or *mother tongue* about their native languages. George Washington was the "father of our country." Even the word *patriot* comes from the Latin word for "father."

On Earth as It Is in Heaven

Jesus taught his disciples that God's Kingdom is not only in Heaven but also in our daily lives on earth. God wants us to help build a society that values truth, justice, freedom, and solidarity. **Society** is a community of people who depend on each other. We support our society by sharing with charities our talents, time, and money. We also need to support the government in its efforts to improve society.

PRAY IT!
Liturgy Connection

Listen closely the next time you're at a Baptism. The rite includes blessings for the child's parents. Your parents may have heard the following or similar words when you were baptized:

"May almighty God, who gives life on earth and in heaven, bless the parents of these children. They thank him now for the gift he has given them. May they always show that gratitude in action by loving and caring for their children."

Families are to be schools of virtue, teaching us those good habits that help us make good choices. Your parents' efforts to nurture your faith are their way of living up to a call they received at your Baptism.

Governments, for their part, are required to respect human rights and protect our ability to live in freedom. We are blessed with many rights, such as the right to gather with other people and the right to express our opinions. We need rights like these if we want to improve our world. We should never take these rights for granted, and neither should our government. Sometimes people question whether their government's laws are actually good for society. When governments take away people's freedom, then they are not following God's law.

When leaders take away our freedom, we can learn from the example of Jesus' first disciples. Things were going pretty well for them until the authorities felt threatened and ordered them to stop preaching about Jesus. Peter and the Apostles had the courage to say, "We must obey God, not men" (Acts 5:29), even though standing up like this might cost them their lives. When society's laws disrespect God's laws, we must resist, even to the point of disobeying the human-made laws.

When governments work well, they help us take care of one another. When our leaders fail to make good decisions, we are called to challenge them.

© Paul Colangelo/CORBIS

We can hope it never comes to that, but it's up to us to make sure our leaders' decisions and actions help lead us to our destiny. Do they lead us closer to or further away from the love and justice Jesus described when he taught about God's Kingdom? We need to speak out, so what the Gospels teach inspires our leaders as they make rules

Live It!

If you wrote an advice book for parents, you might be tempted to push for bigger allowances or later curfews. Your parents can learn from you, but they learned much about parenting from the way they were parented. Likewise, you can learn a lot from them. So pay attention to your parents and how they deal with their joys and pressures.

How do they spend their time? Their work can be demanding but necessary to support your family. How much time do they devote to your activities or helping you with homework? Do they have time for themselves? Do they discipline with love and respect? Do they provide good advice? Are they good listeners? Do they guide you in your faith? Ask them about their prayer lives, or better yet, be part of them. Take time to pray with, and for, your parents.

409

that govern us. If we don't, our leaders might abuse their powers and may even become dictators.

A good example of the need to resist immoral laws is slavery, or treating people like property that can be bought and sold. For centuries many nations, including the United States, had laws allowing slavery. Committed people called abolitionists, often led by Christians, fought to make slavery illegal.

We'd like to think that people have learned from the mistakes of the past.

Are the days gone forever when society allowed people to abuse other people? No, we still see bullying and discrimination in our society, and we know that slavery still exists in some parts of the world, including the United States. Again, we must lift up the moral law that forbids slavery. We shouldn't allow power or money to warp the way we look at people. Bad things surely happen if we do.

When we broaden our vision and see all people as part of our human family, good things happen. When both neighbors and strangers value and respect each other as children of God, we get a glimpse of the joy that Jesus told us is possible.

Looking Back

When Jesus Was a Kid

Jesus was twelve years of age when he became separated from his
parents for nearly three days. They looked all over for him. When his
mother finally found him, she asked, "Son, why have you done this
to us? Your father and I have been terribly worried trying to find
you" (Luke 2:48). Jesus was hanging out in the Temple, amazing the
teachers. He tried to explain himself: "Didn't you know that I had
to be in my Father's house?" (Luke 2:49). They did not understand
his answer.

Jesus caused his parents stress, just as we may do at times. But
the Scriptures tell us he obeyed them. When we see the love, sacrifice, and patience of the Holy Family, we see a great model for today's
families.

RESPECTING LIFE

It's a recipe for chaos. Take 5-pound sacks of flour and add high school students. Stir up everyone's creative juices by pretending the sacks are babies and the students are their parents. Then let things bake for a week.

What this recipe yields depends on the human ingredients. If teens are not responsible, the "baby" rolls off the car roof as "Mom" drives home from school. Poof! The more caring "parents" guard every teaspoon of their precious bundle. Either way, in this common high school assignment, young people learn that taking care of babies requires a lot of time and effort. Hopefully they also learn that life is a gift to be respected and protected.

Unlike flour "babies," we humans, from the moment we are conceived until the time we die, are sacred. That's because God makes us in his image. This puts us in a special relationship with the living God. He is the sole reason for our being. No one can take away this dignity or make cookies out of us!

People's rights begin before they are born. We are human at our conception. That's when a mother's egg and a father's sperm unite to create life. Unborn children have the rights of any person, starting with the right to life itself. **Abortion** is intentionally ending an unborn child's development. Choosing and performing abortions is a serious sin. In 1973 abortions became legal in the United States. Other nations allow it, as well. As we learned earlier, though, just because something is legal doesn't make it moral. Abortion is a major violation of moral law. Though Catholics lead the fight against abortion, the moral truth about it should be obvious to people regardless of their faith backgrounds.

As mentioned, people's rights exist before they are born. So an unborn baby must be cared for like any human. This includes medical care for the baby and its mother. This can be as simple as a mother's eating properly and getting enough rest. On the other extreme, doctors can perform procedures to protect or heal an unborn child. The Church supports this.

PRAY IT!

Dear Lord,
You created us in your image.
You made us good.
Help us do good by respecting and protecting all life.
Let us be life giving in our words and actions.
Let us speak out for those who can't speak for themselves
and make our world a better, safer place for all people to live.

Amen

Pictures from inside the womb help us realize how beautifully made babies are—long before birth.

Shutterstock

From Womb to Tomb

We learn a lot about life early in the Bible. God creates Adam and Eve, and he is proud of his work. He calls them good. After all, they're like him. Then they have two children. God is not pleased when Cain kills Abel. He makes it clear to Cain that killing is wrong. God even protects Cain from being killed by someone else in revenge (see Genesis 4:1–15).

> Then God said, "And now we will make human beings; they will be like us and resemble us."
> (Genesis 1:26)

In God's eyes, and ours, every human life is sacred from the moment a person is conceived until his or her natural death. The key word here is *natural*. Murder, the act of killing someone on purpose, is a sin against the sacredness of life. It's a rejection not only of the victim but also of the holiness of God, who made them good.

Simple steps can lead to the extreme action of murder. Our respect for life can be eroded by violent video games and TV shows. We need to be careful not to let outside influences lead us to believe that violence is okay.

There's just one situation when a person may kill another person. That's when there's no other way to stop someone from hurting the person or someone else. If someone is in a kill-or-be-killed situation, then **legitimate defense** makes it necessary to protect oneself or others. Of course, we need to avoid taking the life of someone who threatens us. For example, if a thief threatens to hurt you and demands your MP3 player, it's best to let him have it instead of fighting for it. Your tunes are less valuable than your life or the thief's life.

FUN FACT

Hearing is one of the last senses to develop in an unborn baby. But babies can hear us in there. Experts say babies recognize their mother's voice immediately after birth. Babies will respond to stories and songs they heard in the womb. In studies of great musicians, it is often found that exposure to good music began in the womb.

The Fifth Commandment: Living and Dying with Dignity

The Fifth Commandment, "You shall not kill," deals with many more situations than you'll see on a prime-time crime show on TV.

God made life good, but the paradise he created for us seems to wither with every bad choice people make. Sometimes life can seem out of control, too hard to live. But **suicide,** the taking of your own life, is not the answer. It rejects God's great love, the gift of hope, and the call to respect our lives and the lives of others. "You shall not kill" includes not killing yourself. Suicide goes way beyond the person who commits it. It hurts God and our neighbors. It tears up the victim's family and friends. It deprives the world of the victim's many gifts.

Suicide is a permanent solution to temporary problems. Telling a trusted adult about someone (including yourself) who is in great emotional pain can save a life!

© Kelly Redinger/Design Pics/Corbis

Sometimes people with fatal diseases or those who are suffering great pain seek the wrong kind of help. They may feel they have the right to die. Sometimes patients may be incapable of making their own decisions, but family members may want to alleviate a patient's suffering by ending his or her life. Putting an end to the lives of people because they are suffering is wrong. It is called **euthanasia.** Regardless of how or why it is done, euthanasia is murder. Remember that for an action to be moral, the act itself, not just the intention, must be good. (See chapter 33.) Euthanasia is a sin against the Fifth Commandment. Choosing to end life denies the dignity of the person and the respect due to God, who created them. Prayer, hospice programs, and pain medicines make it possible to avoid the temptation of euthanasia. They allow people to die with dignity.

Sometimes a decision is made to not use extraordinary means to keep a person alive. Deciding not

PRAY IT!
Liturgy Connection

Listen closely at Mass to the many ways we refer to God's creative power, such as the following:

- "Maker of Heaven and Earth"
- "The Giver of Life"
- "Lord, God of All Creation"

One special practice is to bow during the profession of faith when we say "by the power of the Holy Spirit he was born of the Virgin Mary, and became man."

This bow shows our great respect and thanks to Jesus who, even though he is God, lived among us as a human. He came to save us from sin and restore us to friendship with God.

At Christmas and on the Feast of the Annunciation, we show even greater respect by genuflecting as we pray these words.

to offer this help is not the same as euthanasia. Discontinuing certain medical treatments can be moral when the intention is not to cause death, even if such a decision means that the person will die sooner than they would with the treatment.

Think About It!

Even if you've never taken care of a baby or even seen a baby, you once were a baby. We all have been vulnerable and have depended on others to meet our needs. What are some of a baby's greatest needs? food? protection? love? What gifts does God provide us to take care of babies, elderly people, or people with special needs?

The World We Live In

Wedged in between the Bible's first stories of life and death is a story of the first scandal. It's a big one.

The story of a woman and a man eating an apple may not seem scandalous compared to today's tabloid news. But **scandal** is simply an action or an attitude—or the failure to act—that leads someone to sin. It's a serious problem, and perhaps no story captures this better than Adam and Eve.

"If anyone should cause one of these little ones to lose his faith in me, it would be better for that person to have a large millstone tied around his neck and be drowned in the deep sea." (Matthew 18:6)

This story is called the Fall, and it's where we first witness the sinful nature of humans. Adam represents all of us, and in the story we see temptation harm his relationship with God. Our spiritual lives are hurt today when we see cigarette companies enticing youth to smoke, celebrities wearing sexy clothing, or adults scheduling youth sports on Sunday mornings. Respect for life means caring for our spiritual lives too.

Nothing is more harmful to the human spirit than war. We discussed earlier that at times a person, or even a nation, must defend itself from someone who threatens it. These situations must be avoided however possible. "War is not always inevitable," Pope John Paul II said in 2003. "It is always a defeat for

Live It!

There are many ways to help prevent abortion. For starters, you and your friends can promote chastity. A single person who is chaste does not have sex outside marriage. You might go public with your beliefs by joining a Life Chain event or writing a letter to your legislator.

What would you do if a girl you know became pregnant? What could you do if she thought abortion was her only option?

First, listen. Don't judge. Offer your friendship. Strongly encourage her to tell her parents, a pastor, or a school counselor. Contact an organization like Birthright. Help her learn more about adoption. Many loving families are eager to adopt.

Consider donating money to an agency that helps teenage mothers. You might also organize a baby shower to collect needed baby items.

Above all, pray that expectant mothers always choose life.

humanity" ("Address of His Holiness Pope John Paul II to the Diplomatic Corps"). Because of the many evils and injustices war brings, we must avoid it if at all possible.

Even if nations can't—or won't—avoid war, they must follow the requirements of moral law as they fight the war. This means they must follow universally accepted laws. These include giving respect and humane treatment to wounded soldiers, to prisoners, and especially to people who aren't fighting. Such laws protect the innocent and prevent forces from wiping out entire nations or ethnic minorities. This wiping out is called genocide, and no matter the risk to themselves, soldiers must resist orders calling for such brutal use of force.

As military superpowers in the 1960s built up huge stockpiles of weapons that could wipe out huge cities and their people, the Church spoke out. "The arms race is one of the greatest curses on the human

The "seamless garment" approach to life includes opposition to the death penalty as well as to abortion. Read more about this consistent ethic of life in the "Looking Back" sidebar on the next page.

© Reuters/COR

Looking Back

Weaving the Seamless Garment

Cardinal Joseph Bernardin of Chicago was a strong advocate for the protection of all life, from conception to a natural death. He described a "seamless garment" of life. A garment without seams is made from just one piece of cloth. This image is meant to convey the importance of protecting all life. He believed that being prolife included opposing abortion, the death penalty, war, poverty, and other issues affecting a person's dignity and right to life. It is not enough to focus on one issue only.

His own dignity was threatened when a man falsely accused him of sexual abuse. Cardinal Bernardin did not respond with anger. He reached out to the man with compassion. The man later admitted to lying.

Soon after that, the cardinal was diagnosed with terminal cancer. He lived his final days bravely, praying with other cancer victims as their spiritual friend.

race and the harm it inflicts on the poor is more than can be endured" (CCC, number 2329). Decades later, we still see people lacking food, shelter, medicine, education, and other necessities while their leaders invest in weapons and warfare. This is sinful. The Church is well known for protecting unborn babies. We also want to improve the world into which they're born.

"I was hungry and you fed me, thirsty and you gave me a drink;
I was a stranger and you received me in your homes, naked
and you clothed me; I was sick and you took care of me,
in prison and you visited me." (Matthew 25:35–36)

PEOPLE OF FAITH

Jean Vanier

© 2009 Saint Mary's Press/Illustration by Vicki Shuck

Jean Vanier's great respect for life has opened doors. Many people with mental disabilities who might be in institutions now live in loving homes because of what he calls "a yearning for love." It has grown with him from his youth into old age, as he changes the world one heart at a time.

Jean was a young naval officer, focused on war and discipline, when he first felt the yearning. He set out to "find what was most important inside of myself, which was my heart."

Jean met a priest who made him aware of thousands of people with disabilities living in institutions. In 1964, Jean felt God call him to invite two men, Raphael and Philippe, to leave their institutions and live with him in a house in France.

Their home was named "L'Arche" after Noah's ark. L'Arche has grown to 130 communities worldwide, where caregivers and people with mental challenges live in loving, faith-based homes.

Jean's ministry honors God, but it also has helped him grow: "To be human is that capacity to love which is the phenomenal reality that we can give life to people," he says. "We can transform people by our attentiveness, by our love, and they can transform us."

Respecting Truth and Property

Have you ever worried about forgetting your school locker combination? That's normal but nothing to lose sleep over. But imagine if you arrived at your locker tomorrow and all your stuff was gone. Or what if someone wrote something nasty about you on your locker door? In both cases you'd feel violated because you were robbed of something.

Since you were little, you've heard messages like "Keep your hands to yourself" and "Share with the whole class." As we grow older, and the things we own become more valuable, these messages seem even more important.

The Seventh Commandment: Take It to the Limit

The Seventh Commandment, "You shall not steal," forbids theft, or taking someone's belongings without

How would you feel if someone trashed your locker and stole your things? Why is the Seventh Commandment, "You shall not steal," so important?

© Jeffrey Coolidge/Corbis

that person's permission. There are many kinds of things to steal and many ways of stealing them. We need to explore how far this commandment reaches.

For example, just as you'd be hurt if your locker were raided, your favorite band is hurt when people copy their recordings without paying for them. It doesn't matter if the band isn't aware it's happening or if the band members are superrich. They and others involved in making and selling the recording are still being stolen from.

If you studied hard for a test, anyone who might copy your answers is not only cheating but also stealing from you. It's your work. Others have no right to take it from you.

PRAY IT!

Lord,
It can be easy to
find words to tear
people down,
cheap words that
find flaws in
others or hurt
the people I envy.
Forgive me when I use
words to harm others.
Help me find words
to heal and to forgive
when I've been hurt.
Help me find words to
lift up the good gifts in
others and to praise you
for all you've done for me.
Amen

Illegal music downloads are a form of stealing. "Everybody's doing it" arguments make it more tempting, but that doesn't make it right.

© Anna Peisl/zefa/Corbis

Every way you can imagine of taking and using someone's property unjustly is a sin against the Seventh Commandment. No matter what was stolen or how it was taken, the thieves need to make the situation right. They need to make **restitution,** which means returning what they took. If they damaged someone's property, they need to make **reparation,** which means somehow fixing or replacing it.

Live It!

If you're anxious about how your life fits into God's big plan, read Matthew 6:24–34. Following are some ways to apply its advice to your life:

- You cannot serve both God and money. Add up what you spend your money on. How much could you afford to give to your parish and other charities?
- Don't worry about food or clothes. Could this be a call to fast, either from junk food or designer clothing?
- Don't worry. When you're worried, try praying instead.
- Seek God's Kingdom and his holy ways. Spend less time with technology or other things that distract you from talking with God.

Try living out the call to holiness found in this passage. Your results may vary, but see if it brings you more peace. You might become more content with the good gifts God provides.

We must balance our right to own and protect our property with the principles of justice. The right to have everything we could possibly want seems trivial when weighed against the needs of people who own little or nothing. Charities try to grab our attention with TV commercials of starving children. Some studies say that about 16,000 children die every day due to hunger-related diseases. Meanwhile, Americans, who make up only 5 percent of the world's population, consume 30 percent of its resources. There's something wrong with this picture.

"Much is required from the person to whom much is given." (Luke 12:48)

Imagine that one person in this group of twenty gets one-third of the pizza. The other nineteen have to split the rest. The world's resources are divided in a similar way. How fair is that?

PRAY IT!
Liturgy Connection

Have you ever wondered why the priest washes his hands at Mass? A lot of people think it has something to do with Pontius Pilate. They are wrong.

In the early Church, people sometimes offered gifts such as live chickens. These were brought up with the bread and wine at the offertory. So it was necessary for the priest to wash up after this. Now the priest washes his hands to symbolize his desire for purity of heart.

It's still important that we share what we have with the Church. Consider how your gifts can help make the Church stronger. Bring cash or checks, but please, no chickens!

God created the world's resources for everyone to share. The need to share the world's resources is more important than our right to own as much property as we can get. The unequal distribution of the world's resources could be reversed if each of us tried harder to live simply so others may simply live. The Seventh Commandment calls us to be fair and charitable in the way we share earthly goods and the fruits of human labor. Saint Basil, a great leader of the Church in the fourth century, made this connection long ago:

> When someone steals another's clothes, we call that person a thief. Should we not give the same name to one who could clothe the naked and does not? The bread in your cupboard belongs to the hungry; the coat unused in your closet belongs to the one who needs it; the shoes rotting in your closet belong to the one who has no shoes; the money you hoard up belongs to the poor.

How often do you contribute your own money to the collection at Mass?

i-stock

The Tenth Commandment: The Danger of Envy

Despite how much you might have, it's likely that someone else has more or better stuff than you. Just as it's wrong to steal what belongs to others, it's also wrong to become obsessed with it. The Tenth Commandment, "You shall not covet your neighbor's goods," forbids an unhealthy desire for wealth and the power that comes with it.

Envy, one of the capital sins (see chapter 33), is being jealous about the things other people have to a point of wanting their stuff for yourself. As Christians, we can humbly accept the reality that we all have different gifts and material things. We can even thank God for another person's good fortune. While those attitudes may be hard to reach, we start by trusting that God will provide all we need.

"So do not start worrying 'Where will my food come from? or my drink? or my clothes?' . . . Your Father in heaven knows that you need all these things. Instead, be concerned above everything else with the Kingdom of God and with what [God] requires of you, and he will provide you with all these other things." (Matthew 6:31–33)

FUN FACT

You can't take your possessions to Heaven, but you can take your team loyalty to the grave. Casket makers now produce models featuring the logos and colors of your favorite football or baseball teams. For a few hundred dollars more than a normal casket, you can customize your casket, and you can stand out among everybody buried at your cemetery!

Think About It!

What's the one item you own that would hurt the most to have taken by a thief? Why is that? Is it because of its material value or its sentimental worth?

What would hurt more—to lose that item to a thief or to have your reputation damaged by gossip or rumors?

Jesus told his disciples to travel lightly (see Matthew 10:9). That's good advice for us as we head for Heaven. Not only is it impossible to bring our stuff to Heaven, but we must let go of our desire for riches if we're to enter God's Kingdom. As Jesus said, "It is much harder for a rich person to enter the Kingdom of God than for a camel to go through the eye of a needle" (Luke 18:25).

The Eighth Commandment: What's in a Name?

Words can damage a person. Let's say someone stole everything you own. If you have a good reputation, you can still hold your head high. But imagine if someone damages your reputation by, let's say, spreading false gossip about you. That can hurt worse than losing all your material possessions. Tearing down people, especially with false or mean words, is sinful. Even if the gossip is true, spreading it lessens the person's honor and reputation, which we must respect.

The Eighth Commandment, "You shall not bear false witness against your neighbor," means practicing the virtue of truthfulness. We must be true in what we say and what we do. We must avoid saying one thing and doing another. Jesus tells a story of a man with two sons. One son promises to go work in the vineyard but doesn't, while the other son says he won't work but does (see Matthew 21:28–32). In this story, Jesus makes clear that it's important to be true to your word. Lying is nothing more than saying something false to deceive someone.

Just as when we rob others of their possessions, we also need to make reparation when we commit a sin against the truth, especially when it hurts someone's honor or reputation.

The Sacrament of Penance and Reconciliation always restores our relationship with God. The sacrament can also help in the hard work of making things

LIVE IT!

"Don't believe everything you read in the newspaper" used to be a common warning. It's still good advice, but with the growth of the Internet, blogs, online encyclopedias, and other information sources, we should be more careful than ever. Society has a right to information based on truth and rooted in justice. Whichever side of the media you're on—providing information or using it—you should be cautious and fair.

For example, the Internet gives everyone the opportunity to be a reporter or to be news. Be truthful if you use Web sites that allow you to post personal pages. Don't give too much information or make yourself out to be someone you're not. Be cautious about believing or responding to what others say.

right with people we've hurt. A priest can help you figure out the best way of making reparation to others.

Telling the truth does not mean sharing private information that could hurt another person. For example, a priest must always keep secret everything we

PEOPLE OF FAITH

Archbishop Oscar Romero

© 2009 Saint Mary's Press/Illustration by Vicki Shuck

Imagine being a poor farmer in a land ruled by the rich. They could force you off your farm. If you protested, you might be kidnapped, tortured, or killed. This was El Salvador in the 1970s.

In 1977 Oscar Romero became archbishop of San Salvador, the capital city of El Salvador. Soon his friend Fr. Rutilio Grande was killed. Father Grande had spoken boldly on behalf of the poor. Romero realized that Jesus was executed for the same reason.

Every Sunday, poor El Salvadorans found hope as they listened to Romero preach on the radio.

confide to him when we make our confession. You also must not share confidential information with people who might use that information to hurt another person or group.

"How beautiful will be the day when a new society, instead of selfishly hoarding and keeping, apportions, shares, divides up, and all rejoice because we all feel we are children of the same God!" he said. "What else does God's word want in El Salvador's circumstances but the conversion of all, so that we can feel we are brothers and sisters?" (Brockman, *The Violence of Love*, page 186).

Thousands of El Salvadorans, including many priests and catechists, died in the struggle for rights and dignity.

"Anyone committed to the poor," Romero said, "must suffer the same fate as the poor. And in El Salvador, we know the fate of the poor: to be taken away, to be tortured, to be jailed, to be found dead" (Brockman, *The Violence of Love*, page 192).

On March 24, 1980, Romero was killed while celebrating Mass. Those behind his murder may have hoped to silence him. But his spirit lives on in the El Salvadoran people.

RESPECTING SEXUALITY

You don't have to look far to see sexuality on display. Ads use it to sell burgers and blue jeans. TV shows treat sex as a competition. Music stars wear outfits that leave little to the imagination. It's all out there.

Sexuality is more than sex. **Sexuality** is your identity as a male or female, your interest in and desire for sexual activity. Sexuality is one of the greatest of life's gifts. As your body grows and changes, this gift becomes a stronger influence in your life. You'll find it challenging to respond to outside temptations and inner urges in a way that respects the gift and its giver—God.

People today are constantly bombarded with sexual messages. Read this chapter to learn about sexual integrity in a sex-saturated society.

iStockphoto

Our bodies are evidence of God's great love. This is because through our bodies, we are able to love God and others. Jesus tells us that the way we love others shows our love for God. He tells us to love others as we love ourselves.

How do you want to be loved? Do you think your desire pleases God?

> The body is not to be used for sexual immorality, but to serve the Lord.
> (1 Corinthians 6:13)

The Sixth Commandment: Sexuality Is a Gift

God was pleased by the way he made us: "God created human beings, making them to be like himself. He created them male and female" (Genesis 1:27). Your gender, that is, whether God created you as a male or as a female, is a gift. Both males and females reflect God's image in ways that are unique to each gender. By embracing and living our roles as males or females, we give glory to God. We are able to reach the full potential God wants for us.

Pray It!

Everybody's
 doing it, Lord.
Everybody's doing a lot of
 wondering about sex.
Some people are worrying.
Some people are tempting,
 and it seems everybody
 is tempted.
Some people are feeling weak.
Keep me strong, Lord.
Give me temperance
 and patience,
with myself and others,
to save the gift of my body,
 that I may someday
 share it with my spouse
 and celebrate love in a
 way that honors you.
 Amen

God also gave us personal dignity by creating us with different genders. Each of us should realize and accept our identities as males or females.

Like many gifts, the gift of our sexuality can be misused. Jesus came to free people from the death that sin causes. The Bible tells many tales of how sexual sins damage our relationships with God, others, and ourselves. Jesus restores proper relationships simply by being a model of sexual wholeness and purity, or **chastity.** He calls us to be honest and healthy by respecting his gift, the sexuality of ourselves and others.

The Sixth Commandment challenges us to "not commit adultery." Adultery is sexual relations between two people, at least one of whom is married to another. But every person is called to be sexually pure, married or not.

Did You Know?

Marriage

The Sacrament of Matrimony is important in God's plan. Married people have a responsibility to protect their relationship from all things that would hurt or destroy it. Obviously adultery is a big threat to marriage. Having more than one spouse, or polygamy, also goes against God's plan for true marriage.

Marriage is one man and one woman sharing a love that is total, unique, and exclusive. Living together in a sexual relationship without being sacramentally married is another offense to marriage.

Sometimes married couples aren't able to resolve conflicts, and they separate or divorce. Divorce, however, is not part of God's plan. It separates what God has joined together and creates upheaval that can harm families and even society.

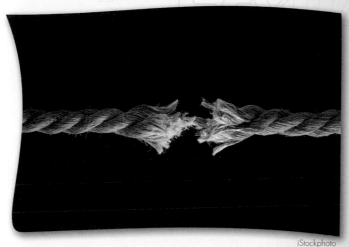

A rope unravels a little bit at a time. So can someone's sexual integrity. What are some of the consequences of giving in to sexual temptations?

iStockphoto

It's important not to let our body's urges overwhelm our minds and spirits. Our bodies, minds, and spirits weave together into our personal integrity. Chastity holds us together when temptations threaten to unravel our integrity. Discipline, prayer, and an awareness of God's commandments and virtues help. We also need patience and persistence. Remember that becoming the master of our desires is a lifelong process.

Sexual Integrity

Before we explore ways people struggle with self-control, let's see why the Church cares so much about sex taking place only in marriage. God created sex for three purposes: to make new life, to express a loving union between a husband and wife, and to give joy to the married couple. These purposes must be woven into the minds, bodies, and spirits of a couple.

When one or two of these purposes is missing, sex fails to reflect our love for God. Sometimes young

PRAY IT!
Liturgy Connection

When you hear "Let us offer each other the sign of peace" at Mass, most folks shake hands pretty casually. This sign goes back to the early Church, when Christians exchanged a kiss of peace before Communion. Paul encouraged these Christians often to "greet one another with the kiss of peace" (Romans 16:16).

This simple embrace, also called a holy kiss, reflected the caring love of God, not romantic, human love. Then, and now, it's how we show we're at peace before we receive Jesus, the Prince of Peace. Jesus teaches us to "make peace with your brother" (Matthew 5:24) before we come to the altar. Remember this as you share the gift of peace.

people get lost in lust and then engage in sex. Lust, the intense and uncontrolled desire for sexual pleasure, is different from love. Unfortunately, people caught up in pursuing only pleasure have little commitment to their partners. They also don't think about the baby that could result or the people who would share the challenge of raising it.

For these reasons, sex shouldn't be treated as a plaything. Sex outside marriage, which the Bible calls fornication, dissolves our sexual wholeness. It may seem like everybody's doing it, but studies show that the majority of teenagers are not. That false perception, or using it as an excuse to sin, is just wrong.

God wants you to be holy and completely free from sexual immorality.
(1 Thessalonians 4:3)

Another challenge to chastity is masturbation. This is genital activity alone or with another person that stops short of sexual intercourse. It's a selfish pleasure that can easily become addictive. There's no possibility of creating life, so people just use—or abuse—themselves. It's also

Why is it more special to wait until your birthday or Christmas to open your gifts? Imagine the joy of a bride and groom who wait until their wedding day to give each other the gift of sex.

iStockphoto

no way to prove love to another person. Oral sex, for example, not only exploits the other person but also can cause sexually transmitted infections. The greatest damage, though, is the cost of quick pleasure today to that priceless bond with your spouse in the future.

Pornography—explicit images or written descriptions meant to stimulate sexual feelings—cheapens our sexuality and is costly to human dignity. Pornography is more widespread than ever. The exploitation that once was limited to magazines now floods the Internet. Some young people, perhaps trying to be cool, even post sexual photos of themselves online. Porn is dangerous because it's so addictive. It warps a person's view about the true goodness of sexuality.

KEY WORDS

sexuality
chastity
pornography
homosexuality

Homosexuality

Homosexuality requires special focus and care as we discuss sexuality. Some people have strong sexual attractions to people of the same gender. This is sometimes called having a homosexual orientation. Our Church affirms that people with homosexual orientations are children of God. They must be treated with respect and compassion.

While our Church welcomes people with homosexual orientations, homosexual acts are sinful because they are contrary to natural law and because new life can't result from them. As we said earlier, all people are called to be sexually pure, according to their states in life. Homosexual people face a lifelong challenge of self-control. God's grace and their own prayers, along with the prayers and support of all in the Church community, will help them on their journey.

FUN FACT

The Church uses the image of the loving bond between a man and a woman in marriage to describe its relationship with Christ. Jesus calls himself the bridegroom. His love is so strong that he gave up his life for the Church. That's why you may hear the Church referred to as the Bride of Christ.

Before You Say "I Do"

No other commitment we can make to a person compares to marriage. God knows this. He created sexual intercourse to be an expression of love only between married partners.

Before a couple takes marriage vows, the two people are asked the following: "Have you come here freely and without reservation to give yourselves to each other in marriage?" They make a free choice to enter into a faithful love, and for the rest of their lives they uphold this covenant to be faithful in their marriage. Right after the vows, you'll hear the following words: "What God has joined, men must not divide." This applies to all who hear it, including the couple.

A married couple faces many challenges, including keeping the vow to "accept children lovingly from God." The two people in a couple usually have an idea of how many kids they'll have and when they'll have them. So does God.

The two people in a couple share in God's creative power, and that gives them a powerful responsibility. They may wish to space the births of their children, but they must do this through natural methods. Though the two may have good reasons to avoid pregnancy, this is not an excuse to use morally wrong methods. These methods include being surgically sterilized, using chemical contraceptives, or using barrier methods such as a condom or diaphragm.

THiNK About It!

Some people are okay with being just friends with each other, while others always feel like they need to be going out with somebody. Some classmates may say that going on dates or experimenting sexually is a sign you're cool. Ads and media seem to rush you into relationships before you are ready.

How do you tune out the outside pressures and be yourself? How can you be sure your comfort level with relationships pleases God?

The Ninth Commandment: Keeping Your Heart Clean

The Wise Choice

A little knowledge can be risky. Consider the story of Adam and Eve. When they ate from the tree of knowledge, they "realized they were naked; so they sewed fig leaves together and covered themselves" (Genesis 3:7).

You're wise enough to know that lust arises when people dress or act immodestly. You know what can happen if you have sex.

The only sure way you can avoid pregnancy and please God is not having sex. Sexual abstinence—not having sex until you are married—is your wise choice. You'll find plenty of advice about sex and birth control. It mostly comes from agencies that profit from birth control and abortions.

Abstinence is 100 percent safe and moral. As you get ready to wed, the Church can teach you natural family planning. For now, rest assured that abstinence is the right choice.

There's more to the Sixth Commandment than meets the eye, and even more guidance in the Ninth, "You shall not covet your neighbor's wife." This goes beyond wanting someone's wife or husband. It speaks toward the tendency in all of us to sin, as a result of Original Sin. This is called concupiscence, or when we're talking about intense desire for sexual pleasure, it's called lust. This desire can overwhelm us, as the body rebels against the spirit. Lust messes up our ability to make good moral decisions. It becomes a daily struggle.

My friends, fill your minds with those things that are good and that deserve praise: things that are true, noble, right, pure, lovely, and honorable. (Philippians 4:8)

We're not alone. The Holy Spirit gives us temperance, a virtue that helps us overcome our passions (see chapter 32). It's a wonderful case of God's providing a virtue to fight a sin. With sexual temptation all around us, avoiding it is not always so simple. Chastity has to be our lifestyle, and it begins as we purify our hearts by focusing our desires on God's plan for sexuality.

Live It!

Keeping our hearts pure means we must keep the rest of our bodies clean too. Following are some clean thoughts:

Your eyes. Watch what you watch. Avoid TV shows and movies that trivialize or cheapen the gift of love.

Your ears. Now hear this! Tune out songs with sexually tempting or abusive lyrics.

Your mouth. Don't tell jokes or use obscene language that cheapens sex or makes fun of people's bodies.

Your hands. Keep them to yourself, and while you're at it, fold them as you pray for strength against temptation.

Jesus says that if our eyes or hands make us lose our faith, we should get rid of them. He is exaggerating to make a point. If people really did this, there'd be a lot of blind people named "Lefty"! But Jesus wants us take seriously our call to keep our hearts and bodies pure.

What you wear sends a message about who you are. Choosing clothes that are attractive yet modest can help protect your sexual integrity.

Shutterstock

Our moral personalities are centered in our hearts. Jesus teaches us that "from your heart come the evil ideas which lead you to kill, commit adultery, and do other immoral things" (Matthew 15:19). On a more positive note, he also tells us "Happy are the pure in heart; they will see God!" (Matthew 5:8).

Purity of heart lets us see things from God's perspective. We see the body—ours and our neighbor's—as a dwelling of the Holy Spirit and evidence of God's beauty. Don't you hope other people see you in the same way? Trendy clothes, cosmetics, perfumes, or body sprays can't change your heart. Wouldn't you rather that people be attracted to who you are and what's inside you?

The virtue of modesty protects our intimate centers. The clothes we wear, what we say, and the way we act sexually send signals to others. When your shirt doesn't say or show too much, when your pants don't sag too low, or when you avoid using curse

words, you've chosen modesty. It's a choice not to
follow the crowd or rush toward a false sense of ma-
turity. Patience and self-discipline are keys to modesty,
which leads to purity of heart, and that puts us on the
two-way road to sexual respect.

LOOKING BACK

Fresh Start for a Good Heart

David was young when God sent Samuel to find a new king among
Jesse's sons. Seven sons were rejected. Finally came David, who was
out with the sheep. He was the youngest, but he had a good heart.

And a great life. He killed Goliath, wrote the Psalms, was Israel's
king for forty years, and was King Solomon's father and an ancestor
of Jesus.

Lust later devastated David. He committed adultery with Bath-
sheba, a married woman, and she became pregnant. Then he sent her
husband off to certain death in battle.

David realized his sin. "Create a pure heart in me, O God," he
prayed, "and put a new and loyal spirit in me" (Psalm 51:10).

Our hearts are sometimes weak. When we sin, we must show our
sorrow. Like David, we must seek a new start with God.

WORKING FOR JUSTICE

Hopeful voices often rise up on dark days. People hear about human tragedies or natural disasters and respond generously. "I just want to do my part," they'll say. Then they roll up their sleeves or open their wallets to help strangers.

But are folks always so willing to help others?

Imagine if they were. When we learn to love as God loves, we see strangers as neighbors. Our sacrificial actions can break down walls of hate and replace them with bridges of hope. Incredibly, we can help prevent future tragedies from happening.

When Hurricane Katrina happened, millions of people wanted to help. Are people always so willing to help others?

© Jerry McCrea/Star Ledger/Corbis

That We All May Be One

To love as God loves, it helps to understand what God is like. The Bible reveals that God is three Persons—Father, Son, and Holy Spirit—in one God. These three divine Persons are a communion of perfect love and peace. We must follow the example of the Holy Trinity by being a community that loves and cares for all people.

"I pray that they may all be one. Father! May they be in us, just as you are in me and I am in you. May they be one, so that the world will believe that you sent me." (John 17:21)

The Church works to transform our world into a loving community where people respect each other, share the earth's goods, and settle conflicts peacefully. Our goal is **social justice**—a respect for all creation and human rights that allows people to get what they need to live in dignity.

What do people need? It's more than just things such as food, shelter, clothing, and health care, although these

PRAY IT!

Lord,
When do we see you
hungry or thirsty?
When do we see you as
a stranger or an
outcast?
Open my eyes, Lord,
to help me see you
in the eyes of my sisters
and brothers in need.
Let my eyes shine with
welcome for the
strangers among us.
Let my eyes run with tears
of compassion for the
hurting.
Let my eyes focus more sharply
on the path that leads
to justice.
So that someday I'll gaze
forever in your eyes.
Amen

447

life goods are important. We need respect and the freedom to shape our own destinies. We also need life-giving relationships with other people. Sound complicated?

Suppose some bullies took your friend's lunch money. Would you offer her half your sandwich or just the crumbs left after you ate it? If you split the sandwich, how would you feel later in the day about being hungry? Would you consider forming a group to prevent bullying, so your friend isn't victimized every day?

Paul tells us we are Christ's body. Each of us is a unique part. "If one part of the body suffers, all the other parts suffer with it" (1 Corinthians 12:26). As a Christian you feel your friend's pain, and hopefully you respond with compassion, just as you'd hope she would if you needed help. We should see ourselves in other

Did You Know?

Charity and Justice

Imagine being hungry every day of your life. You don't need just food; you need also to change whatever is causing your hunger. The Church takes on both needs through works of charity and justice.

We begin with **charity,** which means working to meet people's immediate physical needs. But we also work for justice, which means challenging society to eliminate the things that cause people to be hungry, homeless, jobless, and so on.

Feeding someone is a work of charity. But you don't have enough food to share with every hungry person in the world. That's where justice comes in. Working for justice starts by asking, "Why are people hungry?" The hungry people might need jobs. If we bring people together to support job training programs, we help make the Good News happen.

What does sharing a lunch have to do with bullying? Read the story on these two pages. Then read the "Did You Know?" sidebar to find out how the story relates to charity and justice.

people, whether they're friends or strangers, and give them the same dignity and rights we hope they'll give us.

> "Love your neighbor as you love yourself."
> (Matthew 22:39)

Together for Good

If you decided to work to stop bullying in your school, you would be working for the **common good.** The common good happens when all people, either as individuals or groups, have the opportunity to fulfill all their needs more fully and easily. All groups—whether it's your parish, your school student council, or the U.S. Congress—must put people first. Catholic social teaching tells us we all have a duty to work together for the common good.

Our society should make it easier, not harder, to live in freedom and to practice virtues—the good habits that help us accomplish good things. A

The laws of every nation must be in keeping with God's law. What if they are not?

Shutterstock

PRAY IT!

Liturgy Connection

Be an intense listener at Mass. When you hear a reading from a prophet like Isaiah, think about his words of hope and to whom he was giving hope. Close your eyes when you listen to the Gospel and think about the people in the stories. What kind of fear or despair did they feel? What did these victims, outcasts, and sinners hope Jesus would do or say?

At its root, compassion means "to suffer with." Listen with compassion, feel the pain, and experience the joy Jesus brings.

country's laws should reflect God's law. And human laws must never require people to do anything against God's law. Sometimes we wish we could do our own thing, without having people tell us what to do. But as Pope John XXIII reminds us, we need people in authority "to work and care for the good of all."[1] (CCC, number 1897). Paul says that authorities are established by God and are "God's servants working for your own good" (Romans 13:4).

It doesn't always seem that way. Political leaders often are described as greedy, power hungry, or corrupt. They're not alone. All the way back to Adam, we see humans, including ourselves, making self-centered choices. The challenge for leaders is to be truly committed to the common good. Political leaders have to work for the good of all people and do it by respecting God's commandments—God's moral law.

Helping poor people is everyone's responsibility, but Jesus tells us to "not make a big show of it" (Matthew 6:2). We should give people what they need without taking away their pride. Giving poor people money and respect is pleasing to God.

Each person has God-given dignity. To maintain that dignity, we all must work to improve the common good. We must create and support organizations and institutions that improve human conditions. Society works for the common good and helps bring about social justice when it provides what people need to live out their God-given dignity.

People in Haiti, one of the poorest countries in the world, knew they needed to come together to overcome corruption, poverty, and hunger. Many Haitians united around a

FUN FACT

Saint Vincent de Paul was a French priest in the 1600s who helped poor people. A group named for him continues his great work. It's a wonder he ever got to do any good. Pirates captured Vincent soon after was ordained, and he was sold into slavery for seven years. But after this rough start, he still had plenty of time to do God's work of charity and justice.

© Shepard Sherbell/CORBIS SABA

Helping people in Haiti is an example of charity. Why is it important to also work for justice for the people of this poor country?

451

Give people fish, and they eat for a day. Teach them to fish, and they eat for a lifetime. How does this photo illustrate this saying?

© Rick D'Elia/Corbis

popular slogan: "Alone we are weak, together we are strong, all together we are the flood of justice."

Today, people continue to struggle for justice in Haiti and countries around the world. Their problems are complex and far bigger than any one person— or even the people of one country—can overcome alone. Though local, state, and national governments must work for the common good, we also need to organize society to work for justice on a global level. Organizations such as the United Nations (UN) and Catholic Relief Services (CRS) offer hope that injustice can be overcome when people come together.

The Secret Is Out

Catholic social teaching has been called our Church's best-kept secret, but its wisdom comes alive when we learn and live it.

Our moral vision of society begins with respect for human life and dignity. We are made in God's image, gifted with a soul, and redeemed by Jesus. So we all share an equal dignity, and we are all entitled to all the rights God intended humans to have. That goes for unborn babies, people dying in hospitals, even criminals in jail.

Catholic social teaching is concerned with making sure all people have what they need—food, clothing, shelter, health care, respect, education, work, freedom, and so forth—to live out the vocation God calls us to.

"Happy are you poor; the Kingdom of God is yours! . . . But how terrible for you who are rich now; you have had your easy life!" (Luke 6:20,24)

A good test for our society is to see how its poorest and weakest, or most vulnerable, members are doing. It is a social sin when the gap between the rich and poor is so great that some people live in extreme luxury while others go without food, jobs, homes, and health care. The gap between people who are rich and those who are poor in our world grows bigger every day, so we must work hard to bridge that sinful gap. We say the Church has an "option for the poor and vulnerable." This means the Church, like Jesus, who loved and helped so many people in need, must get involved when people's rights or well-being are

THINK ABOUT IT!

In the Creation story found in Genesis, God gives humans power, or dominion, over creation. What are some examples of choices humans have made that help preserve the environment? What are some examples of choices that have hurt the environment? What are some choices you can make to help care for God's creation?

453

being damaged. Jesus tells us he was sent "to bring good news to the poor" (Luke 4:18).

It's great news when good jobs and wages bring people out of poverty. Work should be more than something people do for a paycheck. It's a way we join God in the work of creation. This brings dignity to work, and workers should never be taken for granted. They should have fair wages, the right to join unions, and the ability to start their own businesses.

Key Words

social justice
charity
common good
solidarity

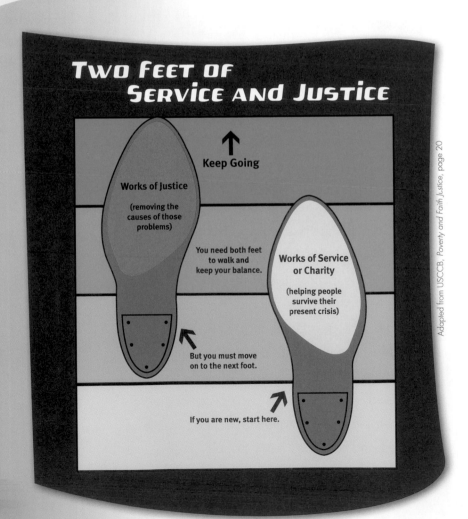

TWO FEET OF SERVICE AND JUSTICE

Keep Going

Works of Justice

(removing the causes of those problems)

You need both feet to walk and keep your balance.

Works of Service or Charity

(helping people survive their present crisis)

But you must move on to the next foot.

If you are new, start here.

Adapted from USCCB, Poverty and Faith Justice, page 20

LiVE IT!

There are so many needs in the world. How can our efforts make a lasting difference? Remember the following:

- **Don't go it alone.** Work with friends who care about the problems you do.

- **Ask why.** For example, don't do a food drive every year without asking why people are hungry. Ask your elected leaders what they're doing to help. Ask if people are hungry at other times of the year and do a food drive then too.

- **Dig deeper.** Before you do service, read about the issue you're taking on (hunger, for example) online or in the newspaper. See what the Bible and Church teachings say about it. Then when you serve, you'll be more aware.

- **Smile.** Even though the work may be hard or seem hopeless, your smiles offer the gift of hope to the people you serve. You're making a difference.

Whether it's a child laborer stitching soccer balls in China, an unborn child in a womb, or an old woman in Africa suffering from hunger, these are all our brothers and sisters. Their needs are ours. Living in **solidarity** means not only that we share our material goods though charity but also that we share our friendship and prayers with other people. Pope Paul VI taught us, "If you want Peace, work for Justice" (*"Message of His Holiness Pope Paul VI for the Celebration of the Day of Peace"*). Our efforts for justice can prevent wars and bring unity in a divided world.

We also need to be one with the earth itself. In the Book of Genesis, God tells us to care for all creation. It's time to be good stewards of the land, water, plants, and animals. Keep in mind the wisdom of the Iroquois, American Indian people who advocate for making decisions based on how they will affect the next seven generations. The changes we make now to conserve energy, water, and other resources will have a lasting effect on generations of people to come after us.

Remember the brave Apostles who wouldn't let society's laws keep them from preaching? They would

People of Faith

Dorothy Day

© 2009 Saint Mary's Press/Illustration by Vicki Shuck

If changing the world seems impossible, get to know Dorothy Day. She was your age about a century ago, but her legacy of compassion lives on today.

An earthquake rocked Dorothy's family in 1906, and they moved to Chicago's slums. She overcame poverty but never forgot the pain it causes. She wanted to help others in need. "From that time on my life was to be linked to theirs . . . ," she recalled. "I had received . . . a direction in life" (Forest, "The Living Legacy of Dorothy Day").

have been killed if not for Gamaliel, a Phari-see, who told his fellow leaders, "Leave them alone! If what they have planned and done is of human origin, it will disappear, but if it comes from God, you cannot possibly defeat them" (Acts 5:38–39). What the Apostles planned did come from God. Now it's your turn to be part of God's plan.

Recycling is one way to care for God's creation. Can you name other ways you can be a good steward?

Dorothy was a great writer with a strong sense of compassion and vocation. She prayed to find ways to use these gifts.

She met Peter Maurin, a man with a mind for social change. He wanted to start a newspaper, so they launched *The Catholic Worker*. Each edition applied the Gospel to modern problems.

Writing was not enough, and Dorothy led the way in taking direct action. Catholic Worker houses opened their doors to hungry, homeless people. Catholic Workers marched with striking workers and went to jail for war protests.

Today, more than 185 Catholic Worker communities promote nonviolence, voluntary poverty, prayer, and hospitality for people in need. Dorothy's desire became a revolution.

"The greatest challenge of the day is: how to bring about a revolution of the heart," she said, "a revolution which has to start with each one of us" (Egan, *Dorothy Day and the Permanent Revolution*, page 22).

PART 6
PRAYER

PRAYER

Our Father who art in heaven,
hallowed be thy name.
Thy kingdom come.
Thy will be done on earth, as it is in heaven.
Give us this day our daily bread,
and forgive us our trespasses,
    as we forgive those who trespass against us,
and lead us not into temptation,
but deliver us from evil.

                                    Amen

PRAYER: CONVERSATIONS with God

Messages to God

Do you ever wish you could text-message God? In today's world of cell phones and instant messaging, we are used to communicating with other people quickly. No matter where you go, you can reach friends and family by using technology. Cyberspace has brought us closer together by giving us the tools to be in constant touch with each other.

Talking to God is as simple as having a conversation with a best friend. If you could send a text message to God, what would you say?

Write new

Dear God, My lyf S confusing. Hlp me thru 2day. Tlk2U L8R. Love, me.

Continue   More

© Lars Langemeier/A.B./zefa/Corbis

Prayer is our way of staying in touch with God at all times. When you pray, you strengthen your relationship with God as you would with your BF (best friend).

What Is Prayer?

When you were a young child, your parents probably chose your friends for you. You played together, sharing toys and doing fun things. Now that you are older, friendships mean something different. You can choose your own friends, and the conversations go beyond the sandbox or playground to deeper subjects. The more time you spend with a person, the more you have to talk about: movies, sports, school, people you know. You share good times, as well as problems you have. Good friends never run out of things to say to each other.

Likewise, when you were a young child, your parents introduced you to God. Since then, you have been learning more about God the Father, Jesus Christ, and the Holy Spirit, through the Church. Like a loving parent, the Holy Spirit has been

PRAY IT!

Jesus,

Remember when you got lost at the Temple? At least your parents thought you were lost. When you were only twelve, you knew what your Father wanted you to do. Send us your Spirit so we can know God's will for us too. Teach us to pray constantly so we may grow as close to the Father as you are.

Amen

teaching the children of God to pray for thousands of years. The Holy Spirit operates through **Tradition,** the living transmission of God's truth to us. The Holy Spirit in the Church keeps the lines of divine communication open between us and God. God is always inviting us to be on his wavelength through prayer. Any time you take a moment to raise your heart and mind to God, you are praying. When you take the time to tell God about your day, share your worries, or ask advice, God is listening. You can ask favors of God and know he wants the best for you. Like any good relationship, the more time you spend with God in prayer, the easier the conversation. You never run out of things to say to each other.

Did You Know?
The Psalms: Great Prayers for All Ages

The Scriptures tell us that people have been talking to God since he breathed life into Adam and Eve. In every book of the Bible, you will find both saints and sinners who call out to God for help. You can hear their voices praising God, giving thanks for all he has done for them. Check out the Psalms for some of the greatest prayers of all time. Like different types of music, they help us express some of the same emotions and concerns people had three thousand years ago. The following are a few psalms and their subjects:

Psalm 3: Morning Prayer for Help

Psalm 10: A Prayer for Justice

Psalm 59: A Prayer for Safety

Psalm 85: A Prayer for the Nation's Welfare

Psalm 95: A Song of Praise

Psalm 102: The Prayer of a Troubled Youth

Psalm 141: An Evening Prayer

© image100/Corbis

When friends spend a lot of time together, they get to know each other pretty well. Likewise, spending time with God can make your relationship stronger.

Tuning In to God

The key to a growing relationship is spending time together, talking, and listening to each other. God never gets tired of wanting to be with us. Starting with Genesis, the first book of the Bible, we hear the stories of God calling and humans responding. Abraham and God made a sacred agreement, or **covenant,** with each other. Moses argued with God because he did not like the assignment to lead God's people out of Egypt. The prophets complained to God too but responded to his call. We know Jesus and his Father talked with each other throughout Jesus' life on this earth. The history of God's people shows us that prayer is always a back-and-forth exchange. God reaches out to get our attention, and we respond.

Today God might use other ways to get our attention. Remember that God's love is like sound waves broadcasting during every nanosecond of our lives. Prayer is something like the radio that helps us

KEY WORDS

Tradition

covenant

grace

conversion

463

PRAY IT!

Liturgy Connection

Have you ever considered that Mass is a prayer? In fact, it is the ultimate prayer of the Church. Just as you get together with your friends to share stories, music, and a meal, so we gather as the People of God. From the opening Sign of the Cross, we are talking with God, who is present with us in a real way. God is with us when we hear the proclamation of the Scriptures and when we share the Body and Blood of Jesus. Because Jesus Christ is really present with us, Communion is the perfect communication between God and us.

tune in so we can experience this love. Like our favorite stations, God is always available to us, but unless we take the time to tune in, we fail to recognize the power of **grace**—God's presence in our lives.

Tuning in to God may take just a few moments, or we might spend a longer time, as we would when we listen to our favorite songs or artists. When we pray, we can take a few seconds to check out how God is playing in our lives. We may want to linger longer, listening and experiencing the divine music that plays constantly in our souls.

When we take time to give thanks to God for a new day, we are praying. When we stop to admire something in nature, we praise God, our Creator. Any time we acknowledge that God is the source of blessings in our

You can't hear a radio until you tune in. You can't experience God unless you tune in to his love.

Shutterstock

lives, we raise our minds and hearts to God. We are tuning in and paying attention to God, who is trying to get our attention. Because God blesses us, we bless him in return.

When to Pray

> Be joyful always, pray at all times, be thankful in all circumstances. This is what God wants from you.
> (1 Thessalonians 5:16)

Because God is always communicating with us, are we supposed to pray nonstop? That is exactly what Paul tells us. We are to pray constantly. Prayer is as essential to our souls as air is to our bodies. Because nothing can separate us from the love of God, it is always possible to pray.

If you are always praying, when would you go to school, spend time with other friends, or get your homework done? How about sports or other activities or just having fun? How can you pray when you are sleeping? Isn't it impossible to tune in to God at every moment of every day?

Because God is always communicating with us, just being open to his presence is an

FUN FACT

Humans breathe more than 23,000 times each day. Without that air coming into and leaving our bodies, we cannot live. Just being aware of our breathing can be an act of prayer. Imagine inhaling God's life 23,000 times a day!

Live It!

The Jugular Prayer

Praying constantly may seem impossible, but prayer can be as close as your fingertips. You can easily raise your mind and heart to God by actually feeling the connection between your brain and your heart. Do this by praying the "Jugular Prayer."

First, place your first and second fingers on the side of your neck until you locate the pulse of your jugular vein. Feel the blood flowing from your brain to your heart. Be aware of God's life within you.

Just practicing this act of touch can remind you of God's presence. Use it to slow yourself down during the day. Try it in the middle of an argument or to ask God's inspiration during a stressful moment. It is an "anytime, anywhere prayer" (Hays, *Prayer Notes to a Friend*, page 33).

act of prayer. We grow in our faith and our spirituality by being aware that God is loving us throughout our day. The more often we tune in, the more we experience the benefits of an active prayer life. Just as your mind and heart are always working even when you are not thinking about it, your soul is always at work too.

Check out the Jugular Prayer in the "Live It!" article above. God dwells within you. You can feel it!

When Prayer Is Difficult

Sometimes it's difficult to pray. Life can be crazy, and we may feel overloaded at times. With TV, computers, magazines, and radio, we are often bombarded with TMI (too much information). So many distractions can keep us from tuning in to God as often as we should. At other times, we may feel as though we experience a dropped call when we pray. Do you ever wonder if God is listening? Do you sometimes just feel like not talking to God?

Some of the greatest friends of God—the saints—have described similar difficulties with prayer. Even before the kind of technology we have in our lives today, some people throughout the ages have felt distracted. Others have described feeling separated from God. They talk about a kind of dryness in their relationship.

Like any friendship, our relationship with God will have ups and downs. But God is amazingly patient. He wants us to keep calling, just as he keeps calling us. Our desire to be faithful through these difficult periods is all he asks of us. When we keep turning back to God even when we seem to get a busy signal, we experience **conversion,** a change of heart that keeps us in touch with the one who loves us beyond all our understanding.

Think About It!

Who taught you to pray? What was your favorite prayer as a small child? What would you say to God in an instant message? What kind of message would God send back to you?

467

Lord, you have examined me and you know me.
You know everything I do; from far away you
understand all my thoughts. You see me, whether
I am working or resting; you know all my
actions. . . . Your knowledge of me is too deep;
it is beyond my understanding. (Psalm 139:1–3,6)

People of Faith

Saint Teresa of Ávila

© 2009 Saint Mary's Press/Illustration by Vicki Shuck

In the Harry Potter book series, J. K. Rowling has created a school in the form of a magical castle, Hogwarts, where Harry, Hermione, and Ron live out their adventures. They explore secret rooms and find both treasures and horrors within the walls. The deeper they go, the more they discover.

Teresa of Ávila used the image of a castle to describe her prayer life. She was born in 1515 in Ávila, Spain, where some of the great castles of Europe still remain. In her book *The Interior Castle*, Teresa pictured the soul as a beautiful castle where God lives in the innermost chamber. Some of the rooms are up above, others down below, others to the sides. But in the center and middle is the main dwellingplace where the secret exchanges between God and the soul happen. Only through prayer can a person enter this secret place.

Although she was a saint, Teresa did not always find it easy to pray, to explore her interior castle. She compared prayer to physical exercise. At first, it is hard and does not seem to produce immediate results. But those who practice prayer often experience feelings of excitement, joy, and peace. Life seems to come alive for them. God invites you to visit him in your interior castle. Will you go on this adventure (adapted from Broughton, *Praying with Teresa of Ávila*, pages 31 and 33)?

TUNING IN TO GOD

Do you have a favorite radio station? Do you listen to some singers or bands more than others? Does a particular kind of music appeal to you more than others? Perhaps you like rock or rap, country or classical. Whatever your taste, music can touch your soul. Remember that prayer is the way we get in touch with the divine music in our souls. God is always broadcasting his love to us and asking us to tune in. God invites us to be in relationship with him every nanosecond of our lives. Prayer is our response to that invitation.

What kind of music is on your playlist? Try putting different kinds of prayer on your "pray list."

iStockphoto

I urge you, friends, by our Lord Jesus Christ and by the love that the Spirit gives: join me in praying fervently to God for me.
(Romans 15:30)

Forms of Prayer

God is open to all kinds of prayer, but there are a few tried-and-true ways of listening and talking to God. The Holy Spirit makes sure the Church is true to the message of Jesus and teaches her how to pray in different ways. In your life as a Christian, you have probably been using all of these five basic forms of prayer without even realizing it: petition, blessing, intercession, praise, and thanksgiving. Let's take a look at the different types of prayer the Church recommends as ways to talk with and listen to God.

Petition. How many times a day do you ask God for something you want? Perhaps you have prayed for the answer to a test question or the ability to do well when you compete. Such prayers are good. They remind us of God's presence in our lives. Have you considered making deeper requests of God—for things you truly need? Consider praying for help with an important decision,

PRAY IT!

Loving God,
The gift of your presence is like divine music that I can hear every moment of my life. Through the Holy Spirit, teach me the ways to download your love so I can recognize your divine power. With the earphones of faith, help me tune out the background noise of my life so I can tune in to your constant love for me. Help me share with others the music of your love.
Amen

FUN FACT

Ever wonder why we say "God bless you" when someone sneezes? In the sixth century, when Gregory the Great was Pope, he asked people to pray as a way to combat the bubonic plague. Because a sneeze could signal the start of the disease, the people would say "God bless you," hoping that the person who sneezed would not get sick.

comfort during tough times, or forgiveness when you have hurt someone. Whenever we ask God for something, we use a form of prayer called **petition.** Asking is the most common kind of prayer, but there are different ways to ask.

Blessing. When we pray for God's loving care for a particular person, place, or activity, we are using a type of prayer called a **blessing.** We are able to pray blessings because God has first blessed us. We pray blessings before meals ("Bless us, O Lord, and these thy gifts . . .") or when someone sneezes ("God bless you"). During Mass we bless God ("Blessed be God forever"), and God blesses us ("Bow your heads and pray for God's blessing").

Intercession. When people ask you to pray for them, they are asking you to put in a good word for them. They must think pretty highly of your relationship with God. Any time you pray on behalf of someone else, it is a prayer of **intercession.**

Every Mass includes prayers of intercession. When we "pray to the Lord" for the intentions of the world, the Church, people in need, or members of our community, we are asking for God's help for others.

Praise. Prayer is not just about petitions, or asking God to take care of our needs and wants. We also need to tell God how much we appreciate all he

Shutterstock

Saying grace before meals is a type of prayer called a blessing. What other kinds of prayer can families do together?

does for us. These are prayers of **praise.**

Prayers of praise can be as simple as noticing the beauties of creation or as powerful as the prayers of Mass. Do the following prayers sound familiar to you?

* Lord God, heavenly King, almighty God and Father, we worship you, we give you thanks, we praise you for your glory.

Did You Know?

Schools of Spirituality

School spirit. From elementary schools through college, each school has a different way of expressing the enthusiasm and strengths of its students. School spirit is handed down through traditions like mascots and school songs.

The Church has different schools of spirituality that share the living tradition of prayer. Many of these have developed from the lives of the saints. Franciscans—those inspired by the life of Saint Francis of Assisi—are especially aware of nature as a place to encounter God. Ignatian spirituality encourages followers of Saint Ignatius of Loyola to use their imaginations when praying. As you grow in your prayer life, schools of spirituality can be precious guides along the way.

- May the Lord accept the sacrifice at your hands for the praise and glory of his name, for our good, and the good of all his Church.

- Father, you are holy indeed, and all creation rightly gives you praise.

We hear these and many more prayers of praise at Mass.

Thanksgiving. It is right for all creation to give God praise. It is also right to tell God how thankful we are. We do not have to wait for a special day of the year for thanksgiving. We are called to be grateful throughout every day. During Mass, we pray in union with the priest when he says, "We do well always and everywhere to give you thanks." As Catholics, we gather to give thanks in a special way through the Eucharist. In fact, the word *Eucharist* comes from a Greek word that means "thanksgiving."

Learning to Pray

Do you remember how you learned to pray? Like learning to talk, you may not have a specific memory. You just started picking up the words and the gestures from others. A simple prayer before meals or before

PRAY IT!
Liturgy Connection

Many people start and end their days with TV news. Although headlines are available to us anytime, the most popular times to tune in are morning and evening.

The Church has official morning and evening "prayer-casts," called the Liturgy of the Hours. Bishops, priests, monks, and religious sisters and brothers have practiced this form of prayer since the earliest centuries of the Church. More recently, lay-people have rediscovered this ancient cycle of prayers. The Liturgy of the Hours is another way the Holy Spirit helps us hear the Good News.

bedtime became daily prayer. Through these daily prayers and the Sunday Eucharist, you grew in your prayer life. Year after year, through liturgical feasts and seasons, you learn more and more the language and practice of prayer.

Prayer does take practice. But like anything else in our lives, the more we practice, the easier prayer becomes. Participating in the liturgy of the Church helps us develop good habits of prayer. Reading the Bible and hearing the Word of God proclaimed at Mass are also big helps to our prayer life.

The virtues of faith, hope, and love also help us pray. Without the gift of faith, prayer would not make much sense. The virtue of hope keeps us from being disappointed when God may not seem to answer our prayers exactly the way we expect. Paul teaches us that love is the greatest virtue of all. Love is the motivation of all prayer. God loves us; we love God in return.

> Hope does not disappoint us, for God has poured out his love into our hearts by means of the Holy Spirit, who is God's gift to us.
>
> (Romans 5:5)

KEY WORDS

petition
blessing
intercession
praise
thanksgiving

© Nice One Productions/Corbis

Just like any sport, learning to pray takes practice. The more you do it, the better you get at it.

Who first taught you to make the Sign of the Cross or say the Hail Mary? Prayers you learn by heart will stay with you for a lifetime.

Bill Wittman

We first learn about God's love through the love of others. Even before babies can speak, they experience God through the love of their families. Often one of the first sentences a child learns is "I love you." These simple words become the basis for all relationships. They also become the starting point for prayer. Parents, grandparents, siblings, and other members of a Christian family teach children that God loves them and listens to them.

By living and teaching about love, families nurture the seeds of prayer that God implanted in the human heart. Eventually, children begin to learn prayers "by heart." From watching and listening to others, you probably learned how to make the Sign of the Cross and say grace before meals. Later came longer prayers that are part of the treasury of our faith: the Hail Mary, the Lord's Prayer, the Act of Contrition. Like the oldies station on the radio, there is a place in our prayer lives for these traditional prayers. Memorized prayers are the family traditions that are passed on from generation to generation. They help us remember who we are and whom we belong to.

Personal Prayer

Remember that God is open to all types of prayer that come from the heart. But Christians have practiced three major expressions of Christian prayer through the ages: vocal prayer, meditation, and contemplation.

Vocal prayer uses words to speak to God. The words can be spoken aloud or silently, and we can pray them alone or in a group. Memorized prayers are one kind of vocal prayer. So are prayers you make up yourself. This kind of prayer is also sometimes called spontaneous prayer. You can always use your own words to tell God what you are feeling or thinking.

There are other kinds of personal prayer. Like instrumental music, meditation and contemplation are powerful ways to pray. Meditation

THINK ABOUT IT!

Computers let you set favorites for links you visit often. Which memorized prayers would you list as your favorite links to God? Art, music, and drama can help us to tune in to God. Think of specific examples of art, music, or drama (including movies and TV shows) that might help your prayer life. How might some art, music, or drama be an obstacle to prayer?

uses our thoughts, imagination, and emotions, to get in touch with God. Using the Scriptures, the rosary, pictures, or creation, meditation is a way to focus our minds and hearts on what God is trying to tell us.

Contemplation, sometimes defined as resting in God, is a wordless prayer. It is another way of listening for God's movement in our lives. By being silent long enough to hear the divine music, we enter in union with God, Father, Son, and Holy Spirit. All these expressions of prayer—vocal prayer, meditation, and contemplation—are ways to remember that we live in the heart of God, and God lives in our hearts.

Saying the rosary is a popular prayer. What other devotions in the "Live It!" sidebar on the next page have you tried?

© Philippe Lissac/Godong/Corbis

Live It!

In addition to liturgy, other forms of piety,
or special expressions of devotion to God,
can help us in our prayer lives. These popular
forms of devotion are not "one size fits all." Different
cultures have various devotions that have received the
Church's seal of approval. They all help spread the Good
News of Jesus Christ.

How many of these are familiar to you? Do some research to find out more about those that you have never heard
of or practiced. Pick one of the following and try it as a new
form of prayer for you:

- Eucharistic Adoration
- The Rosary
- Posadas
- The Angelus
- Novenas
- Stations of the Cross
- Devotions honoring Our Lady of Guadalupe
  Scapulars
- Miraculous Medal
- Devotion to the Sacred
  Heart of Jesus

THE LORD'S PRAYER: THE PERFECT PRAYER

Imagine being one of Jesus' best friends. You have traveled with him, watched him perform miracles, and heard him teach crowds of people. You have been in his inner circle, so you have shared meals with him, spoken with him, and been part of his daily life. You have noticed that Jesus often goes off to pray. Because of who he is, you figure he must be a master at praying. You want him to teach you how to pray.

In Luke's Gospel, this scenario is just what happens with Jesus' friends. They recognize how impor-

Jesus' friends figured that he knew the best way to pray. When they asked him to teach them how, he gave them the Lord's Prayer.

© Brooklyn Museum/Corbis

tant prayer is in Jesus' life, and they want to know the best way to pray. In response to their request, Jesus gives them a prayer that expresses everything they need to live as one of his followers. Two thousand years after Jesus first taught it to his disciples, Christians all over the world still pray the Lord's Prayer, also called the Our Father.

Throughout the history of the Church, the Lord's Prayer has been handed on from generation to generation. *The Catechism of the Catholic Church* calls it the "quintessential prayer of the Church" (CCC, number 2776). That means it is the perfect example of our ongoing conversation with our God, who created us.

What makes the Our Father—the Lord's Prayer—the perfect way for God's people to pray? Let's take a look at ten reasons why the Church makes this extraordinary claim.

> One day Jesus was praying in a certain place. When he had finished, one of his disciples said to him, "Lord, teach us to pray, just as John taught his disciples." (Luke 11:1)

fun fact

Quintessential. This impressive word comes from two Latin words: *quint* ("five") and *essential* ("essence"). Ancient philosophers thought that nature contained four essences, or elements: earth, fire, water, and air. Something perfect had a fifth element from the heavens. What a perfect word to describe the prayer that came from God.

1. Jesus Himself Gave Us the Lord's Prayer

Who would know better how to pray than Jesus? He gives us the words the Father gave him. Because Jesus is both fully divine and fully human, he also knows in his human heart our needs, the needs of all of his human brothers and sisters. He is the best model for our prayer.

2. The Lord's Prayer Teaches Us How to Pray

Live It!

If there are at least ten reasons why the Lord's Prayer is the perfect prayer, there are at least ten different times daily when you could say this prayer. Consider the following times when you might stop and pray the Lord's Prayer:

1. first thing in the morning when you wake up
2. when you go outside and notice the beauty of God's creation
3. when you are hungry
4. when you see someone else who may be hungry
5. when someone says something to hurt you
6. when you say something that hurts someone else
7. when you are tempted to do something you know is wrong
8. when you are scared, upset, or worried
9. when something bad happens to you
10. before you go to bed

When Jesus taught his disciples to pray, he did not give them some kind of secret formula to repeat without thinking. He taught them a way of praying. Remember the terms *praise* and *petition?* Jesus began by addressing God and praising

iStockphoto

Do you ever wonder what to say when you pray? The Lord's Prayer is the perfect prayer under any circumstances.

PRAY IT!

his name and then petitioning, or asking, for what we need in life. Although the exact words of the Lord's Prayer have been translated in different ways through many generations, the way of praying that Jesus gave us has not changed.

God, our Father,
Sometimes I am not
sure what I need. Or
I don't know what
is best for me. I have
a hard time putting
it into words. Thank
you for the gift of the
words that your Son,
Jesus Christ, gave us when
he taught his friends how
to pray. When I say these
words, I want to pray. I want
to say them as if I had been
there, hearing them for the
first time from Jesus himself.
Help me love and appreciate
the gift of the Lord's Prayer.
Amen

3. The Lord's Prayer Is Addressed to the Father

Praying to God as a father may seem like a no-brainer. This is because we know that all prayer is primarily addressed to God the Father. But to the people of Jesus' time, calling upon God as our Father must have sounded a bit strange. They were not used to thinking of God in such a personal way.

PRAY IT!

Liturgy Connection

"Let us pray with confidence to the Father the words our Savior gave us." Right after the Eucharistic Prayer and before Communion, the priest invites us to stand and pray the Lord's Prayer. When we stand to pray, we are saying the prayer of the whole Church. Because we are the Church, the Our Father is most meaningful and effective when we pray it together. The Lord's Prayer sums up everything we have asked for in the Eucharistic prayer and gets us ready to receive the Body and Blood of Christ in Communion. Mass is the perfect place for the perfect prayer.

When you pray the Lord's Prayer at Mass, do you pray with confidence because you know these are the words our Savior gave us?

4. The Lord's Prayer Helps Us Know Who God Is

We can call on God as Father because Jesus revealed to us who God is. Jesus wants us to know that God is not some distant being who hurls thunderbolts from on high. Instead, God is a personal, loving God. Jesus shows how to relate to God—as an approachable, loving Father. That must have been an amazing concept for Jesus' disciples. If we stop to think about it, it is still an amazing thought—that God wants to be as close to each of us as is an ideal and loving father.

Bill Wittman

5. The Lord's Prayer Helps Us Know Who We Are

When Jesus instructs us to say "Our Father," he invites all of us into relationship with his Father. When we pray to the Father, we are in communion with him and with his Son, Jesus Christ. To be in **communion** with someone means we share the closest kind of relationship possible. The Lord's Prayer clearly tells us we are sons and daughters of God. How awesome is that?

Looking Back

Sound Familiar?

The prayer Jesus shared with his disciples may have seemed familiar to them. Many of the words and phrases Jesus used were part of the Kaddish, an ancient Jewish prayer recited at the end of the synagogue service. As a Jewish boy, Jesus attended **synagogue**—the place where Jews met to pray and study. He would have heard phrases like "Exalted and hallowed be his great name in the world which he created according to his will" and "May he let his Kingdom rule in your lifetime and in your days and in the lifetime of the whole house of Israel."

Though Jesus used words familiar to his friends, the prayer he gave us was different. He told them to address God as Father, sharing with them and us the Good News of who we are and whose we are.

6. The Lord's Prayer Helps Us Be More like God Our Father

Have you ever watched small children try to act like their parents? When they play, they often try to speak and act like their mothers and fathers. It is natural for children to want to grow up to be "just like Mom or Dad." When we pray to our Father, we should develop the will to become like God, our Father. We ought to behave like sons and daughters of God.

So Jesus called a child to come and stand in front of them, and said, "I assure you that unless you change and become like children, you will never enter the Kingdom of heaven." (Matthew 18:2–3)

When Jesus began teaching his friends to pray, he told them to say, "Our Father." He wanted to tell them that God loves all people. And we should too.

© David Turnley/CORBIS

7. The Lord's Prayer Helps Us Have Humble and Trusting Hearts

Have you ever been told, "Stop acting like a little child"? It might seem strange that when Jesus wanted to make a point with his adult followers, he told them to be like little children. Jesus recognized that children are humbler and more trusting than adults. Their hearts are more open to the love God offers them. The Our Father reminds us that we are children of God, and we ought to act like it.

8. The Lord's Prayer Is About "We," Not "Me"

When referring to someone who thinks only about herself or himself, you may have heard the expression "It's all about me." When Jesus taught us to pray to our Father, not my father, he was reminding us that being in relationship with God means we are also in relationship with each other. If God is our Father, we must be concerned with all members of the human family. God's love has no limits, and neither should our prayers. When we pray, our focus should extend to all people.

9. The Lord's Prayer Is *the* Prayer of the Church

In the early days of the Church, Jesus' disciples prayed the Lord's Prayer three times a day. Ever since then, the People of God have prayed the Our Father as part of their liturgical lives. It is an essential part of the Liturgy of the Hours (see the "Pray It!" Liturgy Connection in chapter 41). Of course, we pray the Lord's Prayer at every Mass. Next time you stand and pray as Jesus taught us, remember you are continuing the two-thousand-year-old prayer of the Church.

10. The Lord's Prayer Sums Up Everything Jesus Taught

Could you summarize in 30 seconds or less everything Jesus came to teach us about living the Christian life? In the middle of his Sermon on the Mount, Jesus does just that when he stops to teach us the Our Father (see Matthew 6:9–15).

Almost four hundred years later, Saint Augustine, one of the most important saints of the Church, said, "Run through all the words of the holy prayers [in the Scriptures] and I do not think that you will find anything in them that is not contained and included in the Lord's Prayer"[1] (*CCC*, number 2762). That is a pretty incredible statement about a 30-second prayer.

KEY WORDS

quintessential
communion
synagogue

Did You Know?

More than Food

When we pray for our daily bread, we are not asking God just for food. We are asking also for everything we need to live. That includes things we might take for granted like vaccines, those shots you often dread to get. Vaccines do not cure disease. They prevent it, which is even better. If a hundred people get vaccinated, they do not get sick and they cannot infect thousands more. Did you know that millions of children around the world cannot get the shots they need? Did you know we do not have vaccines for AIDS, tuberculosis, or malaria? These three diseases take six million lives worldwide each year. As you pray for "daily bread," pray for the scientists and doctors who are working to save millions of lives.

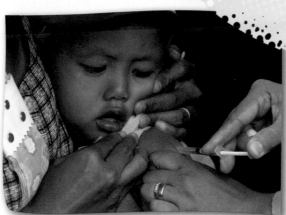

© Mast Irham/epa/Corbis

Read the "Did You Know?" sidebar above to find out how vaccines are part of our "daily bread."

THE LORD'S PRAYER: A PRAYER FOR ALL TIME

Many people think of the number 7 as a lucky number. There are seven days of the week and seven seas. The ancient world considered it the perfect number because it was the sum of two perfect shapes: a triangle with three sides and a square with four sides.

J. K. Rowling, who wrote seven Harry Potter books, used the number 7 in several symbolic ways. Harry was born in the seventh month and wore the number seven on his quidditch jersey. Video game characters often have multiples of seven different challenges on their quests.

The number 7 is significant in the Bible too. There, it represents completeness. God created the world in seven days (see Genesis 1:1—2:3). Jesus tells us to forgive seventy times seven (see Matthew 18:22). He expels seven demons from Mary Magdalene (see Luke 8:2). The

Shutterstock

In this chapter you will discover how the number 7 and the Lord's Prayer are related.

Gospel of Matthew tells us that when Jesus stops in the middle of his Sermon on the Mount to teach the crowd how to pray, he gives them a prayer with seven petitions (see Matthew 6:9–13). Seven is the perfect number for the perfect prayer. In this chapter we will explore the seven petitions, or requests, in the Lord's Prayer.

3 + 4 = 7

Like the Ten Commandments, the Lord's Prayer consists of two parts. In the Ten Commandments, the first three commandments are directed toward our relationship with God. The last seven are about our relationships with others. Similarly, the Our Father contains three petitions that focus on the glory of God the Father. Then there are four requests that name our human needs and desires.

Before we begin the seven petitions, we address God as Father. This name reminds us of the close, personal relationship we enjoy as children of God. By saying "Our Father," Jesus tells us that God's love extends to all people. When we say the words "who art in heaven," we are not naming a physical, faraway place.

PRAY IT!

God, our Father,
When we pray for ourselves and our needs, we know you listen to us. Today we pray for the needs of those who do not know how to pray or have no one to pray for them. We ask that you grant our brothers and sisters in every corner of the world all they need to be well fed, to be safe, and to have the opportunity to know you and love you as your Son, Jesus, has taught us to do.

Amen

Our prayer is not a long-distance call. Heaven is a way of life or state of being. When we address our Father in Heaven, we recognize his nearness to us, and we pray for even greater closeness with God. We are something like the child who stretches out her arms and cries out because she wants to be picked up and held.

1. "Hallowed Be Thy Name"

Did You Know?

The Hail Mary

Have you ever heard of a "Hail Mary" pass in football? In 1975 Roger Staubach, a devout Catholic playing quarterback for the Dallas Cowboys football team, threw a desperation pass, then closed his eyes and said a Hail Mary. His receiver caught the ball and ran into the end zone for the game-winning touchdown. Although Mary, the Mother of God, is not partial to any sports team, this play shows how popular the Hail Mary is among Catholics.

Based on the Scriptures, the Hail Mary begins with the announcement of Jesus' birth (see Luke 1:28) and ends with a prayer for the "hour of our death." When we pray to Mary, we ask her to ask Jesus for whatever we need—from touchdowns to matters much more serious. Both the Hail Mary and the Our Father are part of the playbook of Catholic prayers.

When you first learned the Lord's Prayer, you may have thought that you were saying "Hello be your name"! This innocent mistake occurs because the word hallowed is not commonly heard today. It means "holy." The first of the seven petitions sounds more like praise of God's name than a petition to ask for something. But "hallowed be thy name" is actually a

492

request for help in keeping God's name holy. When we show deep reverence for God's name, we draw closer to him. When we use God's name lightly or abuse it, we are saying he is not important in our lives. "Hallowed be thy name" is a request to be in awe of our awesome God.

2. "Thy Kingdom Come"

You'll notice when you read the Gospels that the term *Kingdom of God* keeps coming up. It is the central theme of Jesus' mission on earth. It is the Good News, because God's Kingdom, or God's Reign, is

God, our Father, reaches out to tenderly comfort one of his children. The words "*hallowed* be thy name" remind us how close God wants to be to each of us.

Illustration by Elizabeth Wang, 'The Father's tender touch in Prayer', copyright © Radiant Light 2008, www.radiantlight.org.uk

a time of justice, peace, and love. In this second petition, Jesus teaches us to ask God for the final coming of his Kingdom. But we don't have to wait for the end of the world. We can also be part of the Kingdom of God right here, even if the world is not perfect yet. When we pray this petition in the Lord's Prayer, we ask God to help us put our priorities in order. The world often tells us happiness can be found primarily in material things. Jesus' message is just the opposite.

Key Words
Kingdom of God
trespass
temptation

"Your Father in heaven knows that you need all these things. . . . Be concerned above everything else with the Kingdom of God and with what he requires of you, and he will provide you with all these other things." (Matthew 6:32–33)

3. "Thy Will Be Done on Earth, as It Is in Heaven"

Whenever a parent, teacher, or coach gives you a task, it helps to be clear about what they want you to do. You have to know their will, or what they want and how they want it done. If you don't know, you might not finish the job properly. On the night before he dies, Jesus is clear in his instructions to us. He does not make a suggestion. He gives us a command: "As I have loved you, so you must love one another" (John 13:34). When we pray the third petition, we ask God to help us understand how to do his will by loving the way Jesus showed us and taught us. The experience of giving and receiving love is a taste of Heaven on earth.

> "As I have loved you, so you must love one another." (John 13:34)

4. "Give Us This Day Our Daily Bread"

The words "Give us this day our daily bread" make an excellent grace before meals. In every culture on earth, people eat some form of bread. We ask for our daily bread for ourselves, our families and friends, and everyone in the world.

FUN FACT

Jesus taught his friends to pray in Aramaic, the common language of the time. Today, the Our Father is prayed in more than 1,400 languages. The Convent of the Pater Noster in the Holy Land keeps track of all these languages. The walls of this church contain 140 large tiles, each inscribed with the Lord's Prayer in a different language.

This photo was taken in the Convent of the Pater Noster (which is Latin for "Our Father"). Read the "Fun Fact" above to discover how many translations of the Lord's Prayer there are.

© Sandro Vannini/CORBIS

We are reminded there are millions of people who do not have enough to eat. We also remember millions who are hungry for God.

Think About It!

Adam and Eve wanted to taste the forbidden fruit. Calling something "forbidden fruit" is a way of referring to temptation. It is something that looks good but goes against God's will. What are some of the most common temptations young people face today?

5. "Forgive Us Our Trespasses, as We Forgive Those Who Trespass Against Us"

Just as each of us needs daily nourishment, we all need forgiveness. Jesus encourages us to recognize our sins and ask for mercy.

A **trespass** is another name for sin. In this fifth petition, there is a big condition. We must first forgive those who have hurt us. This can be a tall order. However, if we seek revenge rather than reconciliation, the cycle of sin or hurt becomes more difficult to stop. If we are unwilling to forgive others, our hearts remain closed to God's love and forgiveness.

6. "Lead Us Not into Temptation"

This may sound like an odd request for God—not to lead us into temptation. But the sixth petition helps us recognize that although we are good, made in the image and likeness of God, we also possess the tendency to do wrong. We coexist with millions of people who also have this tendency; together we are often misguided about God's will for us. A **temptation** is an invitation to do something wrong. Too often the invitation is hard to resist. This petition asks God to help us avoid saying yes to people and situations that could ultimately lead to sin or tragedy.

How can the Internet lead us into temptation?

© Erik Freeland/Corbis

7. "But Deliver Us from Evil"

Listening to almost any news report can remind us of how much evil exists in this world. It is easy to become discouraged and to

Live It!

When you pray the words "lead us not into temptation," do you ever consider how many temptations you face daily? Often temptations exist side by side with good things in your life. For example, on the Internet, you can find both treasures and trouble. E-mails and personal Web pages are a fun way to communicate with friends, but they can lead to destructive gossip that ruins reputations. YouTube can take you to media images that can be entertaining, but some can be harmful.

Internet policies at school or home can help you make good choices every time you log on to your computer. Praying the words of the Our Father can help you avoid cyberspace temptations.

believe that the forces of evil will overcome all that is good. However, the concluding words of the Lord's Prayer are a petition that God will deliver us from those things that would harm us because they attempt to turn us away from God. We pray this last petition in the same way we pray all of the Lord's Prayer: in communion with the whole Church for the needs of

PEOPLE OF FAITH

Pope Benedict XVI

© 2009 Saint Mary's Press/Illustration by Vicki Shuck

It may be hard to imagine what any Pope must have been like as a boy, but each of the more than 260 men who have followed Peter in the role comes with a life story. Did you know the following facts about Pope Benedict XVI's life?

- He was born and baptized Joseph Ratzinger on the same day: April 16, 1927, the day before Easter.
- His father was a policeman, and his mother was a housewife.
- He had a brother named Georg and a sister named Maria.
- His family lived through the horrors of World War II in Germany.

the whole human family. We pray with confidence that good will ultimately triumph over evil.

We end the Lord's Prayer with "Amen," meaning "so be it" or "it is true." Jesus uses this term frequently throughout the Gospels. The last book of the Bible refers to him as the Amen (see Revelation 3:14).

- He joined the Hitler Youth as a teen (a requirement for young Germans) and later became a prisoner of war.
- He became a priest in 1951 on the feast of Saints Peter and Paul (June 29).
- He earned a doctorate in theology and taught at universities and seminaries for many years.
- He was an influential cardinal during the papacy of his friend Pope John Paul II.
- He has many published writings, including a recent book called *Jesus of Nazareth*, which includes a reflection on the Lord's Prayer.

On World Youth Day in 2006, he had the following message for the young people of the world:

> My dear young friends, love the word of God and love the Church, and this will give you access to a treasure of very great value. . . . Love and follow the Church, for it has received from its Founder [Jesus] the mission of showing the people the way to true happiness. ("Message of the Holy Father Benedict XVI to the Youth of the World on the Occasion of the 21st World Youth Day")

Appendix A: Catholic Prayers

Act of Contrition

My God, I am sorry for my sins
with all my heart, and I detest them.
In choosing to do wrong and failing to do good,
I have sinned against you,
whom I should love above all things.
I firmly intend, with your help,
to do penance, to sin no more,
and to avoid whatever leads me to sin.
Our savior Jesus Christ suffered and died for us.
In his name, my God, have mercy.

Act of Faith

My God, I firmly believe you are one God in three
Divine Persons, Father, Son, and Holy Spirit.
I believe in Jesus Christ, your son, who became man
and died for our sins, and who will come to judge the
living and the dead.
I believe these and all the truths which the Holy Catholic
Church teaches, because you have revealed them, who
can neither deceive nor be deceived.
Amen.

Act of Hope

O my God, trusting in your infinite goodness and promises, I hope to obtain pardon of my sins, the help of your grace, and life everlasting, through the merits of Jesus Christ, my Lord and redeemer. Amen.

Act of Love

My God, I love you above all things, with my whole heart and soul, because you are all-good and worthy of all my love. I love my neighbor as myself for love of you. I forgive all who have injured me, and I ask pardon of all whom I have injured. Amen.

Angelus

The angel of the Lord declared unto Mary,
And she conceived of the Holy Spirit.
    Hail Mary . . .
Behold the handmaid of the Lord,
Be it done unto me according to your word.
    Hail Mary . . .
And the Word was made flesh,
And dwelt among us.
    Hail Mary . . .
Pray for us, O Holy Mother of God, that we may be made worthy of the promises of Christ. Let us pray: Pour forth, we beseech you, O Lord, your grace into our hearts that we to whom the incarnation of Christ, your Son, was made known by the message of the angel may, by his passion and cross, be brought to the glory of his resurrection, through Christ our Lord.

Apostles' Creed

I believe in God, the Father Almighty, creator of heaven and earth. I believe in Jesus Christ, his only son, our Lord. He was conceived by the power of the Holy Spirit, and born of the Virgin Mary. He suffered under Pontius Pilate, was crucified, died, and was buried. He descended to the dead. On the third day he rose again. He ascended into heaven and is seated at the right hand of the Father. He will come again to judge the living and the dead.

I believe in the Holy Spirit, the holy Catholic Church, the communion of saints, the forgiveness of sins, the resurrection of the body, and the life everlasting. Amen.

Confiteor ("I Confess")

I confess to almighty God, and to you, my brothers and sisters, that I have sinned through my own fault in my thoughts and in my words, in what I have done and what I have failed to do; and I ask blessed Mary, ever virgin, all the angels and saints, and you, my brothers and sisters, to pray for me to the Lord our God. May almighty God have mercy on us, forgive us our sins, and bring us to everlasting life.

Glory Be

Glory be to the Father, and to the Son, and to the Holy Spirit, as it was in the beginning, is now, and will be forever. Amen.

Grace Before Meals

Bless us, O Lord, and these your gifts,
which we are about to receive
from your bounty,
through Christ our Lord. Amen.

Grace After Meals

We give you thanks, almighty God,
for these and all your gifts
which we have received
through Christ our Lord. Amen.

Hail Mary

Hail Mary, full of grace,
the Lord is with you;
blessed are you among women,
and blessed is the fruit of your womb, Jesus.
Holy Mary, Mother of God,
pray for us sinners
now and at the hour of our death.
Amen.

The Lord's Prayer
(also called the Our Father)

Our Father who art in heaven,

hallowed be thy name.

Thy kingdom come.

Thy will be done on earth, as it is in heaven.

Give us this day our daily bread,

and forgive us our trespasses,

as we forgive those who trespass against us,

and lead us not into temptation,

but deliver us from evil. Amen.

Magnificat (Mary's Song)
(see Luke 1:46–55)

My being proclaims the greatness of the Lord,

my spirit finds joy in God my savior.

For he has looked upon his servant

in all her lowliness.

All ages to come shall call me blessed.

God who is mighty

has done great things for me, holy is his name;

his mercy is from age to age

on those who fear him.

He has shown might with his arm;

he has confused the proud

in their inmost thoughts.

He has deposed the mighty from their thrones

and raised the lowly to high places.

The hungry he has given every good thing
while the rich he has sent empty away.
He has upheld Israel his servant,
ever mindful of his mercy,
even as he promised our fathers,
promised Abraham and his descendants
forever.

Memorare

Remember, O most gracious Virgin Mary, that never was it known that anyone who fled to your protection, implored your help, or sought your intercession was left unaided. Inspired by this confidence, we fly unto you, O virgin of virgins, our mother. To you do we come, before you we stand, sinful and sorrowful. O mother of the Word Incarnate, despise not our petitions, but in your mercy, hear and answer us.

Morning Prayer

Almighty God, I thank you for your past blessings. Today I offer myself—whatever I do, say, or think—to your loving care. Continue to bless me, Lord. I make this morning offering in union with the divine intentions of Jesus Christ who offers himself daily in the holy sacrifice of the Mass, and in union with Mary, his Virgin Mother and our Mother, who was always the faithful handmaid of the Lord. Amen.

The Nicene Creed

We believe in one God, the Father, the Almighty, maker of heaven and earth, of all that is, seen and unseen.

We believe in one Lord, Jesus Christ, the only Son of God eternally begotten of the Father, God from God, Light from Light, true God from true God, begotten, not made, one in Being with the Father. Through him all things were made. For us men and for our salvation he came down from heaven: By the power of the Holy Spirit he was born of the Virgin Mary, and became man.

For our sake he was crucified under Pontius Pilate; he suffered, died, and was buried.

On the third day he rose again in fulfillment of the Scriptures; he ascended into heaven and is seated at the right hand of the Father. He will come again in glory to judge the living and the dead and his kingdom will have no end.

We believe in the Holy Spirit, the Lord, the giver of life, who proceeds from the Father and the Son. With the Father and the Son he is worshiped and glorified. He has spoken through the Prophets. We believe in one holy catholic and apostolic Church. We acknowledge one baptism for the forgiveness of sins. We look for the resurrection of the dead, and the life of the world to come. Amen.

LIVE IT!

Prayer of Saint Francis

Lord, make me an instrument of your peace:

> where there is hatred, let me sow love;
>
> where there is injury, pardon;
>
> where there is doubt, faith;
>
> where there is despair, hope;
>
> where there is darkness, light;
>
> where there is sadness, joy.

Divine Master,

> grant that I may not so much seek
>
> to be consoled as to console,
>
> to be understood as to understand,
>
> to be loved as to love.

For it is in giving that we receive,

> it is in pardoning that we are pardoned,
>
> it is in dying that we are born to eternal life.

Prayer to the Holy Spirit

Come, Holy Spirit, fill the hearts of your faithful. Enkindle in them the fire of your love. Send forth your Spirit, and they will be created. And you will renew the face of the earth.

> Let us pray:
>
> Lord, by the light of the Holy Spirit, you have taught the hearts of the faithful. In the same Spirit, help us to relish what is right and always rejoice in your consolation. We ask this through Christ our Lord. Amen.

The Rosary

The rosary is perhaps the most popular devotion to Mary, the Mother of God. The central part of the rosary consists of the recitation of five sets of ten Hail Marys (each set is called a decade). Each new decade begins by saying an Our Father, and each decade concludes with a Glory Be. Individuals keep track of the prayers said by moving from one bead to the next in order.

The recitation of the rosary begins with a series of prayers, said in the following order while using as a guide a small chain of beads and a crucifix.

1. the sign of the cross
2. the Apostles' Creed
3. one Our Father
4. three Hail Marys
5. one Glory Be

After these introductory prayers, the recitation of the decades, as described above, begins.

The saying of a five-decade rosary is connected with meditation on what are called the mysteries of the life of Jesus. These mysteries too are collected into series of five—five joyful, five luminous, five sorrowful, and five glorious mysteries. The mysteries of the rosary are listed below. Individuals who are praying devote one recitation of the rosary to each set of mysteries. She or he chooses which set of mysteries to meditate on while saying the decades of Hail Marys. Therefore, the complete rosary consists of twenty decades.

With a little practice, the regular praying of the rosary can become a source of great inspiration and consolation for the Christian.

Joyful Mysteries

- The Annunciation
- The Visitation
- The Birth of Our Lord
- The Presentation of Jesus in the Temple
- The Finding of Jesus in the Temple

Mysteries of Light

- The Baptism of Jesus
- Jesus Reveals Himself in the Miracle at Cana
- Jesus Proclaims the Good News of the Kingdom of God
- The Transfiguration of Jesus
- The Institution of the Eucharist

Sorrowful Mysteries

- The Agony of Jesus in the Garden
- The Scourging at the Pillar
- The Crowning of Thorns
- The Carrying of the Cross
- The Crucifixion

Glorious Mysteries

- The Resurrection of Jesus
- The Ascension of Jesus into Heaven
- The Descent of the Holy Spirit on the Apostles (Pentecost)
- The Assumption of Mary into Heaven
- The Crowning of Mary as Queen of Heaven

Sign of the Cross

In the name of the Father, and of the Son, and of the Holy Spirit. Amen.

Stations of the Cross

1. Jesus is condemned to death.
2. Jesus takes up his cross.
3. Jesus falls the first time.
4. Jesus meets his mother.
5. Simon helps Jesus carry the cross.
6. Veronica wipes the face of Jesus.
7. Jesus falls the second time.
8. Jesus meets the women of Jerusalem.
9. Jesus falls the third time.
10. Jesus is stripped of his garments.
11. Jesus is nailed to the cross.
12. Jesus dies on the cross.
13. Jesus is taken down from the cross.
14. Jesus is laid in the tomb.

Appendix B:

Catholic Beliefs and Practices

This section provides brief summaries of major Catholic beliefs and practices. Many items that are only listed here are explored in more depth in the main part of this book. If you would like more information about these beliefs and practices, consult the index found at the end of the book.

Two Great Commandments
(see chapter 11)

- You shall love the Lord your God with all your heart, with all your soul, and all your mind, and with all your strength.

- You shall love your neighbor as yourself.

(See Matthew 22:37–40, Mark 12:29–3, Luke 10:27.)

Ten Commandments
(see chapters 34–38)

1. I am the Lord your God: you shall not have strange gods before me.
2. You shall not take the name of the Lord, your God, in vain.
3. Remember to keep holy the Lord's Day.
4. Honor your father and mother.
5. You shall not kill.
6. You shall not commit adultery.
7. You shall not steal.
8. You shall not bear false witness against your neighbor.
9. You shall not covet your neighbor's wife.
10. You shall not covet your neighbor's goods.

Beatitudes (see chapter 32)

- Blessed are the poor in spirit, the kingdom of heaven is theirs.
- Blessed are they who mourn, they will be comforted.
- Blessed are the meek, they will inherit the earth.
- Blessed are they who hunger and thirst for righteousness, they will be satisfied.
- Blessed are the merciful, they will be shown mercy.
- Blessed are the clean of heart, they will see God.
- Blessed are the peacemakers, they will be called children of God.
- Blessed are they who are persecuted for the sake of righteousness, the kingdom of heaven is theirs.

Corporal Works of Mercy
(see chapter 12)

- Feed the hungry.
- Give drink to the thirsty.
- Shelter the homeless.
- Clothe the naked.
- Care for the sick.
- Help the imprisoned.
- Bury the dead.

Spiritual Works of Mercy
(see chapter 12)

- Share knowledge.
- Give advice to those who need it.
- Comfort those who suffer.
- Be patient with others.
- Forgive those who hurt you.
- Give correction to those who need it.
- Pray for the living and the dead.

Theological Virtues (see chapter 32)

- Faith
- Hope
- Love

Cardinal Virtues (see chapter 32)

- Prudence
- Justice
- Fortitude
- Temperance

Seven Gifts of the Holy Spirit
(see chapter 16)

- **Wisdom.** A wise person recognizes where the Holy Spirit is at work in the world.

- **Understanding.** Understanding helps us recognize how God wants us to live.

- **Right judgment (Counsel).** This gift helps us make choices that will lead us closer to God rather than away from God. The gift of right judgment, sometimes called counsel, helps us figure out what God wants.

- **Courage (Fortitude).** The gift of courage, also called fortitude, is the special help we need when faced with challenges or struggles.

- **Knowledge.** This gift helps us understand the meaning of what God has revealed, particularly the Good News of Jesus Christ.

- **Reverence (Piety).** This gift, sometimes called piety, gives us a deep sense of respect for God and the Church. A reverent person honors God and approaches him with humility, trust, and love.

- **Wonder and awe (Fear of the Lord).** The gift of wonder and awe makes us aware of God's greatness and power.

Fruits of the Holy Spirit
(see chapter 15)

- Charity
- Joy
- Peace
- Patience
- Kindness
- Goodness

- Generosity (or Long-suffering)
- Gentleness (or Humility)
- Faithfulness
- Modesty
- Self-control (or Continence)
- Chastity

Four Marks of the Catholic Church (see chapter 18)

- One
- Holy
- Catholic
- Apostolic

Liturgical Year (see chapter 22)

- Advent
- Christmas
- Ordinary Time
- Lent
- Easter Triduum
- Easter
- Pentecost
- Ordinary Time

Seven Sacraments (see chapters 22–31)

- Baptism
- Confirmation
- Eucharist
- Penance and Reconciliation
- Anointing of the Sick
- Matrimony
- Holy Orders

Precepts of the Church

- Keep holy Sundays and holy days of obligation and attend Mass on these days.

- Confess your sins in the Sacrament of Penance and Reconciliation at least once a year.

- Receive Communion at least during the Easter season.

- Follow the Church's rules concerning fasting and abstaining from eating meat.

- Strengthen and support the Church by providing for the material needs of the Church according to your ability.

Holy Days of Obligation

- Christmas (December 25)

- Solemnity of the Blessed Virgin Mary, the Mother of God (January 1)

- Ascension of the Lord (the Thursday that falls on the fortieth day after Easter, though in some places the celebration is moved to the following Sunday)

- Assumption of the Blessed Virgin Mary (August 15)

- All Saints' (November 1)

- Immaculate Conception of the Blessed Virgin Mary (December 8)

Parts of Mass (see chapters 24–27)

Introductory Rites

- Entrance

- Act of Penitence

- Kyrie

- Gloria

- Collect (opening prayer)

Liturgy of the Word

- First Reading
- Responsorial Psalm
- Second Reading
- Gospel Acclamation
- Gospel
- Homily
- Profession of Faith
- Prayers of the Faithful

Liturgy of the Eucharist

- Preparation of the Altar and the Gifts
- Prayers over the Gifts
- Eucharistic Prayer
- Communion Rite:
    Lord's Prayer
    Rite of Peace
    Breaking of the Bread
    Communion
    Silence/Song of Praise
- Prayer After Communion

Concluding Rites

- Greeting and Blessing
- Dismissal

Appendix C:

Glossary of Key Words

A

Abba. The Aramaic word for "father" that Jesus uses to address God the Father.

abortion. The intentional ending of an unborn child's life. Choosing abortion and performing abortions are serious sins.

absolution. Freeing from guilt. Absolution takes place during the Sacrament of Penance and Reconciliation, when the priest pardons sins in the name of God and the Church.

Advocate. One who helps and supports another person. In the Gospel of John, Jesus refers to the Holy Spirit as the disciples' Advocate. *See also* Holy Spirit.

age of reason. The age when a young person is old enough to understand the difference between right and wrong. This is generally regarded to be the age of seven.

alb. A white liturgical garment.

ambo. The reading stand where the Scriptures are proclaimed during the liturgy.

anamnesis. A special kind of remembering. When we recall a past event, it happens again in the present. In the Eucharist we recall what Jesus did in his life, death, and Resurrection, and we celebrate that his saving action is present today.

angel. A servant or messenger of God. Angels glorify God without ceasing and watch over each us every moment of our lives.

Annunciation. The angel Gabriel's announcement to Mary that she was to be the mother of Jesus Christ.

apostolic. One of the four marks of the Church, along with one, holy, and catholic. The Church is apostolic because she was founded on Jesus' Twelve Apostles. *See also* marks of the Church.

Ascension. The event forty days after the Resurrection of Jesus Christ, when he was taken up to Heaven.

assembly. The people that come together to celebrate the liturgy.

Assumption. The belief that God took Mary directly into Heaven at the end of her life on earth.

atheism. The denial of God's existence.

B

Baptism. The first of the Seven Sacraments of the Church. Through Baptism, people become united to Christ and to the Church. See sacrament.

belief. Something considered to be true.

bishop. One who has received the fullness of the Sacrament of Holy Orders. A bishop takes care of the Church in a particular geographical area called a diocese. He is a sign of unity in his diocese and a member of the College of Bishops.

blessing. A form of prayer in which we ask for God's loving care for someone.

C

catechumenate. The process through which unbaptized adults and children who have reached the age of reason are initiated into the Church.

catholic. Along with one, holy, and apostolic, catholic is one of the four marks of the Church. Catholic means "universal." The Church reaches throughout the world to all people. *See also* marks of the Church.

charity. Working to meet people's needs out of love for God and neighbor. Charity, or love, is a Theological Virtue. *See also* virtue.

chastity. The virtue of living your sexuality in a pure and healthy way, particularly by obeying the Sixth and Ninth Commandments.

Chrism. Perfumed olive oil that has been consecrated. It is used for anointing in the Sacraments of Baptism, Confirmation, and Holy Orders.

Chrism Mass. The annual celebration during which bishops bless the oils to be used in their dioceses during the coming year. This Mass usually takes place on Holy Thursday.

Christians. The name for the followers of Jesus Christ.

Commandments, Ten. *See* Ten Commandments.

common good. A social condition that enables all people to fulfill their human and spiritual needs.

common priesthood of the faithful. The name for the priesthood shared by all who are baptized. The baptized share in the priesthood of Jesus Christ by participating in his mission.

Communion. The sharing of Christ's Body and Blood in the liturgy.

communion. The closest type of relationship shared among people and between people and God.

communion of saints. The whole community of now-living faithful people united with all those who have died but are alive with God.

contrition. Sorrow for one's sins.

conversion. A change of heart that turns us away from sin and toward God.

covenant. A sacred agreement among people, or between God and a human being, where everyone vows to keep a promise forever.

creation. God's actions though which all that exists has come into being.

creed. A statement of what one believes. The Nicene and Apostles' Creeds are the Church's most important creeds.

D

discipline. Self-control.

doctrine. Official teaching of the Church based on God's Revelation by and through Jesus Christ.

E

ecumenism. The work of Catholics and other Christians aimed at restoring unity among Christians.

Emmanuel. A name for Jesus that means "God with us."

envy. Jealousy or sadness because someone else has more possessions, success, or popularity.

epiclesis. A Greek word that means "invocation" or "calling upon." The epiclesis during the liturgy occurs when the priest calls upon the Holy Spirit.

Eucharist. Mass or the Lord's Supper. Eucharist is based on a Greek term for "thanksgiving."

Eucharistic Prayer. The Church's great prayer of thanksgiving to the Father. It includes the consecration of the bread and wine.

euthanasia. Ending the life of a sick, handicapped, or dying person. Though some may view this as mercy, it is murder.

evangelize. To actively work to spread the Good News of Jesus Christ.

F

faith. Believing and accepting that God made himself known to us through his words and actions, especially through Jesus Christ. It is accepting God's truth with our minds and allowing it to guide our entire lives.

free will. The gift from God that allows us to choose what we do. It is the basis for our moral responsibility.

G

Gifts of the Holy Spirit. Special gifts or graces we receive from God that help us live the way God wants us to live. The Seven Gifts of the Holy Spirit are wisdom, understanding, counsel (or right judgment), fortitude (or courage), knowledge, piety (or reverence), and fear of the Lord (or wonder and awe).

God the Father. The first divine Person of the Holy Trinity.

Gospels. The Good News of God's Revelation. The four Gospels—Matthew, Mark, Luke, and John—tell us about the person, life, teachings, death, and Resurrection of Jesus Christ.

grace. The gift of God's loving presence in our lives that enables us to share in God's own divine life and love.

H

Heaven. The state of being in perfect friendship and unity with God for eternity.

Heaven and earth. A phrase that refers to everything that exists, the entire universe.

hell. The state of being separated from God forever.

Holy Spirit. The third divine Person of the Trinity. *See also* Advocate.

homosexuality. Sexual attraction to people of one's own gender.

honor. To show great respect or courtesy.

human person. A living being made up of both a physical body and an immortal, spiritual soul. All human persons are created in God's image.

I

idolatry. The worship of such things as money, possessions, or popularity as if they were God.

Immaculate Conception. The belief that Mary was conceived without Original Sin.

Incarnation. The truth that Jesus Christ, the Son of God and the second Person of the Trinity, is both fully God and fully man.

inspiration. The guidance the Holy Spirit gave to the authors of the Bible. This enabled them to record without error what God wants us to know for our salvation.

intercession. A form of prayer in which we ask for God's help for others.

J

Jesus. A Hebrew name that means "God saves." The Son of God was named Jesus, signifying his role as Savior of the world.

judgment. An assessment of how we've lived our lives.

justification. A process through which God restores our broken relationships after we have sinned.

K

Kingdom of God. The Reign of God, which Jesus announced. It is characterized as a time of justice, peace, and love. The seed or the beginning of the Kingdom is present on earth right now. When the Kingdom is fully realized in the future, God will rule over the hearts of all people.

L

laying on of hands. A gesture used in the liturgy that signifies that the priest is calling upon the Holy Spirit.

Lectionary. The book that contains the readings that have been selected for proclamation during the Church's liturgies throughout the year. All the readings are from the Bible.

legitimate defense. The teaching that it is permissible to take action that causes harm to another person if it is necessary to protect yourself or others.

litany. A litany is a form of prayer, spoken or sung, involving a dialogue between a leader and the people assembled. The people respond to each phrase said or sung by the leader with a constant refrain or acclamation.

liturgy. The Church's official, public, communal prayer. It is God's work, in which the People of God participate. The Church's most important liturgy is the Eucharist, or Mass.

Liturgy of the Eucharist. One of two major parts of Mass. It includes the Eucharistic Prayer and the Communion Rite.

Liturgy of the Word. The first major part of Mass. It includes Scripture readings, a responsorial psalm, a homily, the saying of the Creed, and Prayers of the Faithful.

Logos. A Greek word that is translated as "word." It means "thought," "logic," or "meaning." Jesus is the *Logos*, because when we see Jesus and listen to him, we can begin to see the mind of God and understand God's logic.

Lord's Prayer. Another name for the Our Father, the prayer Jesus taught his disciples.

M

Magi. The wise men who, upon discovering a strange star in the sky, traveled to Bethlehem to greet the newborn Jesus.

Magisterium. The official teaching authority of the Church.

marks of the Church. The four essential features or characteristics of the Church: one, holy, catholic (universal), and apostolic. See also apostolic; catholic.

mediator. A person in a middle position who facilitates communication and relationship between two people or groups. Because Jesus Christ is both God and man, he is the one and perfect mediator between us and God.

Messiah. Hebrew word for "anointed one." The equivalent Greek term is christos. Jesus is the Christ and the Messiah because he is the Anointed One.

ministerial priesthood. Received in the Sacrament of Holy Orders by bishops and priests, the ministrial priesthood is a means by which Jesus Christ builds up and guides the church.

miracles. Special signs beyond our understanding of the normal laws of human and physical behavior that make God's power and presence known in human history.

monotheistic. Describing the belief that there is only one God.

mortal sin. *See* sin, mortal.

mysteries. A term used by early Christians to refer to the sacraments.

mystery. A truth that is so big and profound that no human being can completely know or understand it. We encounter mystery and enter into it.

N

natural law. The God-given instinct to seek out what is good. It is called natural because it is part of human nature.

O

orans. A prayer posture that involves raising one's eyes and extending both hands upward. It resembles the stance of a young child wanting to be picked up.

Original Sin. The sin that Adam and Eve committed and the sinful condition that all human beings have from birth.

P

parables. Types of stories Jesus often used that draw on situations known to the listeners and surprise elements to teach about the Kingdom of God.

Paschal Mystery. The entire process of God's plan of salvation by which Christ saves us from sin and death through his Passion, death, Resurrection, and Ascension. We enter the Paschal Mystery by participating in the liturgy and being faithful followers of Christ.

Passion. Jesus' suffering and death.

Passover. The Jewish feast that commemorates the release of the Jewish people from captivity in Egypt.

Penance. A reference to the Sacrament of Penance and Reconciliation, one of the Seven Sacraments of the Church. Through this sacrament sinners are reconciled with God and the Church.

Pentecost. The biblical event after Jesus rose from the dead and ascended to Heaven, when the Holy Spirit came on the disciples as Jesus had promised. The Church celebrates the feast of Pentecost fifty days after Easter every year.

People of God. An image of the Church from the Bible.

petition. A prayer form in which we ask God for forgiveness or for help with something.

Pope. The name for the leader of the Church. *Pope* comes from a word meaning "father." Sometimes the Pope is called the Holy Father. He is the successor of Saint Peter, the first Pope and Bishop of Rome.

pornography. Visual images or writings that describe sexual activity, created with the intent to arouse sexual feelings.

praise. A form of prayer in which we tell God how much we appreciate all he does for us.

presides. Directs or leads the liturgical activity of a community. Only ordained priests and bishops can preside at Mass.

Q

quintessential. An adjective that means "the best example of something." The Lord's Prayer is the quintessential prayer of the Church, because it is the perfect example of Christian prayer.

R

reconciles. Restores relationships among ourselves and with God.

reparation. Making up for the damage to property or the harm to another person as a result of one's sin.

restitution. Returning property that was taken from someone unfairly.

Resurrection. The passage of Jesus through death to new life after he had been crucified.

Revelation. God's communication about himself and his plan for humanity. Throughout history God's Revelation has been made known through creation, events, and people, but most fully through Jesus Christ.

Rite of Peace. The part of Mass when the people are invited to share a sign of Christ's peace with one another.

S

Sabbath. In the Jewish tradition, the Sabbath is from sundown Friday to sundown Saturday. Jews observe the Sabbath through prayer, fasting, and worshiping together on Saturday. Catholics fulfill the commandment to "keep holy the Sabbath" on Sunday, because that is the day Jesus rose from the dead.

sacrament. A visible sign of God's invisible grace. The Seven Sacraments are Baptism, the Eucharist, Confirmation, Penance and Reconciliation, Anointing of the Sick, Matrimony, and Holy Orders.

sacramentals. Sacred signs (the Sign of the Cross, holy water) instituted by the Church. They do not confer grace as sacraments do, but they make us ready to cooperate with the grace we receive in a sacrament.

salvation history. The pattern of events in human history through which God makes his presence and saving actions known to us.

sanctifying grace. A free gift we receive from God. It heals us from sin, makes us holy, and restores our friendship with him.

scandal. An action or attitude—or failure to act—that causes someone to sin.

Scriptures. A term for sacred writings. For Christians, the Scriptures are the books in the Old and New Testaments that make up the Bible. They are the Word of God.

sexuality. Our identities as males and females.

sin, mortal. An action or offense so seriously against God's will that it completely separates a person from God. It is called "mortal" because it leads to eternal death. *See also* sins, venial.

sins, venial. Actions or offenses against God's will that weaken our relationships with God and others and that hurt our personal characters; venial sins are not so serious that they cause complete separation between us and God. *See also* sin, mortal.

social justice. The respect for all creation and human rights that allows people to get what they need to live and to realize their God-given dignity.

society. A community of people who depend on each other.

solidarity. A close relationship or unity with others. Living in solidarity means we share with people who are poor or powerless not only our material goods but also our friendship and prayers.

Son of God. A title frequently given to Jesus Christ, the second Person of the Trinity.

soul. The spiritual element that gives humans life and survives after death. The sould is created by God at the moment of our conception.

stations of the cross. Images of Jesus' Passion found on display in most Catholic churches.

suicide. Taking one's own life.

symbols. Objects, actions, gestures, or words that point beyond themselves to a deeper, more meaningful reality.

synagogue. The place where Jews meet to pray and study.

synoptic. "To see together." Matthew, Mark, and Luke are called the synoptic Gospels due to their similarities.

T

temptation. Something that seems fun, exciting, or even good to do but is actually sinful.

Ten Commandments. The laws God gave Moses that guide human action. Jesus' command to love God and to love our neighbors is a summary of the Ten Commandments.

thanksgiving. A form of prayer in which we express thanks and gratitude for the gifts God has given us.

Theotokos. A Greek term that means "God-bearer." The Church uses this name for Mary, because she is the Mother of Jesus Christ, the second Person of the Trinity.

Tradition. The living transmission of God's truth to us. It means both the central content of the Catholic faith and the way in which that content has been handed down through the centuries under the guidance of the Holy Spirit.

Transfiguration. A mysterious event in which Peter, James, and John see Jesus speaking to Moses and Elijah, two important people from the Old Testament. The event is so called because Jesus' appearance was transformed and revealed his divinity.

transubstantiation. The change that takes place when the bread and wine become the Body and Blood of Jesus Christ during Mass.

trespass. Sin (noun); to sin (verb).

Trinity. The central Christian belief that there is one God in three divine Persons: Father, Son, and Holy Spirit.

V

venerate. To show deep reverence for something sacred.

venial sins. *See* sins, venial.

virtues. Good habits that develop and help us consistently do the right thing. The four Cardinal Virtues are prudence, justice, temperance, and fortitude. The three Theological Virtues are faith, hope, and love (or charity).

vocation. The call from God to live a life of holiness. Some live out God's call as ordained priests, while others are called to marriage, to lives as members of religious communities, or to lives as single people.

W

works of mercy. Acts of charity by which we help others meet their physical and spiritual needs.

Y

Yahweh. The Old Testament name for God that he revealed to Moses. It is frequently translated as "I AM" or "I am who I am."

Index

A

Abba, 28, 395
abolitionists, 410
abortion, 55, 413, 419
Abraham, 64, 66–67, 69, 71, 463
absolution, 345, 347
abstinence, sexual, 442
acclamations, 283, 295, 299
actions. see also morality; works
    Eucharist and, 310
    faith and, 76–77
    grace and, 177, 178–179
    Jesus', 100
    judgment and, 225–226
    liturgy and, 244, 245
    moral, 381–384
    Mother Teresa on, 79, 277
    teaching as, 119
Act of Contrition, 341, 342, 500
Act of Faith, 500
Act of Hope, 501
Act of Love, 501
Acts of the Apostles, 133, 136,
    186–192, 404
Adam and Eve
    overviews, 46, 56–57, 65, 220,
        418–419
    breath and, 55
    clothing and, 442
    goodness and, 414
    names of, 53
    sin and, 177, 317
addictions, 373
adult baptism, 319, 323
adultery, 436, 445
Advent, 109
advertising, 388
age of reason, 331
Agony of Jesus, 509
alb, 363
altar, 334
ambo, 284

ambry, 334
Amen, 301, 499
amnesia, 268
anamnesis, 267–269
Angelico, Fra, 225
angels, 49–50, *108*, 109, 110,
    155, 229, 267
Angelus, 501
Anna, 169
annulments, 359
Annunciation, 109, *229*, 509
anointing, 102, 193, 333,
    334, 366
Anointing of the Sick, 136, 255,
    262, 328, 339, 345, 349–353
Anselm, Saint, 335
Anthony of Padua,
Saint, 288–289
Antichrist, 159
anti-Semitism, 214
apologies, 175
Apostles. see also Acts of the Apostles;
    disciples; Pentecost; *individual*
    Apostles
    overviews, 19, 69, 86, 157
    Church and, 197
    commissioning of, 207
    governments and, 408, 456–457
    healing and, 137
    Holy Spirit and, 167, 170–171
    priests and, 362
Apostles' Creed, 502
apostolic Church, 187, 204
apostolic succession, 205
Aramaic, 28, 495–496
arms race, 421
art, 225, 477. see also individual
    works of art
Ascension, 158–159, 167, 509
Ash Wednesday, 348, 394
assembly, 248, 274–277, 358
Assumption, 234, 509
atheism, 16, 393

Note: italicized page numbers indicate Illustrations.

Acknowledgments

The scriptural quotations marked NRSV are from the New Revised Standard Version of the Bible, Catholic Edition. Copyright © 1993 and 1989 by the Division of Christian Education of the National Council of the Churches of Christ in the United States of America. All rights reserved.

All other scriptural quotations in this publication are from the Good News Translation in Today's English Version, Second Edition. Copyright © 1992 by the American Bible Society. Used with permission.

The prayers, devotions, beliefs, and practices contained herein have been verified against authoritative sources.

All excerpts marked *CCC* are quoted or adapted from the English translation of the *Catechism of the Catholic Church* for use in the United States of America, second edition. Copyright © 1994 by the United States Catholic Conference, Inc.—Libreria Editrice Vaticana. English translation of the *Catechism of the Catholic Church: Modifications from the Editio Typica* copyright © 1997 by the United States Catholic Conference, Inc.—Libreria Editrice Vaticana.

The quotation on page 65 is from *Dogmatic Constitution on the Church (Lumen Gentium)*, number 16, at *www.vatican.va/archive/hist_councils/ii_vatican_council/documents/vat-ii_const_19641121_lumen-gentium_en.html*, accessed October 16, 2008.

The quotation by Mother Teresa on page 79 is from *Faith and Compassion: The Life and Work of Mother Teresa,* by Raghu Rai and Navin Chawla (Rockport, ME: Element Books, 1996), page 158. Copyright © 1996 by Element Books Limited.

The quotations on pages 135, 151, 158, 160, 210, 226, 258, 271, 272, 293, 294, 295, 298, 305, 306, 307, 309, 472, and 474 are from the *Sacramentary,* English translation prepared by the International Commission on English in the Liturgy (ICEL) (New York: Catholic Book Publishing Company, 1985), pages 564, 371, 555, 549, 550, 546, 549, 563, 548, 1102, 1102, 551, 549, 561, 567, 564, 367, 372, 552, and 561, respectively. Illustrations and arrangement copyright © 1985–1974 by the Catholic Book Publishing Company, New York. Used with permission of the ICEL.

The statistics on pages 171, 201, and, 209 are from the *2007 Catholic Almanac,* Matthew Bunson, general editor (Huntington, IN: Our Sunday Visitor, 2007), pages 333, 333, and 430, respectively. Copyright © 2006 by Our Sunday Visitor.

The quotations on pages 181,183, 408, and 441 are from *The Rites of the Catholic Church,* volume 1, prepared by the ICEL, a Joint Commission of Catholic Bishops' Conferences (Collegeville, MN: Liturgical Press, A Pueblo Book, 1990), pages 490, 388, 392, 726, and 728,respectively. Copyright © 1990 by The Order of Saint Benedict, Collegeville, MN. All rights reserved. Used with permission of the ICEL.

The story on pages 238–239 is adapted from "The Story of Our Lady of Guadalupe," by Jack Wintz, at *www.americancatholic.org/Messenger/Dec1999/feature2.asp#5,* accessed October 16, 2008.

The statistics on pages 243 and 244 are from *Soul Searching: The Religious and Spiritual Lives of American Teenagers,* by Christian Smith (New York: Oxford University Press, 2005), pages 62 and 37. Copyright © 2005 by Oxford University Press.

The prayers on pages 251 are from *Benedictine Daily Prayers: A Short Breviary,* compiled and edited by Maxwell E. Johnson (Collegeville, MN: The Liturgical Press, and the Monks of Saint John's Abbey, 2005), pages 903 and 932. Copyright © 2005 by the Order of Saint Benedict, Collegeville, MN. All rights reserved. Used with permission of The Liturgical Press.

The quotations on pages 261 and 274–275 are from *Constitution on the Sacred Liturgy (Sacrosanctum Concilium),* numbers 11 and 14, at *www.vatican.va/archive/hist_councils/ii_vatican_council/documents/vat-ii_const_19631204_sacrosanctum-concilium_en.html,* accessed October 16, 2008.

The excerpt by Mother Teresa on page 277 is from *Finding God at Harvard: Spiritual Journeys of Thinking Christians,* edited by Kelly K. Monroe (Grand Rapids, MI: Zondervan Publishing House, 1996), page 318. Copyright © 2006 by Kelly M. Monroe.

The statistics on page 285 are from the United States Conference of Catholic Bishops' Committee on the Liturgy, *Newsletter,* volume 43, May–June 2007, page 27.

The quotation on page 335 is from *St. Anselm's Proslogion, with A Reply on Behalf of the Fool, by Gaunilo, and The Author's Reply to Gaunilo,* translated by M. J. Charlesworth (London: Oxford University Press, 1965), page 117. Copyright ©1965 by Oxford University Press.

The quotation on page 358 is from a papal greeting by Pope Benedict XVI, March 25, 2007, at *www.zenit.org/article-19488?l=english,* accessed October 16, 2008.

The quotation by Peter Claver on page 401 is from the Knights of Peter Claver Web site, at *www.kofpc.org/pdf/2007PostConvention/KnightsofStPeterClaverHistory.pdf,* accessed October 16, 2008.

The quotation on page 420 is from "Address of His Holiness Pope John Paul II to the Diplomatic Corps," at *www.vatican.va/holy_father/john_paul_ii/speeches/2003/january/documents/hf_jp-ii_spe_20030113_diplomatic-corps_en.html,* accessed October 16, 2008.

The quotations by Jean Vanier on pages 422–423 are from an interview found at *www.csec.org/csec/sermon/vanier_4321.htm,* accessed October 16, 2008.

The excerpt by Basil the Great on page 428 was found at *www.daytonpeacemuseum.org/PEACE%20QUOTES%010108.pdf,* accessed October 16, 2008.

The quotations by Oscar Romero on page 433 are from *The Violence of Love: Oscar Romero,* compiled and translated by James R. Brockman (Farmington, PA: The Plough Publishing House, 1998), pages 186 and 192. Text copyright © 1988 by the Chicago Province of the Society of Jesus.

The quotation on page 455 is from "Message of His Holiness Pope Paul VI for the Celebration of the Day of Peace," at *www.vatican.va/holy_father/paul_vi/messages/peace/documents/hf_p-vi_mes_19711208_v-world-day-for-peace_en.html,* accessed October 16, 2008.

The quotation by Dorothy Day on page 456 is from "The Living Legacy of Dorothy Day," by Jim Forest, at *salt.claretianpubs.org/issues/DorothyDay/legacy.html,* accessed October 16, 2008.

The quotation by Dorothy Day on page 457 is from *Dorothy Day and the Permanent Revolution,* by Eileen Egan (Erie, PA: Pax Christi, 1983), page 22. Copyright © 1983 by Eileen Egan.

The Jugular Prayer on page 466 is adapted from *Prayer Notes to a Friend,* by Edward Hays (Leavenworth, KS: Forest of Peace Publishing, 2002), page 33. Copyright © 2002 by Edward M. Hays.

The information about Teresa of Ávila on pages 468–469 is adapted from *Praying with Teresa of Ávila,* by Rosemary Broughton (Winona, MN: Saint Mary's Press, 1990), pages 31 and 33. Copyright © 1990 by Saint Mary's Press. All rights reserved.

The excerpt on page 499 is from "Message of the Holy Father Benedict XVI to the Youth of the World on the Occasion of the 21st World Youth Day," at *www.vatican.va/holy_father/benedict_xvi/messages/youth/documents/hf_ben-xvi_mes_20060222_youth_en.html,* accessed October 16, 2008.

To view copyright terms and conditions for Internet materials cited here, log on to the home pages for the referenced Web sites.

During this book's preparation, all citations, facts, figures, names, addresses, telephone numbers, Internet URLs, and other pieces of information cited within were verified for accuracy. The authors and Saint Mary's Press staff have made every attempt to reference current and valid sources, but we cannot guarantee the content of any source, and we are not responsible for any changes that may have occurred since our verification. If you find an error in, or have a question or concern about, any of the information or sources listed within, please contact Saint Mary's Press.

Acknowledgments

Endnotes Cited in Quotations from the *Catechism of the Catholic Church*, Second Edition

Chapter 9
1. *Gaudium et spes* 22 § 2.
2. St. Thomas Aquinas, *Opusc.* 57: 1–4.

Chapter 39
1. John XXIII, *Pacem in terris,* 46.

Chapter 42
1. St. Augustine, *Ep.* 130, 12, 22: J. P. Migne, ed., Patrologia Latina (Paris:1841–1855) 33, 503.